Impact maths R

About this book

Impact maths provides a complete course to help you achieve your best in your Key Stage 3 Mathematics course. This book will help you understand and remember mathematical ideas, solve mathematical problems with and without the help of a calculator and develop your mental maths skills.

Exercises you should try without the help of a calculator are marked with this symbol:

Finding your way around

To help you find your way around when you are studying use the:

- **edge marks** shown on the front pages – these help you get to the right chapter quickly

- **contents list** and **index** – these list all the key ideas covered in the book and help you turn straight to them.

- **links** in the margin – these show when an idea elsewhere in the book may be useful:

There is more about fractions on page 154.

Remembering key ideas

We have provided clear explanations of the key ideas you need throughout the book with **worked examples** showing you how to answer questions. **Key points** you need to remember look like this:

■ **The distance around the edge of a shape is its perimeter.**

and are listed in a **summary** at the end of each unit.

Investigations and information technology

Two units focus on particular skills you need for your course:

- **using and applying mathematics** (chapter 19) – shows you some ways of investigating mathematical problems.

- **calculators and computers** (chapter 20) – shows you some ways of using calculators and computers and will help with mental maths practice.

11
12
13
14
15
16
17
18
19
20

Heinemann Educational Publishers
Halley Court, Jordan Hill, Oxford, OX2 8EJ
a division of Reed Educational & Professional Publishing Ltd
Heinemann is a registered trademark of Reed Educational & Professional Publishing Ltd

OXFORD   MELBOURNE   AUCKLAND
JOHANNESBURG   BLANTYRE   GABARONE
IBADAN   PORTSMOUTH   NH (USA)   CHICAGO

© Heinemann Educational Publishers

First published 2000

ISBN 0 435 01758 6

05 04 03 02
10 9 8 7

Designed and typeset by TechSet Ltd, Gateshead, Tyne and Wear
Illustrated by Barry Atkinson, Barking Dog and TechSet
Cover design by Miller, Craig and Cocking
Printed and bound by Edelvives, Spain

Acknowledgements
The authors and publishers would like to thank the following for permission to use photographs:
P1:Robert Harding Picture Library; Science Photo Library/Prof.K.Seddon & Dr.T.Evans, Queen s University, Belfast; Pet Rescue magazine, John Brown Publishing/Channel 4. P15: Corbis. P46: China Span/Keren Su. P55: Holt Studios/Nigel Cattlin. P58 and 60: Robert Harding Picture Library. P61, 62 and 63: Action-Plus/Glyn Kirk; Peter Blakeman; Neil Tingle. P81: Science & Society Picture Library. P91: Action-Plus/Neil Tingle. P134: J. Allan Cash Ltd.; Action-Plus/Richard Francis. P147: Aerofilms. P164: J.Allan Cash Ltd. P178: Action-Plus/Glyn Kirk. P184: Direct Holidays; Robert Harding Picture Library; J.Allan Cash Ltd. P232: J.Allan Cash Ltd. P245: Robert Harding Picture Library. P251: Trevor Hill. P274: Action-Plus/Glyn Kirk.

Cover photo "Synchronicity" by Daniel Culloch © '87, Design Synergy, U.S.A., Tel: 505-986-1215, URL: http://www.dolphin-synergy.com

Publishing team		Author team	
Editorial	**Design**	David Benjamin	David Kent
Philip Ellaway	Phil Richards	Sue Bright	Gina Marquess
Sarah Caton	Colette Jacquelin	Tony Clough	Christine Medlow
Nigel Green	Mags Robertson	Gareth Cole	Graham Newman
Shaheen Hassan		Diana DeBrida	Sheila Nolan
Harry Smith	**Production**	Ray Fraser	Keith Pledger
Deborah Dobson	David Lawrence	Barry Grantham	Ian Roper
Anne Russell	Jo Morgan	Karen Hughes	John Sylvester
Margaret Shepherd	Jason Wyatt	Peter Jolly	

Tel:01865 888058 email:info.he@heinemann.co.uk

Contents

3 Number patterns

4 Probability

5 Multiplication and division

6   Decimals

7   Measuring

8   Fractions and ratio

9   Working with algebra

10 Perimeter, area and volume

11 Formulae and equations

12 Negative numbers

13 Graphs

14 Angles

15 Handling data

16 Percentages

17 Averages

18 Transformations

19 Using and applying mathematics

20 Calculators and computers

Index

1 Shapes

1.1 Why do we study shapes?

The world is full of interesting shapes.

Engineers use shapes to make their structures strong . . .

Designers use shapes to make the page more interesting . . .

Scientists use shapes to help them understand molecular structure . . .

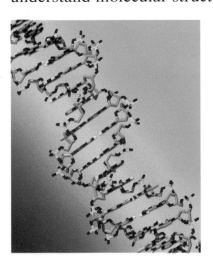

Mathematicians help us understand what is special about different shapes.

This unit introduces some shapes and shows you how to describe them.

1.2 Naming shapes

You name shapes like these by the number of sides they have:

■ Shape	Name	Hint
△	Triangle: 3 sides	**Tri**cycles have 3 wheels. **Tri**plets are 3 babies.
⬠	Quadrilateral: 4 sides	**Quad** bikes have 4 wheels. **Quads** are 4 babies.
⬠	Pentagon: 5 sides	A **penta**thlon has 5 athletic events.
⬡	Hexagon: 6 sides	Six and hexagon both use the letter **x**.
⬡	Heptagon: 7 sides	A **hepta**thlon has 7 athletic events.
⯃	Octagon: 8 sides	An **oct**opus has 8 legs.

Shapes with all straight sides are called **polygons**. Polygon means 'many sided'.

Notice that ⬡ and ⯈ are both hexagons.

Exercise 1A

1   For each polygon:
   - write down the number of sides
   - name the polygon.

   The first shape has 3 sides. It is a triangle.

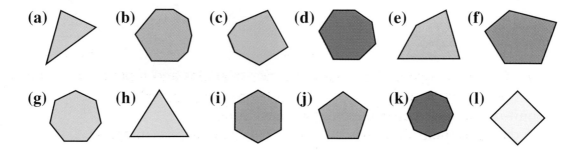

2 On this tile:

(a) how many triangles are there

(b) how many quadrilaterals are there?

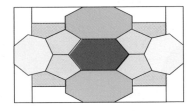

3 In this coloured window:

(a) how many pentagons are there

(b) how many hexagons are there

(c) how many heptagons are there

(d) how many octagons are there?

4 For each of these windows:

- list all the different shapes
- count how many of each shape there are.

(a) 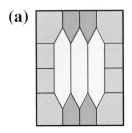 **(b)** 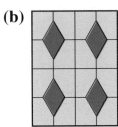 **(c)** 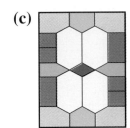 **(d)**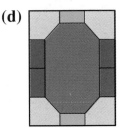

How to sketch a shape
To sketch a pentagon
draw 5 dots like this:
then join them up.

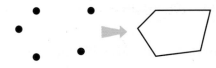

5 **(a)** Sketch a hexagon
Hint: draw 6 dots

(b) Sketch a heptagon

(c) Sketch an octagon

6 **Activity** You need Activity sheet 1. Cut out the triangles and pentagons.

You can use a triangle and
a pentagon to make a
hexagon:

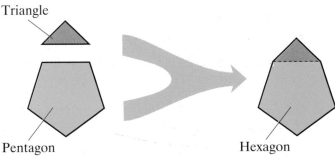

Triangle

Pentagon

Hexagon

(a) Use a triangle and a
pentagon to make:

- two more hexagons
- two quadrilaterals

(b) Use two triangles and a pentagon to make:

- a heptagon (7 sides)
- a triangle
- a different sized pentagon

1.3 Mirror symmetry

This shape has symmetry:

This is a **line of symmetry**.

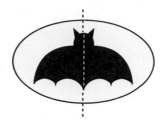

If you folded on the line of symmetry, one half would fit over the other exactly.

You can use a mirror to find the line of symmetry.

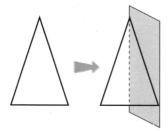

This shape has symmetry

The mirror image fits exactly

This shape doesn't have symmetry

The mirror image does not fit

■ **A shape has symmetry if you can fold it so that one side fits exactly on to the other.**
The fold line is the line of symmetry.
A line of symmetry is also called a mirror line.

Example 1

How many lines of symmetry does this shape have?

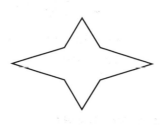

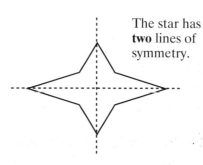

The star has **two** lines of symmetry.

Exercise 1B

1 How many lines of symmetry does each shape have?

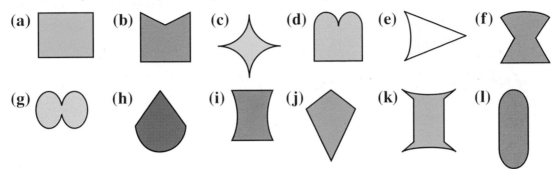

(a) (b) (c) (d) (e) (f)

(g) (h) (i) (j) (k) (l)

2 Copy these letters. Draw any lines of symmetry.
   The first one has been done for you.

A B C D E F H I W X N M O S

3 How many lines of symmetry do these words have?

BOB DAD WOW OXO SOS

4 What is the longest word you can find that has a line of
   symmetry? (Hint: you may need to use your
   dictionary.)

5 You need Activity sheet 2.
   Draw all the lines of symmetry on each shape.

1.4 Symmetry and regular shapes

These shapes are regular:

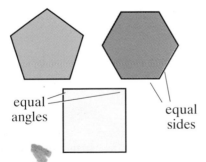

equal
angles

equal
sides

These shapes are not regular:

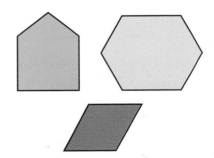

In each shape:
- the sides are equal lengths
- the angles are equal

In each shape the sides and angles
are **not** equal.

■ **A regular shape has equal sides and equal angles.**

Example 2

How many lines of symmetry does
this regular hexagon have?

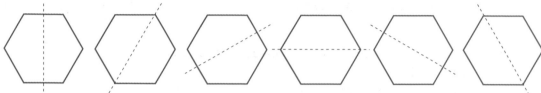

There are 6 lines of symmetry.

■ **A regular shape has the same number of lines of
symmetry as sides.**

Exercise 1C

For each shape:
- Is it regular or not regular?
- How many lines of symmetry has it got?

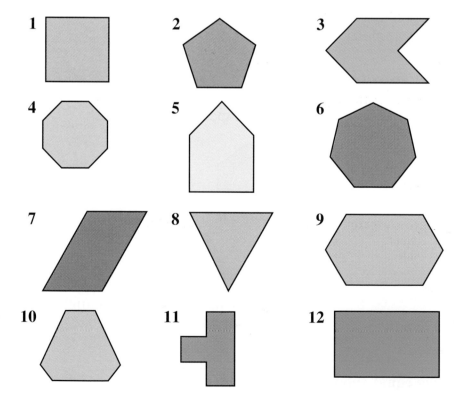

Hint: trace the
shapes into
your book first.

13 Copy and complete the sentences.
The first one has been done for you.

(a) A regular quadrilateral has <u>4</u> equal sides and <u>4</u>
equal angles.
It has 4 lines of symmetry.

(b) A regular hexagon has _____ equal sides and _____
equal angles.
It has 6 lines of symmetry.

(c) A regular pentagon has _____ equal sides and _____
equal angles.
It has _____ lines of symmetry.

(d) A regular triangle has _____ equal sides and _____
equal angles.
It has _____ lines of symmetry.

(e) A regular octagon has   equal sides and _____
equal angles.
It has _____ lines of symmetry.

(f) A regular heptagon has _____ equal sides and _____
equal angles.
It has _____ lines of symmetry.

1.5 Reflecting shapes

You can reflect this shape in a mirror ... to make another shape:

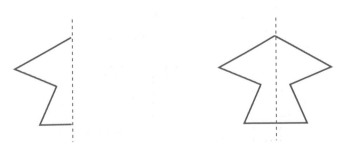

Exercise 1D

Activity You need a mirror. Use it to reflect the shapes below.

What shapes do you make?

Choose your answers from this box.

Triangle	Hexagon	Regular quadrilateral	Regular triangle
Pentagon	Octagon	Regular pentagon	Regular hexagon
Heptagon	Quadrilateral	Regular heptagon	Regular octagon

The first shape is a **quadrilateral**.

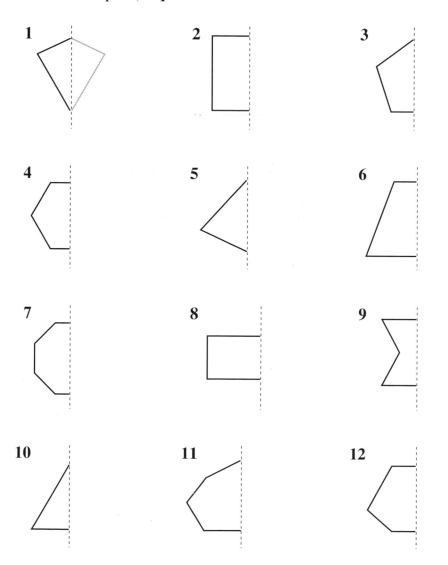

1.6 Symmetry and special triangles

Special triangles have special names:

Equilateral
All sides are equal.

Isosceles
Two sides are equal.

Scalene
No sides are equal.

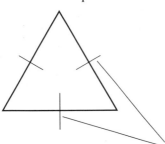

You mark equal sides with a dash.

and special symmetries:

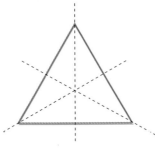

3 lines of symmetry

1 line of symmetry

no lines of symmetry

Exercise 1E

For each triangle write down:

- how many sides are equal
- the name of the triangle
- how many lines of symmetry it has.

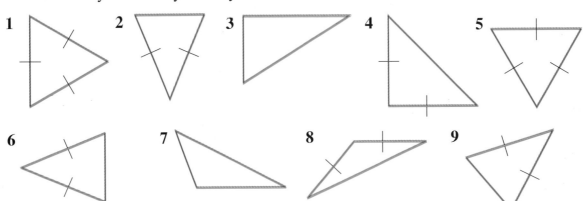

1

2

3

4

5

6

7

8

9

1.7 Symmetry in quadrilaterals

Special quadrilaterals have special names:

Shape:	Properties:	Notes:
Square:	All sides equal. All angles equal.	Angles marked like this: are right angles.
Rectangle:	Opposite sides equal. All angles equal.	
Rhombus:	All sides equal. Opposite angles equal.	You mark equal sides with an equal number of dashes:
Trapezium:	One pair of parallel sides.	Lines that are always the same distance apart are parallel. You mark them with an equal number of arrows:
Parallelogram:	Opposite sides equal and parallel. Opposite angles equal.	
Kite:	Two pairs of adjacent sides are equal.	**Adjacent** just means 'next to'. These sides are adjacent:
Arrowhead:	Two pairs of adjacent sides are equal.	

Exercise 1F

For each shape write down:
- the name of the shape (give the reasons for your answer)
- how many lines of symmetry it has.

The first shape is a parallelogram.
Reason: Opposite sides are equal and parallel.

No lines of symmetry.

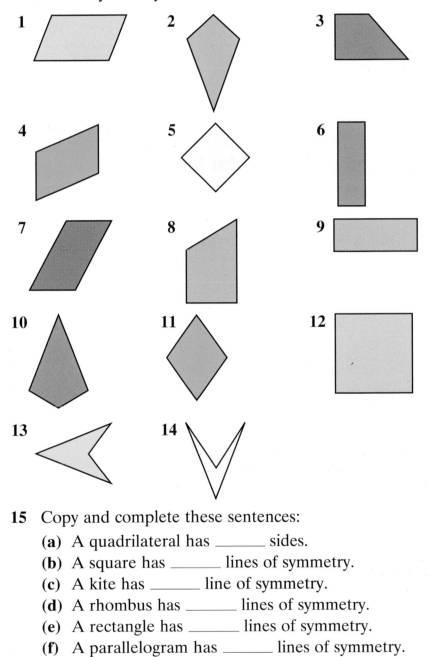

15 Copy and complete these sentences:
(a) A quadrilateral has _____ sides.
(b) A square has _____ lines of symmetry.
(c) A kite has _____ line of symmetry.
(d) A rhombus has _____ lines of symmetry.
(e) A rectangle has _____ lines of symmetry.
(f) A parallelogram has _____ lines of symmetry.

16 Activity Use two equilateral triangles.

- How many different shapes can you make with them?
- Write down the name of any shape you have made.

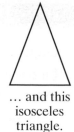

You can trace this equilateral triangle …

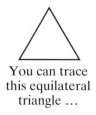

… and this isosceles triangle.

17 Activity Repeat question **16** using:

(a) 3 equilateral triangles **(b)** 4 equilateral triangles
(c) 2 isosceles triangles **(d)** 3 isosceles triangles
(e) 4 isosceles triangles

Make sure that:

The edges line up like this …

… not like this!

No overlapping allowed.

1.8 Drawing parallel and perpendicular lines

Parallel lines are always an equal distance apart. You can draw them with a ruler and set square:

Draw this line …   … slide along   … draw this line

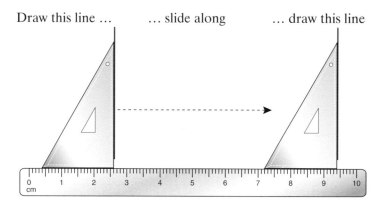

Perpendicular lines are at right angles to each other. You can draw them with a ruler and set square:

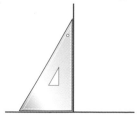

Draw a line with your ruler

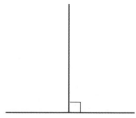

Use a set square to draw the perpendicular

Mark the right angle.

Exercise 1G

1 Draw two lines which meet at a point.
Use a ruler and set square to draw two
more lines to make a parallelogram.

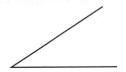

2 Copy the diagram and draw three parallel lines 3 cm apart.

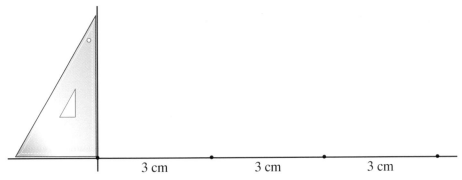

3 cm   3 cm   3 cm

3 Copy the diagram and draw parallel lines from each
point to the opposite side of the triangle.

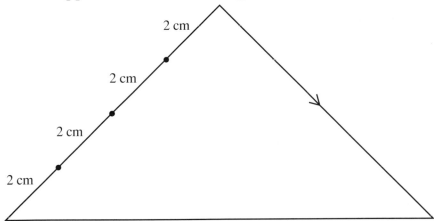

2 cm

2 cm

2 cm

2 cm

4 Use the ruler and set
square method to draw a
4 by 4 grid of rhombuses
with $2\frac{1}{2}$ cm sides.
Do one facing each
way.

5 Use a set square to draw perpendicular
lines from each point to the other line.

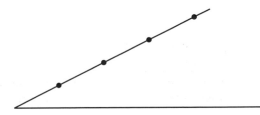

6 Draw a line and label the ends A and B. Draw a line starting at A. Use a set square to draw a perpendicular line that ends at B. Draw several like this:

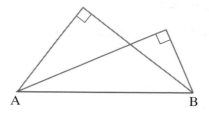

7 Copy this diagram:

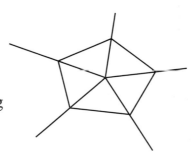

Use the method for drawing parallel lines to draw a 'spiders web'.

1.9 Solid shapes

Here are four types of solid shapes.
You need to be able to recognise them.

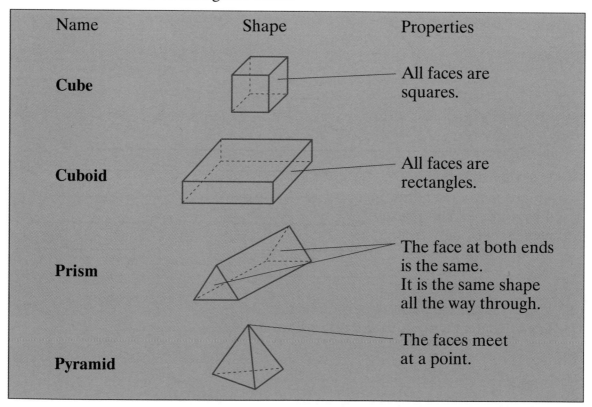

Name	Shape	Properties
Cube		All faces are squares.
Cuboid		All faces are rectangles.
Prism		The face at both ends is the same. It is the same shape all the way through.
Pyramid		The faces meet at a point.

Each part of a shape has a special name:

■ **A face is the flat surface of a solid.**

■ **An edge is the line where two faces meet.**

■ **A vertex is the point where three or more edges meet.**

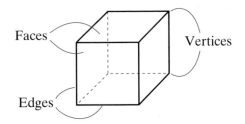

Faces   Vertices

Edges

Vertex is the mathematical name for a corner. The plural is **vertices**.

This cube has:

6 faces, 12 edges and 8 vertices.

Exercise 1H

1 Which of these shapes are:

- cubcs   - cuboids   - prisms   - pyramids?

(a) 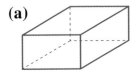   **(b)**   **(c)**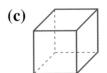

In drawings of 3D shapes, hidden edges and vertices are shown by dotted lines.

(d) 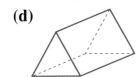   **(e)** 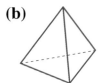   **(f)**

(g) 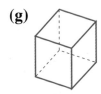   **(h)** 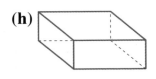   **(i)**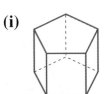

(j) 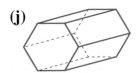   **(k)** 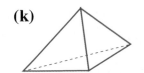   **(l)**

2 For each of these prisms, write down the shape of the end face.

(a) 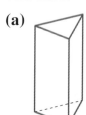 **(b)** 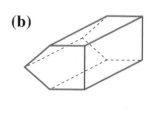 **(c)**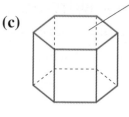

This is the end face

3 For each pyramid, write down the shape of the base.

(a) 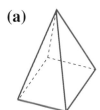 **(b)** 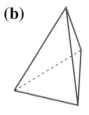 **(c)**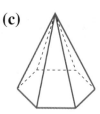

4 Draw a table to show how many faces, edges and vertices the shapes in questions **2** and **3** have.

1.10 Prisms and pyramids

Naming prisms

A prism is the same shape all the way through.

You can cut any prism in two like this:

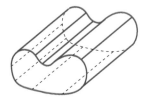  

The middle of a prism looks exactly the same as the end face.
It has a **constant cross section**.

You name a prism by the shape of its cross section.

Triangular prism 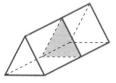 Hexagonal prism 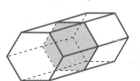 Pentagonal prism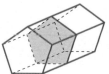

The cross section is a triangle   The cross section is a hexagon   The cross section is a pentagon

Naming pyramids

You name a pyramid by the shape of its base.

Triangular based pyramid   Hexagonal based pyramid   Square based pyramid

The base is a triangle   The base is a hexagon   The base is a square

Exercise 1I

Write down the name of each shape:

1 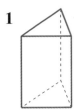   **2** 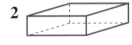   **3**   **4**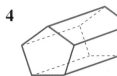

5    **6** 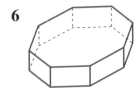   **7**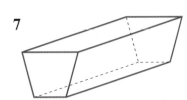

1.11 Plane symmetry

Some solid shapes have symmetry too.

■ **A plane of symmetry cuts a solid shape into two parts that are mirror images of each other.**

This building has plane symmetry.   This car has plane symmetry.   This wedge has plane symmetry.

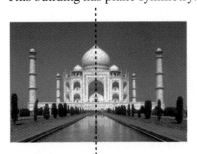      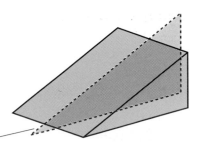

This is the plane of symmetry.

A solid shape can have many planes of symmetry.

Example 3

How many planes of symmetry
does this shape have?

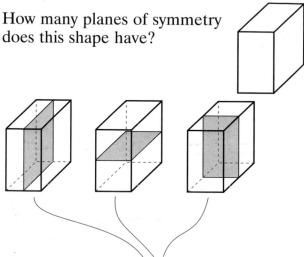

It has 3 planes of symmetry.

Example 4

How many planes of symmetry does this prism have?

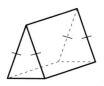

Every prism has this
plane of symmetry......

... but this prism has another
plane of symmetry too.

 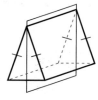

This prism has two planes of symmetry.

Pyramids

If the base has symmetry the pyramid may have plane
symmetry.
It will only have plane symmetry if the top of the pyramid is
above a line of symmetry on the base.

Example 5

How many planes of symmetry does
this square based pyramid have?

The top of the pyramid is over
one corner of the square.

The square has
4 lines of
symmetry:

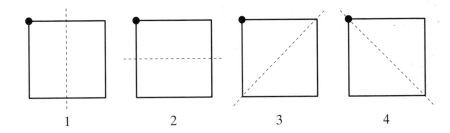

1   2   3   4

Only one line of symmetry passes through the corner.
So the pyramid has 1 plane of symmetry.

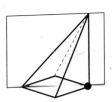

Exercise 1J

1   For each shape, write down the number of planes of
     symmetry it has.

(a)    (b)   (c) 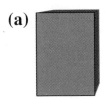   (d)

(e)   (f)   (g)    (h)

2 For each shape, write down:
  - the name of the shape
  - how many planes of symmetry it has.

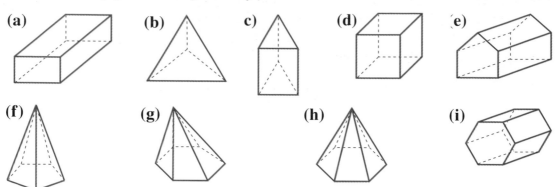

3 How many planes of symmetry does each shape have in Exercise **1I** (on page 17)?

Summary of key points

1

Shape	Name	Hint
	Triangle: 3 sides	**Tri**cycles have 3 wheels. **Tri**plets are 3 babies.
	Quadrilateral: 4 sides	**Quad** bikes have 4 wheels. **Quads** are 4 babies.
	Pentagon: 5 sides	A **penta**thlon has 5 athletic events.
	Hexagon: 6 sides	Six and hexagon both use the letter **x**.
	Heptagon: 7 sides	A **hepta**thlon has 7 athletic events.
	Octagon: 8 sides	An **oct**opus has 8 legs.

2 A shape has symmetry if you can fold it so that one side fits exactly on to the other.
The fold line is the line of symmetry.
The line of symmetry is also called the mirror line.

3 A regular shape has equal sides and equal angles.

4 A regular shape has the same number of lines of symmetry as sides.

5 A face is the flat surface of a solid.

6 An edge is the line where two faces meet.

7 A vertex is the point where three or more edges meet.

8 A plane of symmetry cuts a solid shape into two parts that are mirror images of each other.

2 Understanding numbers

2.1 Digits and place value

Our number system was invented in India over 1400 years ago…

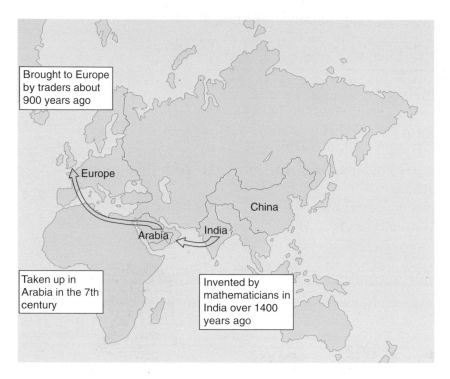

You can use it to make large and small numbers using just ten **digits**:

0 1 2 3 4 5 6 7 8 9

■ **The value of a digit depends on its place in a number.**
You can see this in a place value diagram:

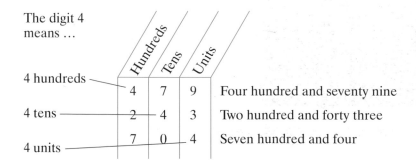

The digit 4 means …

4 hundreds — 4 7 9   Four hundred and seventy nine

4 tens — 2 4 3   Two hundred and forty three

7 0 4   Seven hundred and four

4 units —

■ **82 is a two-digit number because it has two digits.**
704 is a three-digit number because it has three digits.

704 is also called a three-figure number.

Exercise 2A

1 What does the 2 mean in each of these numbers?
   (a) 723 **(b)** 462 **(c)** 291 **(d)** 42 **(e)** 29 **(f)** 206

2 What does the 7 mean in each of these numbers?
   (a) 47 **(b)** 807 **(c)** 79 **(d)** 751 **(e)** 71 **(f)** 597

3 What does the 0 mean in each of these numbers?
   (a) 503 **(b)** 280 **(c)** 204 **(d)** 90 **(e)** 0 **(f)** 601

4 **(a)** These students have each chosen a number from the
   blackboard. Which number has each student chosen?

WHAT'S MY NUMBER?

251   564
   285
4   58   382
   46   406

(b) Choose a number from the blackboard and
describe it.

5 This is a machine for sorting numbers:

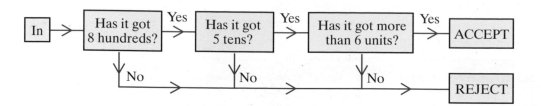

Which of these numbers are accepted and which are rejected?

(a) Eight hundred and fifty nine

(b) Five hundred and eighty nine

(c) Eight hundred and fifty seven

(d) Eight hundred and fifty five

(e) Eight hundred and fifty six

(f) Seven hundred and fifty eight

6 This is another machine for sorting numbers:

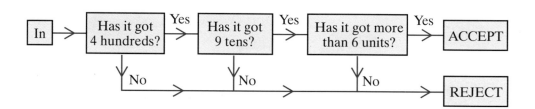

Which three-digit numbers will it accept?

7 Design a number machine to accept only these three-digit numbers

(a) 648, 649   **(b)** 390, 391, 392   **(c)** 867, 877, 887, 897

(d) 873, 973   **(e)** 721, 821, 921   **(f)** 302, 312, 322, 332

8 Design a number machine to accept these three-digit numbers only: 253, 254, 255.

Hint: you will need to ask two questions about the units.

2.2 Reading large numbers

Did you know...

You'll spend over 14 000 hours in school before you leave ...

There are about 690 000 students the same age as you in the UK ...

You'll eat over 28 000 kilograms of food in your lifetime ...

A place value diagram can help you read large numbers:

The digit 5 means ...	Hundred thousands	Ten thousands	Thousands	Hundreds	Tens	Units	
5 thousand			5	0	0	0	Five thousand
50 thousand		5	0	0	0	0	Fifty thousand
500 thousand	5	0	0	0	0	0	Five hundred thousand

You read and write large numbers like this:

67 382 Sixty seven thousand, three hundred and eighty two
324 167 Three hundred and twenty four thousand, one hundred and sixty seven

> A space like this shows you where the thousands end.

Example 1

How many thousands are there in each of these numbers?

(a) 28 394   (b) 407 302   (c) 5 293

(a) 28 thousands   (b) 407 thousands   (c) 5 thousands

Exercise 2B

1 How many thousands are there in each of these numbers?
(a) 7483   (b) 73 803   (c) 39 870   (d) 836 339
(e) 8401   (f) 923 458   (g) 873 994   (h) 47 824

2 How many thousands are there in each of these numbers?
(a) 5089   (b) 50 398   (c) 407 338   (d) 490 704
(e) 120 067   (f) 196 383   (g) 587 934   (h) 196 038

3 What does the 6 mean in each of these numbers?
(a) 26 277   (b) 365 789   (c) 648 925   (d) 960 382
(e) 629 487   (f) 196 383   (g) 69 421   (h) 196 038

4 Write these numbers using digits.
(a) Five thousand two hundred and forty six.
(b) Forty seven thousand three hundred and ninety six.
(c) Three hundred and sixty four thousand nine hundred and fifty six.
(d) Two hundred and five thousand nine hundred and eighty one.
(e) Nine hundred thousand two hundred and fifteen.
(f) Twenty six thousand and thirty eight.

5 This is a number machine for sorting numbers with thousands:

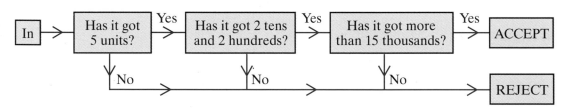

Which of these numbers are accepted and which are rejected by the machine?
(a) 14 225   (b) 31 225   (c) 140 225   (d) 25 252
(e) 280 255   (f) 225 525   (g) 789 225   (h) 15 225

6 Design a number machine to accept these numbers only:
(a) 21 507, 21 508, 21 509
(b) 47 395, 48 395, 49 395
(c) 899 423, 898 423, 897 423

Hint: you will need to ask two questions about the thousands.

2.3 Order, order!

In a lottery six balls are picked.

Then they are sorted in order of size, smallest first.

You can use a number line to help sort numbers into size order.

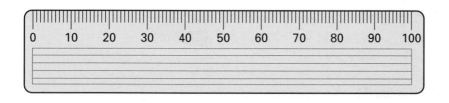

A millimetre ruler makes a good number line.

Example 2

Put the numbers 24, 97, 47, 8, 66 in order of size.
Start with the smallest number.

Find the position of each number on a number line.

So the order is: 8, 24, 47, 66, 97.

Exercise 2C

Put these numbers in size order. Start with the smallest.

1 81, 25, 4, 43	**2** 48, 96, 17, 33	**3** 94, 93, 36, 54
4 24, 38, 56, 15	**5** 50, 0, 49, 100	**6** 26, 14, 11, 84
7 98, 51, 69, 42	**8** 41, 83, 60, 7	**9** 18, 26, 54, 76
10 87, 54, 38, 11	**11** 79, 3, 99, 7	**12** 46, 20, 63, 77

13 Activity You need ten
cards numbered:
0, 1, 2, 3, 4, 5, 6, 7, 8, 9.

Put them in a bag or a
box and pick out two cards.

Can you make a number
less than 50 with your two
cards?

Can you make a number
greater than fifty with
your two cards?

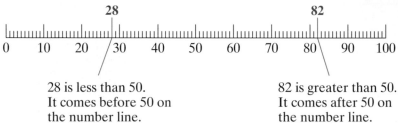

28 is less than 50.
It comes before 50 on
the number line.

82 is greater than 50.
It comes after 50 on
the number line.

Write down your results then put the two cards back in
the bag.

Repeat the experiment until you have done it ten times.

(a) Which pairs of cards can only be used to make
numbers less than 50?

(b) Which pairs of cards can only be used to make
numbers greater than 50?

(c) Which pairs of cards can be used to make one
number less than 50 and one number greater
than 50?

(d) Are there any other possibilities?

14 Activity You need ten cards numbered:
0, 1, 2, 3, 4, 5, 6, 7, 8, 9.

Pick out three cards from the bag.

Make as many different two-digit numbers as you can
with the three cards.

Write them down in order of size, smallest first.

Put the three cards back in the bag.

Repeat the experiment until you have done it five times.

(a) Name three cards that will only make numbers bigger than 50.

(b) Name three cards that will only make numbers smaller than 50.

(c) Name three cards that will only make numbers between 40 and 90.

2.4 Ordering large numbers

To sort large numbers you'd need a huge number line...

Here is another way to put large numbers in order.

Example 3

Put these numbers in order of size, starting with the smallest:

    392   365   589   121   633   583

First sort them using the **hundreds** digits:

Put the smallest first ...   then the next smallest ...   and so on ...

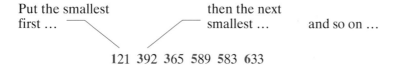

121 392 365 589 583 633

392 and 365 both have 3 hundreds.
Sort them using the **tens** digits.

121 392 365 589 583 633

Put the smallest first ...   then the next smallest ...

121 365 392 589 583 633

589 and 583 both have 5 hundreds and 8 tens.
Sort them using the **units** digits.

121 392 365 589 583 633

Put the smallest first ...   then the next smallest ...

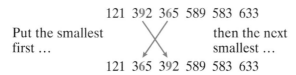

121 365 392 583 589 633

Now the numbers are in size order: 121 365 392 583 589 633.

Exercise 2D

Put each set of numbers in order of size, starting with the smallest.

1 533, 278, 514, 288, 233   **2** 876, 428, 407, 858, 849

65 has 0 hundreds

3 183, 938, 147, 958, 941   **4** 94, 438, 263, 488, 65

5 91, 684, 629, 392, 381   **6** 547, 36, 295, 216, 18

7 257, 838, 469, 472, 829, 437, 238

8 548, 485, 763, 492, 576, 559, 782

9 **Activity** You need ten cards numbered: 0, 1, 2, 3, 4, 5, 6, 7, 8, 9.

Put them in a bag or box and pick out three cards.
Arrange the cards to make the largest three-digit number possible.
Arrange the three cards to make the smallest three-digit number possible.

Write down your results then put the three cards back into the bag. Repeat the experiment until you have done it ten times.

(a) Write a rule to explain how to find the largest three-digit number.

(b) Write a rule to explain how to find the smallest three-digit number.

10 Write down the smallest three-digit number and the largest three-digit number that can be made from each set of cards.

(a) 5 2 9   **(b)** 7 8 3   **(c)** 2 1 7

(d) 4 9 7   **(e)** 4 2 9   **(f)** 1 9 3

(g) 8 4 1   **(h)** 6 7 4   **(i)** 2 4 3

(j) 5 8 7   **(k)** 7 3 7   **(l)** 4 8 0

Remember: you don't write 0 at the front of a number.

11 Write down the second largest three-digit number that can be made with each set of cards.

(a) 4 3 9   (b) 2 9 6   (c) 3 4 0

(d) 3 1 6   (e) 9 8 7   (f) 3 4 5

(g) 7 3 4   (h) 0 8 1   (i) 4 2 7

12 Write down the second smallest three-digit number that can be made with each set of cards.

(a) 5 2 9   (b) 4 8 3   (c) 2 5 1

(d) 4 1 8   (e) 6 7 8   (f) 3 7 6

(g) 8 7 6   (h) 0 9 2   (i) 3 5 7

2.5 Mental maths

The next exercise will help you practise adding and subtracting small numbers in your head.

If you can do these you will be able to add and subtract larger numbers more easily.

 This sign next to an exercise means don't use your calculator!

Exercise 2E

You can use this number line to help you answer the questions:

| 0 | 1 | 2 | 3 | 4 | 5 | 6 | 7 | 8 | 9 | 10 | 11 | 12 | 13 | 14 | 15 | 16 | 17 | 18 | 19 | 20 |

1 Find two numbers next to each other which:

(a) add up to 7   (b) add up to 5   (c) add up to 11
(d) total 9   (e) total 15   (f) add up to 19

2 Find three numbers next to each other which:

(a) add up to 12   (b) total 6   (c) add up to 3
(d) total 15   (e) add up to 9   (f) total 18

3 Find as many pairs of numbers as you can which have a sum of:

(a) 9   (b) 12   (c) 10   (d) 15   (e) 18   (f) 20

4 Find as many pairs as you can which have a difference of:

(a) 5   (b) 8   (c) 16   (d) 20   (e) 1   (f) 10

Remember: sum is another word for the total.

The numbers do not have to be next to each other. For example 19 and 1 make 20.

5   Find as many different ways as you can to fill the square and triangular boxes.

(a) $\square + \triangle = 11$ (b) $2 + \square = \triangle$

(c) $\square - \triangle = 4$ (d) $12 - \square = \triangle$

(e) $\square - 5 = \triangle$ (f) $\square + 7 = \triangle$

(g) $\square + 2 = \triangle + 3$ (h) $20 - \square = 10 + \triangle$

For example:

$\square + \triangle = 11$

$\boxed{4} + \triangle\!\!\!\!/7 = 11$

$\boxed{9} + \triangle\!\!\!\!/2 = 11$

6   Can you make each number from 8 to 20 by adding only threes and fives?

For example:

$11 = 3 + 3 + 5$

7   What numbers can you make by adding twos and threes?

8   Copy or trace this diagram into your book:

Write the numbers

    1, 2, 3, 4, 5, 6, 7, 8, 9

in the circles so that each line of numbers adds up to 15.

Make up your own puzzle like this.

9   This is an arithmogon.
On each side of the triangle the total of the numbers in the circles is shown in the square.

Copy and complete these arithmogons.

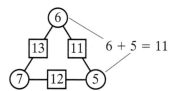

(a)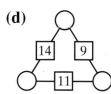

(b)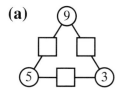

(c)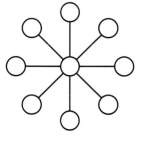

(d)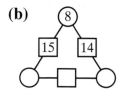

(e)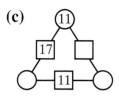

(f)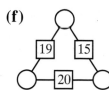

2.6 Mental maths with tens

Mental maths is easier if you can add and subtract 10 quickly.

◼ **When you add 10 the units digit stays the same:**

$$8 + 10 = 18 \qquad \text{or} \qquad \begin{array}{r} 10 \\ 8 + \\ \hline 18 \end{array}$$

◼ **When you subtract 10 from a larger number the units digit stays the same:**

$$37 - 10 = 27 \qquad \text{or} \qquad \begin{array}{r} 37 \\ 10 - \\ \hline 27 \end{array}$$

Exercise 2F

1   **Activity**   You need a calculator to do this question.

> Enter 9 on your calculator.
> Add 10 and keep on adding 10.
>
> **(a)** What do you notice about the way the answers change?
> **(b)** Does it make any difference if you start by entering 19?

> Enter 9 on your calculator.
> Add 20 and keep adding 20.
>
> **(c)** What do you notice about the way the answers change?
> **(d)** Does it make any difference if you start by entering 19?

> Enter 9 on your calculator.
> Add 30 and keep on adding 30.
>
> **(e)** What do you notice about the way the answers change?
> **(f)** Does it make any difference if you start by entering 19?

Do the rest of this exercise mentally.
Do not use a calculator.

2 (a) $26 + 10$ (b) $45 + 10$ (c) $32 - 10$
    (d) $54 - 10$ (e) $87 + 10$ (f) $94 - 10$
    (g) $24 + 20$ (h) $47 + 20$ (i) $54 + 20$
    (j) $35 - 20$ (k) $82 - 20$ (l) $77 - 20$
    (m) $16 + 30$ (n) $32 + 30$ (o) $74 - 30$
    (p) $46 - 30$ (q) $54 + 30$ (r) $94 - 30$

3 (a) $22 + 40$ (b) $34 + 50$ (c) $29 + 70$
    (d) $74 - 40$ (e) $86 - 50$ (f) $98 - 70$
    (g) $15 + 80$ (h) $68 - 50$ (i) $23 + 60$
    (j) $51 + 40$ (k) $79 - 50$ (l) $88 - 60$

4 (a) $14 + 10 + 20$ (b) $47 + 10 + 20$ (c) $33 + 30 + 20$
    (d) $42 + 30 + 10$ (e) $15 + 30 + 40$ (f) $27 + 40 + 20$
    (g) $18 + 40 + 30$ (h) $39 + 30 + 30$

5 (a) $95 \quad 10 \quad 20$ (b) $89 - 10 - 20$
    (c) $67 - 30 - 20$ (d) $76 - 30 - 10$
    (e) $56 - 20 - 30$ (f) $87 - 40 - 30$
    (g) $99 - 40 - 40$ (h) $91 - 50 - 40$

6 (a) $23 + 40 - 10$ (b) $35 + 60 - 20$
    (c) $64 - 30 + 20$ (d) $48 + 50 - 30$
    (e) $62 - 20 + 30$ (f) $41 + 40 - 60$
    (g) $64 - 40 + 10$ (h) $67 - 50 + 80$

7 Pick a number from each cloud and add them together.

How many different answers can you make by doing this?

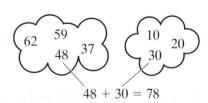

$48 + 30 = 78$

8 Pick a number from each cloud.

Add the first two numbers then subtract the third number.

How many different numbers can you make by doing this?

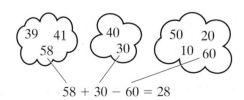

$58 + 30 - 60 = 28$

2.7 Mental maths methods

Here are some easy ways to do mental calculations by adding or subtracting 10:

Two ways to add 9 and 12

$9 + 12 =$

12 is 10 + 2

$9 + 10 + 2$

$19 \quad + 2 = 21$

So $9 + 12 = 21$

$12 + 9 =$

9 is 10 − 1

$12 + 10 - 1$

$22 \quad - 1 = 21$

So $9 + 12 = 21$

Two ways to subtract 11 from 19

$19 - 11$

11 is 10 + 1

To subtract 11, first subtract 10, then subtract 1.

$19 - 10 - 1 = 8$

So $\quad 19 - 11 = 8$

$19 - 11$

11 is 10 + 1

To subtract 11, first subtract 1, then subtract 10.

$19 - 1 - 10 = 8$

So $\quad 19 - 11 = 8$

To remember these methods just remember two examples:

■ **To add 9, first add 10, then subtract 1**

■ **To subtract 11, first subtract 10, then subtract 1**

Exercise 2G

Work these out mentally:

1 $17 + 9$	**2** $25 - 11$	**3** $16 + 8$	**4** $19 - 9$
5 $22 + 9$	**6** $32 - 11$	**7** $29 - 12$	**8** $43 + 8$

9 $51 - 9$ **10** $49 + 8$ **11** $27 + 9$ **12** $40 - 11$

13 $73 - 9$ **14** $26 + 8$ **15** $43 - 8$ **16** $17 - 8$

Copy and complete these sentences:

17 To add 8 you add 10 then take away ___ .

18 To take away 8 you take away ___ then add ___ .

19 To subtract 9 you subtract ___ then add ___ .

20 To subtract 12 you subtract ___ then subtract ___ .

2.8 Mental maths: adding two-digit numbers

■ **You can make adding easier by breaking up numbers.**

Here are two ways to add 31 and 27:

$31 + 27 =$

27 is 20 + 7

$31 + 20 + 7$

$51 \quad + 7 = 58$

So 31 + 27 = 58

$31 + 27 =$

$31 + 7 + 20$

$38 \quad + 20 = 58$

So 31 + 27 = 58

Exercise 2H

You should do this exercise mentally.
Do not use a calculator.

1 **(a)** $34 + 23$ **(b)** $25 + 23$ **(c)** $37 + 21$ **(d)** $31 + 25$
  (e) $46 + 33$ **(f)** $25 + 72$ **(g)** $32 + 55$ **(h)** $76 + 21$
  (i) $37 + 12$ **(j)** $24 + 73$ **(k)** $67 + 22$ **(l)** $26 + 51$

Hint: it might be easier to think of this as $72 + 25$.

2 **(a)** $38 + 24$ **(b)** $49 + 25$ **(c)** $48 + 36$ **(d)** $68 + 23$
  (e) $37 + 55$ **(f)** $28 + 43$ **(g)** $42 + 29$ **(h)** $37 + 23$
  (i) $54 + 36$ **(j)** $29 + 53$ **(k)** $44 + 28$ **(l)** $36 + 36$

3 Activity   You need ten cards numbered:
0, 1, 2, 3, 4, 5, 6, 7, 8, 9.

Put them in a bag or box and pick out four cards.

Arrange the four cards to make two two-digit numbers.

Add them together.

$$\boxed{5}\,\boxed{7} + \boxed{3}\,\boxed{2} = 89$$

Rearrange the cards to make two more
two-digit numbers and add them together.

$$\boxed{3}\,\boxed{7} + \boxed{2}\,\boxed{5} = 62$$

(a) How many different pairs of two-digit
numbers can you make?

(b) How many different totals do you get?

(c) Which arrangement gives the biggest total?

(d) Which arrangement gives the smallest total?

Hint: try to find a
system for writing
down all the pairs of
2-digit numbers

4 Put the cards back in the bag and repeat question **3**.

5 Activity You need a 100 square.

Draw a rectangle on a 100 number square.

Add the numbers in opposite corners of the
rectangle like this:

Do this for other rectangles.

What do you notice?

Explain any pattern you notice.

12 + 35

1	2	3	4	5	6	7	8	9	10
11	12	13	14	15	16	17	18	19	20
21	22	23	24	25	26	27	28	29	30
31	32	33	34	35	36	37	38	39	40
41	42	43	44	45	46	47	48	49	50

32 + 15

2.9 Mental addition: adding a 2-digit to a 3-digit number

If you can add 31 to 27 then you can add 431 to 27.

Here are two ways to add 431 and 27:

431 + 27

431 + 20 + 7

451   + 7 = 458

So 431 + 27 = 458

431 + 27 =

431 + 7 + 20

438   + 20 = 458

So 431 + 27 = 458

Exercise 2I

You should do this exercise mentally.

1 **(a)** $123 + 25$ **(b)** $146 + 32$ **(c)** $263 + 25$ **(d)** $326 + 32$
    (e) $542 + 57$ **(f)** $354 + 23$ **(g)** $613 + 84$ **(h)** $432 + 42$
    (i) $746 + 31$ **(j)** $957 + 32$ **(k)** $823 + 76$ **(l)** $468 + 21$

2 **(a)** $148 + 24$ **(b)** $239 + 45$ **(c)** $127 + 35$ **(d)** $268 + 26$
    (e) $436 + 58$ **(f)** $564 + 27$ **(g)** $319 + 64$ **(h)** $623 + 69$
    (i) $425 + 16$ **(j)** $741 + 39$ **(k)** $867 + 28$ **(l)** $842 + 48$

3 **(a)** $258 + 34$ **(b)** $436 + 27$ **(c)** $347 + 45$ **(d)** $529 + 64$
    (e) $464 + 73$ **(f)** $635 + 81$ **(g)** $853 + 74$ **(h)** $826 + 92$
    (i) $682 + 69$ **(j)** $574 + 48$ **(k)** $748 + 65$ **(l)** $894 + 27$

2.10 Mental maths: subtracting 2-digit numbers

■ **You can make subtracting easier by breaking up numbers.**

Here are three ways to subtract 28 from 65:

$$65 - 28$$

$$65 - 20 - 8$$

$$45 \quad - 8 = 37$$

So $65 - 28 = 37$

$$65 - 28$$

$$65 - 8 - 20$$

$$57 \quad - 20 = 37$$

So $65 - 28 = 37$

Start at 28 and count on to 65:

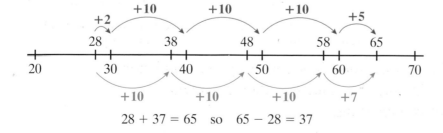

$$28 + 37 = 65 \quad \text{so} \quad 65 - 28 = 37$$

Exercise 2J

Do this exercise mentally. Do not use a calculator.

1 **(a)** 34 − 13   **(b)** 45 − 12   **(c)** 37 − 14   **(d)** 68 − 24
   (e) 53 − 21   **(f)** 78 − 25   **(g)** 64 − 31   **(h)** 86 − 42
   (i) 96 − 52   **(j)** 89 − 63   **(k)** 48 − 31   **(l)** 93 − 71

2 **(a)** 34 − 15   **(b)** 43 − 24   **(c)** 36 − 17   **(d)** 54 − 26
   (e) 44 − 18   **(f)** 67 − 39   **(g)** 56 − 28   **(h)** 63 − 35
   (i) 84 − 57   **(j)** 93 − 47   **(k)** 75 − 27   **(l)** 88 − 59

3 These pupils have each chosen a pair of two-digit numbers from the whiteboard.

Remember: the difference means the largest number take away the smallest number. The difference between 28 and 53 is 53 − 28 = 25

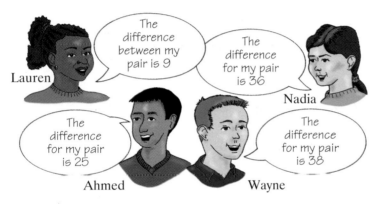

The difference between my pair is 9 — Lauren

The difference for my pair is 36 — Nadia

The difference for my pair is 25 — Ahmed

The difference for my pair is 38 — Wayne

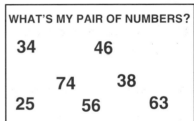

WHAT'S MY PAIR OF NUMBERS?

34   46

74   38

25   56   63

Which pair of numbers has each pupil chosen?

4 Activity

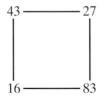

Choose any four two-digit numbers and write them at the four corners of a square.

```
43 ——— 27
 |         |
 |         |
16 ——— 83
```

Work out the difference between the numbers on each edge of the square and write the difference at the middle of that edge.

```
43 — 16 — 27
 |  /    \  |
27         57
 |  \    /  |
16 — 68 — 84
```

Join the four new numbers to make a square.

Work out the difference between the numbers at the ends of each edge of the new square and write the difference at the middle of that edge

```
43 — 16 — 27
 |  11—41  |
27 |    | 57
 |  41—11  |
16 — 68 — 84
```

Join the four new numbers to make a square.

(a) Continue this process until it is obvious you should stop.

(b) Repeat **(a)** using another four two-digit numbers.

(c) Explain what is happening.

(d) Try choosing three two-digit numbers and writing them at the corners of a triangle.

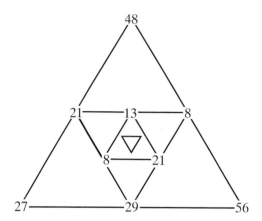

5 Start with 100.

Move along the arrows from start to finish, subtracting the numbers shown on the arrows as you go.

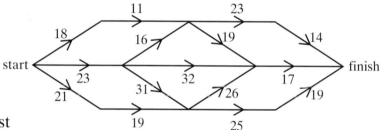

(a) What is the smallest number you can finish with?

(b) What is the largest number you can finish with?

2.11 Subtracting a 2-digit from a 3-digit number

If you can subtract 28 from 65 then you can subtract 28 from 465.

$465 - 28$

$465 - 20 - 8$

$445 \quad - 8 = 437$

So $465 - 28 = 437$

$465 - 28 =$

$465 - 8 - 20$

$457 \quad - 20 = 437$

So $465 - 28 = 437$

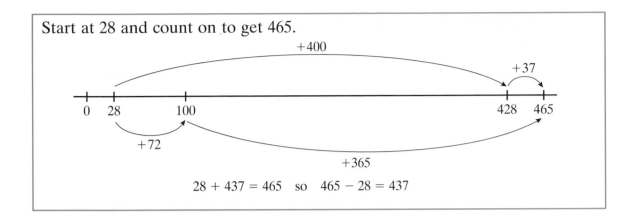

Start at 28 and count on to get 465.

$28 + 437 = 465$ so $465 - 28 = 437$

Exercise 2K

1 (a) $147 - 35$ (b) $158 - 26$ (c) $256 - 43$ (d) $467 - 35$
(e) $425 - 13$ (f) $384 - 23$ (g) $582 - 51$ (h) $649 - 17$
(i) $796 - 54$ (j) $984 - 63$ (k) $878 - 53$ (l) $465 - 53$

2 (a) $254 - 26$ (b) $181 - 64$ (c) $253 - 24$ (d) $372 - 45$
(e) $595 - 67$ (f) $467 - 38$ (g) $458 - 39$ (h) $645 - 17$
(i) $736 - 18$ (j) $874 - 36$ (k) $986 - 48$ (l) $847 - 29$

3 (a) $245 - 61$ (b) $328 - 53$ (c) $463 - 82$ (d) $354 - 92$
(e) $652 - 71$ (f) $543 - 62$ (g) $435 - 43$ (h) $785 - 94$
(i) $942 - 64$ (j) $824 - 36$ (k) $635 - 67$ (l) $723 - 79$

Hint: You might find it best to do question **3** by the number line method.

2.12 Using mental maths to solve problems

You can use mental maths to solve everyday problems.

First decide whether to add or subtract to solve the problem.

These words usually mean you **add**:

total, **sum**, **altogether**, **plus**

These words and phrases usually mean you **subtract**:

minus, **take away**, **less**
How many more?
How much change?
What is the difference between...?

Example 4

Paul bought a bar of chocolate for 38p and a packet of chewing gum for 45p.

How much change did he get from a £1 coin?

The total cost was $38 + 45 = 83p$

The change was $£1 - 83p = 100p - 83p = 17p$.

Exercise 2L

1 In a class of children there are 17 girls and 15 boys.

What is the total number of children in the class?

> **Class 7B**
> Girls 17
> Boys 15
> Total ...

2 Two classes of children went on a trip together.
There were 34 children from one class and 29 children from the other class.
How many children went on the trip?

3 98 children from a school went on a half day visit.
47 children went in the morning.
How many went in the afternoon?

4 A water tank holds 72 litres when full.
There are 44 litres of water in the tank.
How many more litres of water can be put into the tank?

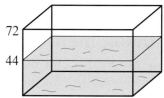

5 Zoe buys a drink for 48p and a bar of chocolate for 36p.

  (a) What is the total cost?

  (b) What change should she get if she pays with a £1 coin?

6 An electricity pylon is 33 metres tall.
A church tower is 25 metres tall.
How much taller is the pylon than the tower?

7   In a pond there are 28 mirror carp and 65 koi carp.

(a) What is the total number of carp in the pond?

(b) How many more koi carp than mirror carp are there?

8   In a class of 32 children, 18 have school dinner and the rest bring packed lunches.
How many children bring packed lunches?

Class 8C
School dinner   18
Packed lunches ...
Total   32

9   In a darts match Morag scored 54 and 18 with her first two darts. After her third dart she had scored a total of 96.
What did she score with her third dart?

10   A computer shop had software for sale at these prices.
Marco bought three items of software for a total cost of £90.
Find all the possible costs of the three items Marco bought.

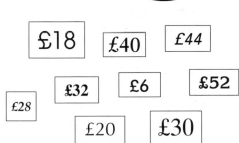

£18   £40   £44

£28   £32   £6   £52

£20   £30

11   Jerry bought a coat for £247 and a pair of trousers for £56.
How much did she pay in total?

12   Gerard drove 83 miles from Exeter to Bristol and 232 miles from Bristol to Hull.
How far did he drive altogether?

13   Jerry bought a pair of shoes for £76 and a jacket.
The total cost was £154.
How much did the jacket cost?

14   Gerard drove 93 miles from Hull to Nottingham.
He then drove from Nottingham to Glasgow.
If the total journey was 379 miles, how far is it from Nottingham to Glasgow?

2.13 Greater or less than?

A computer game costs £37
Stan and Iris each want to buy the game.

Look at this number line:

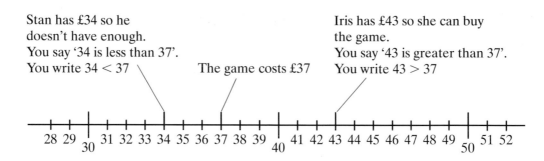

Stan has £34 so he
doesn't have enough.
You say '34 is less than 37'.
You write $34 < 37$

The game costs £37

Iris has £43 so she can buy
the game.
You say '43 is greater than 37'.
You write $43 > 37$

Example 5

Put < or > in the box to make
this statement true:

$$23 + 46 \ \square \ 70$$

$23 + 46 = 69$

69 is to the **left** of 70 on the
number line so 69 is **less** than 70:

$$23 + 46 \ < \ 70$$

Example 6

Choose a digit from the cloud
to make the statement true:

$\square \, 8 > 36$

78 is to the **right** of 36 on the
number line so 78 is **greater** than 36

28 is to the **left** of 36 on the
number line so 28 is **less** than 36:

$$78 \ > \ 36$$

■ **< means 'less than'.
The numbers < 4 are 0, 1, 2, 3**

■ **> means 'greater than'.
The numbers > 4 are 5, 6, 7, 8, . . . and so on**

Exercise 2M

1 Put > or < in each box to make each statement true.

   (a) $34 + 23 \ \square \ 50$ **(b)** $16 + 23 \ \square \ 48$ **(c)** $24 + 37 \ \square \ 72$

   (d) $43 + 38 \ \square \ 79$ **(e)** $58 - 23 \ \square \ 28$ **(f)** $76 - 42 \ \square \ 39$

2 True or false?

(a) $23 + 36 > 50$ (b) $43 + 25 < 82$

(c) $87 - 26 < 54$ (d) $68 - 23 > 40$

(e) $56 + 19 < 70$ (f) $37 + 54 > 85$

(g) $46 - 17 < 33$ (h) $82 - 26 > 58$

3 Choose a digit from the cloud to make the statement true:

(a)  $\square 3 < 52$

(b)  $\square 5 < 34$

(c) 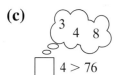 $\square 4 > 76$

(d) 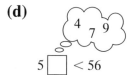 $5 \square < 56$

(e)  $57 < \square 3$

(f) 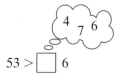 $53 > \square 6$

4 Fill the boxes from the clouds to make statements that are true.

$\square \square$ $\square$ $\square \square$

For example

$65 < 74$

In a fairground game Stan throws one dart at this board. He must score 3 or less to win.

You use the symbol $\leqslant$ to show 'less than or equal to':

3	4	4	4	4	4	3
4	2	5	5	5	2	4
4	5	1	6	1	5	4
4	5	6	0	6	5	4
4	5	1	6	1	5	4
4	2	5	5	5	2	4
3	4	4	4	4	4	3

■ $\leqslant$ **means less than or equal to.**
The numbers $\leqslant 3$ are **0, 1, 2, 3**

■ $\geqslant$ **means greater than or equal to.**
The numbers $\geqslant 3$ are **3, 4, 5, 6, 7, ... and so on.**

Example 7

What sets of numbers are described by:

(a) numbers $\leqslant 7$ (b) numbers $\geqslant 5$

(a) 0, 1, 2, 3, 4, 5, 6, 7   (b) 5, 6, 7, 8, ...

Example 8

Use ≤ or ≥ to describe each set of numbers:

(a) 0, 1, 2, 3, 4   **(b)** 2, 3, 4, 5, . . .

(a) numbers ≤ 4   **(b)** numbers ≥ 2

Example 9

Which numbers from the cloud make the statement true:

(a)   **(b)**

3 9 6   7 9 5
17 2 10   3 8 12

☐ ≤ 6   ☐ ≥ 8

Answer: 2, 3, 6   Answer: 8, 9, 12

Exercise 2N

1   Which set of numbers is described by:

    (a) numbers ≤ 9   **(b)** numbers ≥ 4

    (c) numbers ≥ 7   **(d)** numbers ≤ 8

    (e) numbers ≤ 10   **(f)** numbers ≥ 6

    (g) numbers ≥ 0   **(h)** numbers ≤ 11

2   Use ≤ or ≥ to describe each set of numbers.

    (a) 0, 1, 2   **(b)** 9, 10, 11, 12, . . .

    (c) 0, 1, 2, 3, 4, 5   **(d)** 10, 11, 12, 13, . . .

    (e) 0, 1, 2, 3, 4, 5, 6   **(f)** 0, 1

    (g) 14, 15, 16, 17, . . .   **(h)** 100, 101, 102, 103, . . .

3   Which numbers from the cloud make the statement true:

    (a)   **(b)**   **(c)**

9 3   8 4   6 5 14
2 11 8   2 6 0   11 20
       7

☐ ≤ 8   ☐ ≥ 6   ☐ ≤ 11

    (d)   **(e)**   **(f)**

8 12 0   19 2 5   5 4 2
13 5 10   13 15 11   8 0

☐ ≤ 10   ☐ ≥ 13   ☐ ≥ 4

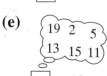

2.14 To the nearest . . .

There are 71 sweets in the jar.

Debra guessed too low but Haidar guessed too high.
Whose guess was the nearest?

Find the difference between each guess and the actual number of sweets:

Debra   Haidar

Debra	Actual	Haidar
58	71	83

71 − 58 = 13   83 − 71 = 12

12 is less than 13 so Haidar's guess was nearest.

Exercise 2O

1   Work out whose guess is the nearest in each case:

   (a) Haidar 58   **(b)** Haidar 37   **(c)** Haidar 34
       Debra 35   Debra 66   Debra 78
       Actual number 46   Actual number 48   Actual number 53

   (d) Haidar 86   **(e)** Haidar 29   **(f)** Haidar 38
       Debra 65   Debra 43   Debra 75
       Actual number 74   Actual number 35   Actual number 56

   (g) Haidar 87   **(h)** Haidar 49
       Debra 64   Debra 76
       Actual number 75   Actual number 62

2   Stan and Iris were asked to guess the distance from Birmingham of some cities. Work out whose guess was nearest for each city.

   (a) Bristol: **(b) Nottingham:**
      Stan 98   Stan 38
      Iris 79   Iris 73

   (c) Oxford: **(d) Shrewsbury:**
      Stan 84   Stan 74
      Iris 49   Iris 23

City	Distance from Birmingham in miles
Bristol	88
Nottingham	54
Oxford	68
Shrewsbury	48

3 In a TV quiz game three contestants each guessed the price of these items.
Whose guess was nearest for each item?

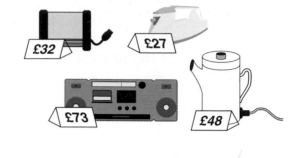

(a) **Radio:**
Jay £58
Milan £64
Dipak £86

(b) **Toaster:**
Jay £24
Milan £54
Dipak £43

(c) **Iron:**
Jay £16
Milan £46
Dipak £34

(d) **Kettle:**
Jay £84
Milan £32
Dipak £53

2.15 Adding numbers on paper

You can add large numbers together on paper.
Sometimes it's easier than adding them in your head.

Line up the units. Use headings to help you.	Add the units together. $4 + 5 = 9$	Now add the tens. $2 + 6 = 8$	Add the hundreds. $1 + 3 = 4$
H T U 1 2 4 +3 6 5	H T U 1 2 4 +3 6 5 9	H T U 1 2 4 +3 6 5 8 9	H T U 1 2 4 +3 6 5 4 8 9

Example 10

Add 35 and 48.

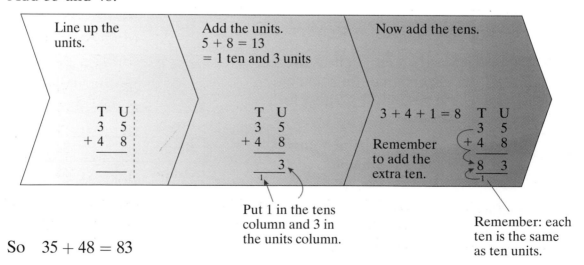

Line up the units.	Add the units. $5 + 8 = 13$ = 1 ten and 3 units	Now add the tens.
T U 3 5 +4 8	T U 3 5 +4 8 3 1	$3 + 4 + 1 = 8$ T U 3 5 Remember to add the extra ten. +4 8 8 3 1

Put 1 in the tens column and 3 in the units column.

Remember: each ten is the same as ten units.

So $35 + 48 = 83$

You can check your answer on a number line.

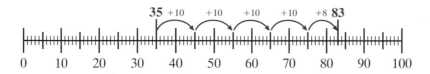

Example 11

Add 28, 17 and 36.

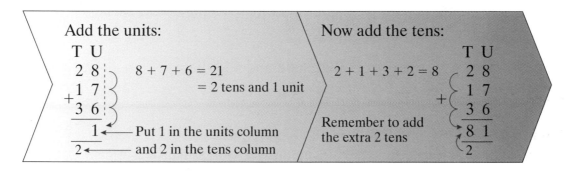

Exercise 2P

Work out:

1   **(a)**   38 + 25   **(b)**   46 + 18   **(c)**   52 + 36   **(d)**   35 + 23
    (e)   49 + 28   **(f)**   33 + 28   **(g)**   73 + 24   **(h)**   64 + 29
    (i)   43 + 27   **(j)**   62 + 28   **(k)**   46 + 46   **(l)**   69 + 29

2   **(a)**   54 + 23   **(b)**   45 + 38   **(c)**   56 + 39   **(d)**   27 + 54
    (e)   32 + 49   **(f)**   43 + 27   **(g)**   26 + 67   **(h)**   38 + 48
    (i)   38 + 38   **(j)**   22 + 47   **(k)**   37 + 27   **(l)**   59 + 24

3   **(a)**   35 + 26 + 23   **(b)**   34 + 37 + 25   **(c)**   27 + 34 + 28   **(d)**   37 + 29 + 28
    (e)   29 + 28 + 36   **(f)**   46 + 28 + 16   **(g)**   39 + 25 + 28   **(h)**   17 + 28 + 37

4   **(a)**   85 + 54   **(b)**   76 + 49   **(c)**   64 + 83   **(d)**   91 + 38
    (e)   87 + 68   **(f)**   55 + 79   **(g)**   89 + 89   **(h)**   67 + 75
    (i)   73 + 67   **(j)**   48 + 52   **(k)**   86 + 95   **(l)**   56 + 49

5   **(a)**   46 + 43 + 34   **(b)**   53 + 65 + 34   **(c)**   36 + 81 + 57   **(d)**   48 + 37 + 39
    (e)   28 + 69 + 36   **(f)**   73 + 80 + 84   **(g)**   89 + 86 + 78   **(h)**   88 + 94 + 79

6   **(a)**   259 + 134   **(b)**   407 + 285   **(c)**   658 + 183   **(d)**   758 + 681
    (e)   679 + 583   **(f)**   398 + 843   **(g)**   564 + 487   **(h)**   672 + 428
    (i)   837 + 163   **(j)**   987 + 689

7 **(a)** $642 + 25$ **(b)** $368 + 24$ **(c)** $49 + 374$

     (d) $465 + 78$ **(e)** $67 + 206$ **(f)** $535 + 85$

     (g) $724 + 79$ **(h)** $563 + 37$ **(i)** $59 + 684$

     (j) $96 + 748$

> Remember to line up the units first.

8 You can use the digits 2, 3, 4 and 5 to make a pair of two-digit numbers that add up to 77.
Using the same digits find other pairs of two-digit numbers that add up to 77.

$$\begin{array}{r} 45 \\ +32 \\ \hline 77 \end{array}$$

9 Using only the digits 3, 4, 5 and 6 find pairs of two-digit numbers that add up to 99.

10 Pick a pair of numbers from this cloud and add them together.

     (a) What is the largest answer you can get?

     (b) What is the smallest answer you can get?

     (c) Which pair of numbers gives an answer closest to 100?

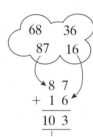

11 Repeat question **10** for each of these clouds.

     (a) 49   53   74   29   **(b)** 38   58   48   69   **(c)** 88   38   17   69   **(d)** 36   63   68   42

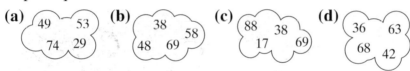

12 Copy and complete these additions:

(a)
$$\begin{array}{r} 5\,\square \\ +\,\square\,5 \\ \hline 7\ 8 \end{array}$$
(b)
$$\begin{array}{r} 3\,\square \\ +\,\square\,2 \\ \hline 8\ 8 \end{array}$$
(c)
$$\begin{array}{r} 4\,\square \\ +\,\square\,7 \\ \hline 8\ 2 \end{array}$$
(d)
$$\begin{array}{r} 2\,\square \\ +\,\square\,4 \\ \hline 6\ 3 \end{array}$$
(e)
$$\begin{array}{r} 8\,\square \\ +\,\square\,2 \\ \hline 9\ 6 \end{array}$$

(f)
$$\begin{array}{r} 2\ 1 \\ 4\,\square \\ +\,\square\,7 \\ \hline 9\ 6 \end{array}$$
(g)
$$\begin{array}{r} \square\,7 \\ 3\,\square \\ +\,1\ 8 \\ \hline 8\ 1 \end{array}$$
(h)
$$\begin{array}{r} 2\ 6 \\ 1\,\square \\ +\,\square\,8 \\ \hline 9\ 3 \end{array}$$
(i)
$$\begin{array}{r} 3\,\square \\ \square\,7 \\ +\,1\ 9 \\ \hline 8\ 4 \end{array}$$
(j)
$$\begin{array}{r} 1\,\square \\ 3\ 5 \\ +\,\square\,4 \\ \hline 9\ 5 \end{array}$$

(k)
$$\begin{array}{r} 3\,\square \\ \square\,2 \\ +\,6\ 3 \\ \hline 1\ 7\ 9 \end{array}$$
(l)
$$\begin{array}{r} \square\,8 \\ 6\ 3 \\ +\,2\,\square \\ \hline 1\ 3\ 7 \end{array}$$
(m)
$$\begin{array}{r} 9\,\square \\ 7\ 2 \\ +\,\square\,5 \\ \hline 2\ 5\ 3 \end{array}$$
(n)
$$\begin{array}{r} \square\,9 \\ 8\,\square \\ +\,3\ 5 \\ \hline \square\,7\ 1 \end{array}$$
(o)
$$\begin{array}{r} 8\ 6 \\ 4\,\square \\ +\,\square\,8 \\ \hline \square\,1\ 3 \end{array}$$

13 Choose any three-digit number.
Reverse the digits.
Add the two numbers together.

$$\begin{array}{r} 528 \\ +825 \\ \hline 1353 \\ {\scriptstyle 1\ \ 1} \end{array}$$

Reverse the digits of the answer.
Add the two numbers.

$$\begin{array}{r} 1353 \\ +3531 \\ \hline 4884 \end{array}$$

4884 is called a palindromic number.
A palindromic number stays the same when you reverse its digits.

Try this for each of these three-digit numbers.

(a) 427 **(b)** 635 **(c)** 834 **(d)** 264 —— Keep reversing the digits and adding until you get a palindromic number.

(e) Try other three-digit numbers.

Do you always get a palindromic number eventually?

2.16 Subtracting numbers on paper

You can subtract two numbers on paper like this:

To find $289 - 153$ first line up the units:

$$\begin{array}{r} \text{H T U} \\ 2\ \ 8\ \ 9 \\ -\ 1\ \ 5\ \ 3 \\ \hline \end{array}$$

Subtract the units:
$9 - 3 = 6$

$$\begin{array}{r} \text{H T U} \\ 2\ \ 8\ \ 9 \\ -\ 1\ \ 5\ \ 3 \\ \hline 6 \end{array}$$

Subtract the tens:
$8 - 5 = 3$

$$\begin{array}{r} \text{H T U} \\ 2\ \ 8\ \ 9 \\ -\ 1\ \ 5\ \ 3 \\ \hline 3\ \ 6 \end{array}$$

Subtract the hundreds:
$2 - 1 = 1$

$$\begin{array}{r} \text{H T U} \\ 2\ \ 8\ \ 9 \\ -\ 1\ \ 5\ \ 3 \\ \hline 1\ \ 3\ \ 6 \end{array}$$

Example 12

Find $172 - 58$

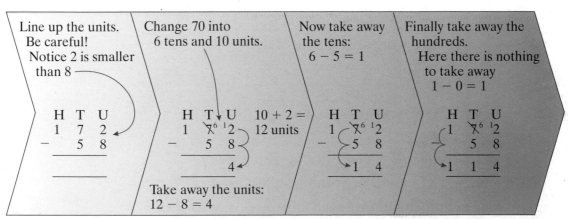

Line up the units.
Be careful!
Notice 2 is smaller than 8

$$\begin{array}{r} \text{H T U} \\ 1\ \ 7\ \ 2 \\ -\ \ \ 5\ \ 8 \\ \hline \end{array}$$

Change 70 into 6 tens and 10 units.

$$\begin{array}{r} \text{H T U} \\ 1\ \ {}^6\!\!\!\!\diagup7\ {}^1\!2 \\ -\ \ \ 5\ \ 8 \\ \hline 4 \end{array}$$
$10 + 2 = 12$ units

Take away the units:
$12 - 8 = 4$

Now take away the tens:
$6 - 5 = 1$

$$\begin{array}{r} \text{H T U} \\ 1\ \ {}^6\!\!\!\!\diagup7\ {}^1\!2 \\ -\ \ \ 5\ \ 8 \\ \hline 1\ \ 4 \end{array}$$

Finally take away the hundreds.
Here there is nothing to take away
$1 - 0 = 1$

$$\begin{array}{r} \text{H T U} \\ 1\ \ {}^6\!\!\!\!\diagup7\ {}^1\!2 \\ -\ \ \ 5\ \ 8 \\ \hline 1\ \ 1\ \ 4 \end{array}$$

Exercise 2Q

1 (a) 85 − 23   (b) 54 − 31   (c) 67 − 46   (d) 38 − 23
   (e) 96 − 21   (f) 47 − 37   (g) 59 − 54   (h) 78 − 48
   (i) 96 − 14   (j) 77 − 25   (k) 48 − 36   (l) 59 − 23

2 (a) 64 − 27   (b) 43 − 29   (c) 56 − 27   (d) 36 − 19
   (e) 80 − 47   (f) 61 − 28   (g) 53 − 45   (h) 90 − 38
   (i) 57 − 38   (j) 70 − 28   (k) 48 − 19   (l) 91 − 25

3 (a) 687 − 543   (b) 496 − 132   (c) 584 − 230   (d) 769 − 345
   (e) 947 − 207   (f) 856 − 653   (g) 478 − 278   (h) 574 − 532
   (i) 769 − 719   (j) 685 − 681   (k) 357 − 351   (l) 113 − 101

4 (a) 546 − 127   (b) 864 − 328   (c) 750 − 416   (d) 457 − 208
   (e) 675 − 467   (f) 947 − 362   (g) 854 − 671   (h) 605 − 294
   (i) 748 − 656   (j) 537 − 492   (k) 537 − 238   (l) 852 − 357
   (m) 645 − 269   (n) 543 − 465   (o) 767 − 689

5 (a) 684 − 23   (b) 567 − 32   (c) 483 − 53   (d) 494 − 60
   (e) 539 − 31   (f) 486 − 28   (g) 563 − 37   (h) 743 − 38
   (i) 646 − 62   (j) 534 − 71   (k) 845 − 75   (l) 736 − 62
   (m) 428 − 59   (n) 942 − 78   (o) 356 − 89

6 Pick a pair of numbers, one from each cloud, and find the difference.

   (a) Which pair gives the largest answer?
   (b) Which pair gives the smallest answer?
   (c) Which pair gives the answer closest to 400?

7 Repeat question **6** for this pair of clouds.

8 Put the digits 4, 5, 6, 7 and 8 in the boxes of this take-away sum and work out the answer.

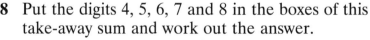

   (a) Which arrangement gives the biggest answer?
   (b) Which arrangement gives the smallest answer?
   (c) Which arrangement gives the answer closest to 500?

9 Take any two-digit number
Reverse the digits to make another two-digit number.

Find the difference between the two numbers.

Do the same for the answer,

and again.

$$\begin{array}{r} 36 \\ 63 \end{array}$$

$$\begin{array}{r} 63 \\ -36 \\ \hline 27 \end{array}$$

$$\begin{array}{r} {}^{6}\!\!\not{7}{}^{1}2 \\ -27 \\ \hline 45 \end{array}$$

$$\begin{array}{r} {}^{4}\!\!\not{5}{}^{1}4 \\ -45 \\ \hline 9 \end{array}$$

Try this for other two-digit numbers.
Do you always get the answer 9 eventually?
Does the same happen for three-digit numbers?

2.17 Rounding to the nearest 10

Kath, Ted and Edna are selling programmes for their school fete.

To find an approximate total they all round their numbers to the nearest 10.

I've sold 74 programmes

I've sold 75 programmes

I've sold 79 programmes

Kath

Ted

Edna

■ **To round to the nearest 10:**
Look at the digit in the units column.
If it is less than 5 round down.
If it is 5 or more round up.

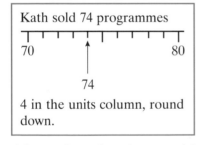

Kath sold 74 programmes
70 ——————— 80
74
4 in the units column, round down.

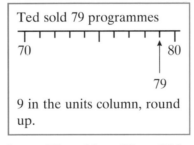

Ted sold 79 programmes
70 ——————— 80
79
9 in the units column, round up.

Edna sold 75 programmes
70 ——————— 80
75
5 in the units column, round up.

Altogether they have sold about $70 + 80 + 80 = 230$ programmes.

Example 13

Find an approximate answer for $76 + 63$.

$$\begin{array}{ll} \text{76 rounds to} & 80 \\ \text{63 rounds to} & \underline{60} + \\ & 140 \end{array}$$

So $76 + 63$ is approximately 140.

Example 14

Ken sold 80 tickets to the school play, rounded to the nearest 10.

How many tickets might he actually have sold?

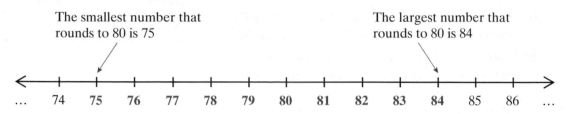

The smallest number that rounds to 80 is 75

The largest number that rounds to 80 is 84

... 74 75 76 77 78 79 80 81 82 83 84 85 86 ...

So Ken could have sold between 75 and 84 tickets inclusive.

'Between 75 and 84 inclusive' means you include 75 and 84.

Exercise 2R

1 Round each of these numbers to the nearest 10.
   (a) 39   (b) 12   (c) 43   (d) 45   (e) 73   (f) 87
   (g) 86   (h) 41   (i) 25   (j) 99   (k) 18   (l) 97

2 Approximate each of these numbers to the nearest 10.
   (a) 138   (b) 452   (c) 783   (d) 235
   (e) 851   (f) 788   (g) 598   (h) 603
   (i) 794   (j) 896   (k) 247   (l) 795

   Hint:
   Round to ...
   Approximate to ...
   Write correct to ...
   all mean the same thing.

3 Write each of these numbers to the nearest 10.
   (a) 1249   (b) 7651   (c) 3487   (d) 4695   (e) 7396   (f) 6997
   (g) 4998   (h) 13 473   (i) 18 635   (j) 19 797   (k) 32 996   (l) 49 997

4 Round each number to the nearest 10 then add or subtract to get an approximate answer.
   (a) 54 + 76   (b) 39 + 85   (c) 96 − 28   (d) 82 − 39
   (e) 94 + 65 + 49   (f) 79 + 68 − 38   (g) 117 + 79 + 83   (h) 297 + 69 − 88

5 Kath, Ted and Edna have been selling programmes again. They each rounded the number of programmes they sold to the nearest ten.
   How many programmes could each have actually sold?

I've sold about 50 programmes

I've sold about 70 programmes

I've sold about 100 programmes

Kath

Edna

Ted

6 This table shows how many calories are in 100 grams of different types of fish, rounded to the nearest 10.

Fish	Calories
Plaice	90
Mackerel	190
Salmon	200
Tuna	120

  (a) How many calories could each actually have?

  (b) Haddock has 96 calories per 100 grams. How would this be written in the table?

  (c) Cod has 94 calories per 100 grams. How would this be written in the table?

7 The distance from Münich to Köln is 580 km to the nearest 10 km.

  (a) What is the least distance it could actually be?

  (b) What is the greatest distance it could actually be?

2.18 Rounding to the nearest 100 and 1000

Alyson, Carolyn and Peter have been rasing money for their youth club.

To find an approximate total they each rounded their amounts to the nearest £100.

Alyson   Carolyn   Peter

- **To round to the nearest 100:**
  Look at the digit in the tens column.
  If it is less than 5 round down.
  If it is 5 or more round up.

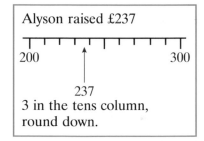

Alyson raised £237

200   300

237
3 in the tens column, round down.

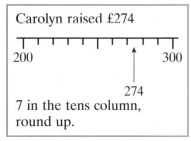

Carolyn raised £274

200   300

274
7 in the tens column, round up.

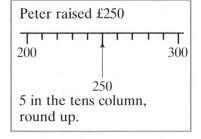

Peter raised £250

200   300

250
5 in the tens column, round up.

Altogether they raised about £200 + £300 + £300 = £800.

Similarly:

- **To round to the nearest 1000:**
  Look at the digit in the hundreds column.
  If it is less than 5 round down.
  If it is 5 or more round up.

Example 15

Find an approximate answer to $674 + 827 + 350$.
Round each number to the nearest 100 then add.

$$
\begin{array}{lr}
674 \text{ rounds up to} & 700 \\
827 \text{ rounds down to} & 800 \\
350 \text{ rounds up to} & \underline{400} + \\
& 1900
\end{array}
$$

So $674 + 827 + 350$ is about 1900.

Example 16

Find an approximate answer to $5823 + 7504 - 6087$
Round each number to the nearest 1000 then add.
Split the calculation into two stages:

$$
\begin{array}{lr}
5823 \text{ rounds up to} & 6000 \\
7504 \text{ rounds up to} & \underline{8000} + \\
& 14\,000
\end{array}
\qquad
\begin{array}{lr}
\text{Answer to first stage} & 14\,000 \\
6087 \text{ rounds down to} & \underline{6000} - \\
& 8000
\end{array}
$$

So $5823 + 7504 - 6087$ is about 8000.

Example 17

There are 3700 different species of cockroaches in the
world, rounded to the nearest 100. How many different
species might there actually be?

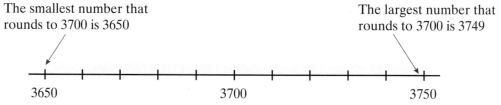

The smallest number that
rounds to 3700 is 3650

The largest number that
rounds to 3700 is 3749

3650   3700   3750

So there are between 3650 and 3749 species of cockroach
in the world.

Exercise 2S

1   Round each of these numbers to the nearest 100.

   (a) 463   (b) 381   (c) 648   (d) 752
   (e) 87   (f) 709   (g) 1437   (h) 2374
   (i) 3482   (j) 2974   (k) 4952   (l) 9983

2 Round each number to the nearest 100, then add or
subtract to find an approximate answer to the
calculation.

(a) $572 + 137$ (b) $258 + 396$ (c) $847 - 583$
(d) $750 - 254$ (e) $748 + 862$ (f) $983 - 314$
(g) $817 - 582$ (h) $809 - 294$ (i) $793 - 243$
(j) $1928 - 493$ (k) $3251 - 905$ (l) $2963 - 572$

3 Write each of these numbers to the nearest 1000.

(a) 4832   (b) 8643   (c) 7378   (d) 8052
(e) 3541   (f) 13 640   (g) 41 502   (h) 202 814
(i) 9724   (j) 842   (k) 489   (l) 99 630

4 Round each number to the nearest 1000, then add or
subtract to find an approximate answer to these
calculations.

(a) $7178 - 2813$ (b) $8921 - 3295$
(c) $7510 + 2043$ (d) $9388 + 2501$
(e) $8279 + 4520$ (f) $8734 + 916 - 2534$
(g) $5068 + 8514 - 6813$ (h) $9365 + 2544 - 4187$
(i) $15 396 - 2911$ (j) $17 289 + 7512$
(k) $36 813 - 13 486$ (l) $29 723 + 6142$

5 Alan, Concie and Bill have been collecting signatures
on a petition. They each rounded their numbers to the
nearest 100. How many signatures might each have
collected?

I've collected about 500

I've collected about 700

I've collected about 2000

Alan

Concie

Bill

6 The table shows the number of species
in some different families of birds.
Write each number rounded to the
nearest 100.

Family	Species
Cuckoo	128
Thrush	305
Warblers	350
Kingfishers	87

7 The table shows the distance from London to some foreign cities rounded to the nearest 1000.

   (a) What is the least distance each city might be from London?

   (b) What is the greatest distance each city might be from London?

City	Distance from London in miles
Cairo	2000
Mexico City	6000
Nairobi	4000
Sidney	11 000

8 The table shows the areas in km² of some American states.

   (a) Write the area of each state rounded to the nearest 100 km^2.

   (b) Write the area of each state rounded to the nearest 1000 km^2.

State	Area in km^2
Massachusetts	8284
New Hampshire	9279
New Jersey	7787
Hawaii	6471
Vermont	9614

2.19 Checking answers by estimating

Omar used his calculator to add $853 + 627 + 2350$
Has he got the right answer?

Round each number to the nearest hundred.

853 rounds up to	900
627 rounds down to	600
2350 rounds up to	2400 +
	3900

The answer is about 3900 so Omar has got the answer wrong.

■ **You can check to see if a calculator answer is correct by rounding to get an approximate answer.**

Rounding to get an approximate answer is called **estimating**.

Example 18

Which number in the cloud is the correct answer to $672 + 247$

672 rounds to	700
247 rounds to	200 +
	900

919
    719
519   1519

So 919 must be the correct answer.

Exercise 2T

1 Which number in the cloud is the correct answer?

(a) 578 + 237

315
815   615
1015

(b) 917 − 482

435
235   735
635

(c) 918 + 654

982   1352
1192   1572

(d) 874 − 519

355   565
785   1305

(e) 891 − 357

734
234
534   914

(f) 376 + 248

424   624
724   934

2 Use rounding to help you see which calculator shows the correct answer.

(a) 7731 − 1213

Calculator 6518 C
Calculator 3418
Calculator 5418
A   B

(b) 8399 + 3527

Calculator 14426
Calculator 11926 C
Calculator 9126
A   B

(c) 10 513 + 7824

Calculator 18337
Calculator 15237 C
Calculator 13237
A   B

(d) 32 591 + 7041

Calculator 45632
Calculator 42532 C
Calculator 39632
A   B

(e) 8936 − 683

Calculator 3253
Calculator 5453 C
Calculator 8253
A   B

(f) 7218 + 869

Calculator 8087
Calculator 6487 C
Calculator 16087
A   B

Summary of key points

1 The value of a digit depends on its place in a number. You can see this in a place value diagram:

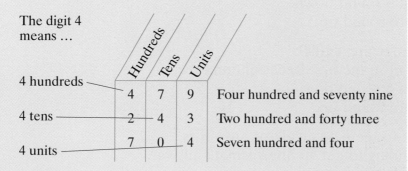

The digit 4 means …

	Hundreds	Tens	Units	
4 hundreds	4	7	9	Four hundred and seventy nine
4 tens	2	4	3	Two hundred and forty three
4 units	7	0	4	Seven hundred and four

2   82 is a two-digit number because it has two digits.
704 is a three-digit number because it has three digits.

704 is also called a three-figure number.

3   When you add 10 the units digit stays the same:

$$8 + 10 = 18 \qquad \text{or} \qquad \begin{array}{r} 10 \\ 8\,+ \\ \hline 18 \end{array}$$

When you subtract 10 from a larger number the units digit stays the same:

$$37 - 10 = 27 \qquad \text{or} \qquad \begin{array}{r} 37 \\ 10\,- \\ \hline 27 \end{array}$$

4   To add 9, first add 10, then subtract 1
To subtract 11, first subtract 10, then subtract 1

5   You can make adding easier by breaking up numbers.

6   You can make subtracting easier by breaking up numbers.

7   < means 'less than'.
The numbers < 4 are 0, 1, 2, 3.

> means 'greater than'.
The numbers > 4 are 5, 6, 7, ... and so on.

8   To round to the nearest 10:
Look at the digit in the units column.
If it is less than 5 round down.
If it is 5 or more round up.

9   To round to the nearest 100:
Look at the digit in the tens column.
If it is less than 5 round down.
If it is 5 or more round up.

10   To round to the nearest 1000:
Look at the digit in the hundreds column.
If it is less than 5 round down.
If it is 5 or more round up.

11   You can check to see if a calculator answer is correct by rounding to get an approximate answer.

3 Number patterns

People have been fascinated by number patterns for centuries.

You will explore some number patterns in this unit.

This altar in China has nine circles, each with a multiple of nine stones.
The ancient Chinese believed that using nine's brought them closer to Heaven.

3.1 Patterns from matchsticks

Here are the first four shapes in a matchstick pattern:

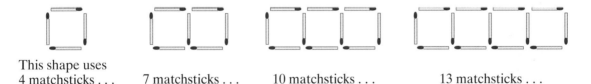

This shape uses 4 matchsticks . . .   7 matchsticks . . .   10 matchsticks . . .   13 matchsticks . . .

Using numbers the pattern is:

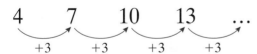

The rule to go from one shape to the next is '**add 3**'.

Exercise 3A

Copy the matchstick patterns on the next page.
For each pattern:

- draw the next two shapes
- write down the pattern using numbers
- write down the rule to go from one shape to the next.

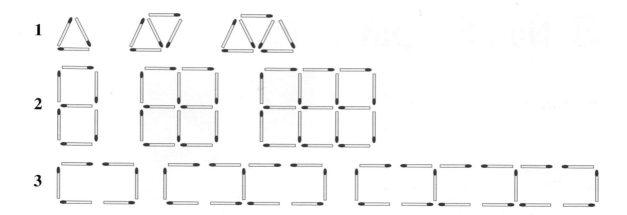

1

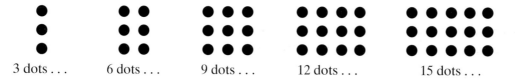

2

3

3.2 Dot patterns

Here are the first five shapes in a dot pattern:

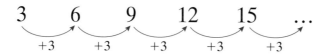

3 dots . . .   6 dots . . .   9 dots . . .   12 dots . . .   15 dots . . .

Using numbers the pattern is:

$$3 \quad 6 \quad 9 \quad 12 \quad 15 \quad \ldots$$
$$+3 \quad +3 \quad +3 \quad +3 \quad +3$$

The rule to go from one shape to the next is '**add 3**'.

Exercise 3B

1 Copy the dot patterns below.
   For each pattern:

   • write down the pattern using numbers
   • write down the rule to go from one shape to the next.

   (a)

   (b)

(c)

(d)

(e)

(f)

2 Draw dots to show these number patterns.
Write down what you notice about them.

   (a) 2, 4, 6, 8, 10

   (b) 0, 5, 10, 15, 20

   (c) 2, 5, 8, 11, 14

   (d) 3, 7, 11, 15, 19

   (e) 1, 7, 13, 19, 25

3.3 Number machines

■ **You can use number machines to make number patterns.**

Here is a number machine for multiplying by 3:

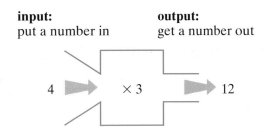

input:
put a number in

output:
get a number out

4    $\times 3$ 12

If you put a number pattern into a number machine, the
output numbers will make a pattern too.

Example 1

(a) Input the number pattern 1, 2, 3, 4, 5, and 6 into this machine:

(b) List the output numbers.

(c) Describe the pattern.

(a)

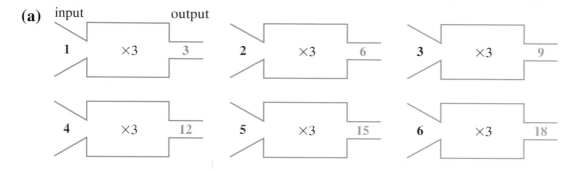

or:

Write your results in a table like this:

×3

input		output
1	×3	3
2	×3	6
3	×3	9
4	×3	12
5	×3	15
6	×3	18

Notice that you can see the pattern if you shade the output numbers on a 100 square. The pattern continues...

(b) The output numbers are 3, 6, 9, 12, 15 and 18.

(c) The pattern is: the output numbers go up in threes.

1	2	3	4	5	6	7	8	9	10
11	12	13	14	15	16	17	18	19	20
21	22	23	24	25	26	27	28	29	30
31	32	33	34	35	36	37	38	39	40
41	42	43	44	45	46	47	48	49	50
51	52	53	54	55	56	57	58	59	60
61	62	63	64	65	66	67	68	69	70
71	72	73	74	75	76	77	78	79	80
81	82	83	84	85	86	87	88	89	90
91	92	93	94	95	96	97	98	99	100

Exercise 3C

For each question:

(a) Input the number pattern 1, 2, 3, 4, 5, 6.

(b) List the output numbers.

(c) Describe the pattern.

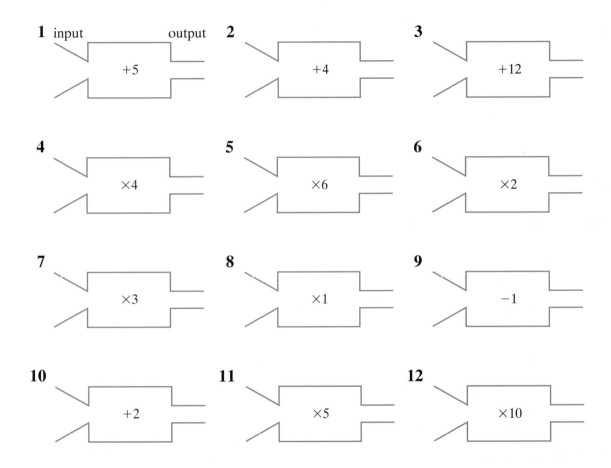

1 input   output   +5

2   +4

3   +12

4   ×4

5   ×6

6   ×2

7   ×3

8   ×1

9   −1

10   +2

11   ×5

12   ×10

3.4 Sequences

Another name for a number pattern is a **sequence**.

■   **A sequence is a number pattern.**
    The numbers are usually written in a row like this:

      2, 4, 6, 8, 10, . . .

              The dots show the sequence goes on forever.

Example 2

(a) Describe this sequence of numbers in words:

1, 4, 7, 10, 13, 16, . . .

(b) Find the next two numbers in the sequence.

(a) The numbers go up in threes. So the sequence is:
Start at 1 and keep adding on 3.

(b) To find the next two numbers you add on three

$$16 + 3 = 19$$
$$19 + 3 = 22$$

The next two numbers are 19 and 22.

Example 3

(a) Find the next number in the sequence:

12, 10, 8, 6, 4, . . .

(b) Write down the rule for finding the next number.

(a) The numbers go down by 2 each time, so you subtract 2 to find the next number:

$$4 - 2 = 2.$$

The next number is 2.

(b) The rule is: subtract 2.

Exercise 3D

For each sequence:
(a) Write down the next two numbers.
(b) Write down the rule for finding the next number.

1 1, 3, 5, 7, 9, . . . , . . .   **2** 0, 3, 6, 9, 12, . . . , . . .

3 0, 5, 10, 15, . . . , . . .   **4** 1, 4, 7, 10, 13, . . . , . . .

5 4, 8, 12, 16, 20, . . . , . . .   **6** 10, 20, 30, 40, . . . , . . .

7 2, 6, 10, 14, . . . , . . .   **8** 0, 7, 14, 21, 28, . . . , . . .

9 9, 18, 27, 36, . . . , . . .   **10** 20, 18, 16, 14, 12, . . . , . . .

11 18, 15, 12, 9, . . . , . . .   **12** 25, 20, 15, 10, . . . , . . .

13 70, 60, 50, 40, . . . , . . .   **14** 20, 17, 14, 11, . . . , . . .

15 8, 7, 6, 5, 4, . . . , . . .   **16** 23, 19, 15, 11, . . . , . . .

17 80, 75, 70, 65, . . . , . . .   **18** 54, 45, 36, 27, . . . , . . .

Example 4

Find the missing numbers in these sequences:

(a) 32, 28, 24, __, __, 12, __

(b) 3, 6, 12, __, __, 96

(a) 32,   28,   24,   **20**,   **16**,   12,   **8**

-4 -4 -4 -4 -4 -4

The rule connecting the numbers is **subtract 4**.

(b) 3,   6   12,   **24**,   **48**,   96

$\times 2$ $\times 2$ $\times 2$ $\times 2$ $\times 2$

The rule connecting the numbers is **multiply by 2**.

Exercise 3E

Find the missing numbers in these sequences:

1 1, 3, 9, __, __, 243, __

2 64, 59, 54, __, __, 39, __

3 108, 96, 84, __, __, 48, __

4 7, 14, 21, __, __, 42, __, 56

5 0, 10, 20, __, __, 50, __

6 38, 34, 30, __, __, 18, __

7 1, 2, 4, __, __, 32

8 90, 80, 70, __, __, 40, __

9 3, 7, 11, __, __, 23, __, __

3.5 Two step number machines

This is a two step number machine.

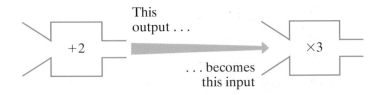

Example 5

For this two step number machine,
find the output if the input is 5.

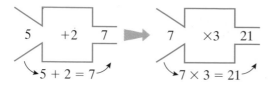

5 +2 7 → 7 ×3 21
5 + 2 = 7 · 7 × 3 = 21   The output is 21.

You can also make patterns with two step machines.

Example 6

(a) Input the number pattern 1, 2, 3, 4 and 5
in this machine.

(b) Show your results in a table.

(c) Describe the pattern of output numbers.

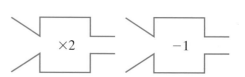

(a)

input 1: **1** ×2 2 → 2 −1 1
1 × 2 = 2   2 − 1 = 1

input 2: **2** ×2 4 → 4 −1 3
2 × 2 = 4   4 − 1 = 3

input 3: **3** × 2 = 6 → 6 − 1 = 5
input 4: **4** × 2 = 8 → 8 − 1 = 7
input 5: **5** × 2 = 10 → 10 − 1 = 9

(b) ×2 → −1

input	output
1	1
2	3
3	5
4	7
5	9

(c) The pattern is: the output numbers go up in twos.
The output numbers are the odd numbers.

■ **In a two step number machine the output from the first
machine becomes the input for the second machine.**

Exercise 3F

1 Write down the output numbers for these two step machines.

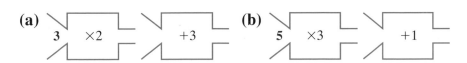

(a) 3 ×2 +3   (b) 5 ×3 +1

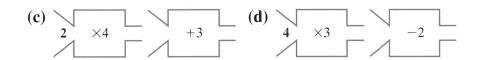

(c) 2 ×4 +3   (d) 4 ×3 −2

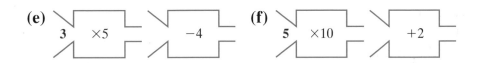

(e) 3 ×5 −4   (f) 5 ×10 +2

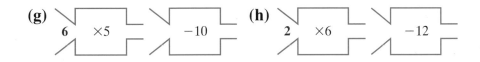

(g) 6 ×5 −10   (h) 2 ×6 −12

2 For each two step number machine:
- Input the numbers 1, 2, 3, 4, 5, 6.
- Show your results in a table.
- Describe the pattern of output numbers.

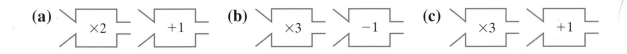

(a) ×2 +1   (b) ×3 −1   (c) ×3 +1

(d) ×5 −2   (e) ×4 −1   (f) ×2 +3

(g) ×5 +1   (h) ×10 −5   (i) ×5 −4

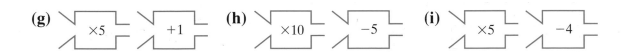

3 Use the numbers 2, 3, 5, 7, 11 in the two step machines in question **2**. Show your results in a table.

3.6 Finding any number in a sequence

Each number in a sequence is called a **term**:

2   4   6   8   ...   ...

the **first term**,   the **third term**,   an unknown number in
or term number 1   or term number 3   a sequence is called
                                            the *nth* term or term
                                            number *n*

There is more
about using letters
like *n* to represent
numbers on
page 179.

To find the 30th term in the sequence you could:

... just keep adding 2:

2   4   6 ...
  +2   +2

This is rather boring!

... OR notice this pattern:

2   4   6 ...
)×2)×2)×2
1   2   3

The rule to find any term is:
multiply the term number by 2

■   **You can write a rule to find any term in a
      sequence from its term number.**

The rule to find
any term in a
sequence is called
the *nth* term rule.

Example 7

Find the *n*th term rule for this sequence: 5, 10, 15, 20, 25, ...
Use your rule to find the 20th term.

Write the sequence and term numbers in a table:

Term number	1	2	3	4	5	
	)×5	)×5	)×5	)×5	)×5	
Sequence	5	10	15	20	25	...

The *n*th term rule is: **multiply the term number by 5.**
The **20th** term is: $20 \times 5 = 100$

Example 8

Find the *n*th term rule for this sequence: 0, 2, 4, 6, 8, . . .

Use your rule to find the 15th term.

Write the sequence next to the term numbers in a table:

Term number	1	2	3	4	5
Sequence	0	2	4	6	8 ...

The rule for finding the *next* term is **add 2 each time**.

+2

Try different number machines to find the rule:

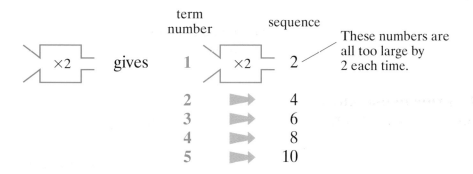

These numbers are all too large by 2 each time.

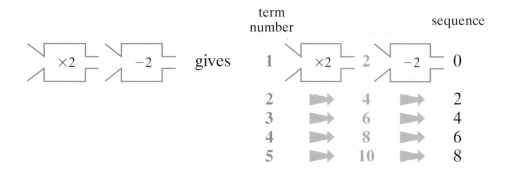

The *n*th term rule is: **multiply the term number by two, then subtract 2.**

The **15th** term is: $(15 \times 2) - 2 = 28$

There is more about calculations involving brackets on page 226.

Exercise 3G

1 For each of these sequences:
- write down the nth term rule
- use the rule to find the 20th term.

  (a) 11, 22, 33, 44, 55, 66, ...
  (b) 12, 23, 34, 45, 56, 67, ... ——————Hint: what should you add to part **(a)**?
  (c) 3, 6, 9, 12, 15, 18, ...
  (d) 5, 8, 11, 14, 17, 20, ... ——————Hint: compare with part **(c)** ...
  (e) 5.5, 9.5, 13.5, 17.5, 21.5, ...

2 Use these nth term rules to find the first 10 terms in each sequence:

  (a) multiply 3 by the term number, then subtract 2
  (b) multiply 7 by the term number, then add 3
  (c) multiply 6 by the term number, then subtract 3
  (d) divide the term number by 2
  (e) multiply the term number by itself

3 Jane's laser printer has smudged this sequence:

  ▓ 12, 16, ▓, 24, ▓ 32

  Find:

  (a) the nth term rule for the sequence
  (b) the three missing terms
  (c) the 20th term

4 The 5th term of a mystery sequence is 7. Find the nth term rule when:

  (a) the first term is 3
  (b) the first term is -1
  (c) the first term is -5

5 Two terms in this sequence are incorrect:

  5, 12, 17, 24, 29, 35

  Write down:

  (a) the correct sequence
  (b) the nth term term rule
  (c) the 20th term

3.7 Some special number patterns

Here are three number patterns you need to be able to recognize:

Square numbers

This dot pattern shows some **square numbers**:

$1 \times 1 = 1$ $2 \times 2 = 4$ $3 \times 3 = 9$ $4 \times 4 = 16$

You can see how to use your calculator for square numbers on page 350.

■ **A square number is the result of multiplying a number by itself.**

Triangular numbers

This dot pattern shows some **triangular numbers**:

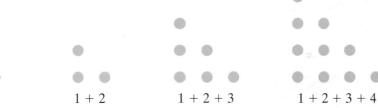

1          $1 + 2$ $1 + 2 + 3$ $1 + 2 + 3 + 4$

Fibonacci sequences

These numbers form a **Fibonacci sequence**:

  1, 1, 2, 3, 5, 8, 13...

Here is how to make the sequence:

The sizes of the diamonds on this pineapple's surface are linked by the Fibonacci sequence.

These two numbers start the sequence.

1   1   2   3   5   8   13   ...   1   1   2   3   5   8   13   ...

Add the first two numbers . . .

Add the next two numbers . . .   . . . and so on

Exercise 3H

1 From this list of numbers:
   9, 6, 8, 1, 3, 13, 2
   write down:
   (a) the square numbers **(b)** the triangular numbers
   (c) the Fibonacci numbers

2 Write down:
   (a) the fourth square number **(b)** the fifth Fibonacci number
   (c) the sixth square number **(d)** the seventh triangular number
   (e) the eighth Fibonacci number

Summary of key points

1 You can use number machines to make number
   patterns.
   Here is a number machine for multiplying by 3:

   input: **output:**
   put a number in   get a number out

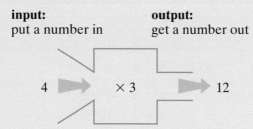

2 A sequence is a number pattern.
   The numbers are usually written in a row like this:
       2, 4, 6, 8, 10, . . .

   The dots show the sequence goes
   on forever.

3 In a two step number machine the output from the
   first machine becomes the input for the second
   machine:

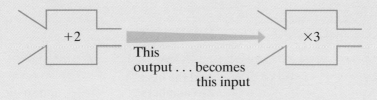

   This
   output . . . becomes
           this input

4 You can write a rule to find any term in a sequence from its term number:

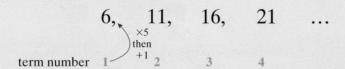

$$6, \quad 11, \quad 16, \quad 21 \quad \dots$$

×5
then
+1

term number 1   2   3   4

The rule for this sequence is: multiply 5 by the term number, than add 1.

5 A square number is the result of multiplying a number by itself.
For example:

$$1 \times 1 = 1 \quad 2 \times 2 = 4 \quad 3 \times 3 = 9 \quad 10 \times 10 = 100$$

square numbers

6 Here is how to make a sequence of triangular numbers:

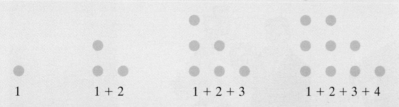

1   1 + 2   1 + 2 + 3   1 + 2 + 3 + 4

7 Here is how to make a Fibonacci sequence:

1   1   2   3   5   8   13   ...

Add the first
two numbers ...

1   1   2   3   5   8   13   ...

Then add the
next two numbers ...   ... and so on.

4 Probability

Philip and Sarah are going to play tennis. Sarah spins her raquet to decide who will serve first.

It has a blue side and a red side.

Spinning the racquet is an **event**.

This event has two possible outcomes: blue and red.

In this unit you will learn how to measure the chance of different outcomes happening.

4.1 Certain, impossible or possible

The outcome of an event may be:

impossible

You will get 12 out of 10 in a Geography test.

possible

It will rain tomorrow.

certain

The sun will rise tomorrow.

Example 1

Write down whether these outcomes are: impossible, possible or certain

(a) A car will break down on the M25 tomorrow.
(b) A dog will have kittens.
(c) Tuesday will be the day after Monday next week.

(a) It is possible that a car will break down on the M25 tomorrow.

(b) It is impossible for a dog to have kittens.

(c) It is certain that Tuesday will be the day after Monday next week.

It is not certain or impossible.

Exercise 4A

Write down whether these outcomes are:
certain, impossible or possible.

1 The school netball team will win their next match.

2 You will throw a 7 with a normal dice.

3 A red car will pass the school this evening.

4 You will have chips for tea tonight.

5 Thursday will be the day after Wednesday next week.

6 A plane will land at Manchester airport tomorrow.

7 Your friend will go to the moon next summer.

8 A cat will have puppies next year.

9 You will have a birthday next year.

10 You will receive a telephone call from a friend tonight.

4.2 Likely or unlikely?

Some outcomes are more likely to happen than others:

It is likely that you will eat breakfast tomorrow   It is unlikely that you will break a leg tomorrow

Example 2

Is this outcome likely or unlikely?
It will snow in Switzerland in
January.
Give a reason for your answer.

It is likely to snow in Switzerland
in January because Switzerland
has very cold winters.

Exercise 4B

Is each outcome likely or unlikely?
Give a reason for your answer.

1   You will break your leg next week.

2   You will see a famous film star in school next week.

3   You will watch Eastenders tonight.

4   Someone in your class will be absent next week.

5   It will rain in England in April.

6   When a card is taken from a normal pack it will be a
    number card.

7   Copy the table. Complete it by filling in 5 likely and
    5 unlikely outcomes.

Outcome	
Likely	Unlikely

4.3 An even chance

At the start of a football match a coin is tossed to decide which team kicks off.

There are two possible outcomes: heads or tails.

Both outcomes are equally likely.

Each outcome has an **even chance** of happening.

■ **When an event has two equally likely outcomes, each outcome has an even chance of happening.**

Exercise 4C

Which of these outcomes have an even chance of happening? Give a reason for each outcome you choose.

1 The next baby to be born will be female.

2 The next car to pass your school will be white.

3 You will have an accident on the way home.

4 The number on the top of an ordinary dice will be odd.

5 The top card in a well shuffled pack will be black.

4.4 How likely is it?

The outcomes of an event can have different chances of happening. This table shows the different chances:

Likelihood	Explanation
Impossible	There is no chance it will happen
Unlikely	It has a greater chance of not happening than happening
Even chance	It has the same chance of happening as not happening
Likely	It has a greater chance of happening than not happening
Certain	It will definitely happen

Example 3

Choose the likelihood which matches the outcome of each event:
impossible, unlikely, even chance, likely or certain.

Give a reason for your answers.

(a) The mountaineer will be hurt if he falls off the mountain.

(b) The number on the top face of an ordinary dice will be less than 7.

(c) Mr Smith will cut the grass on his lawn when it is snowing.

(d) The *Titanic* will float back up to thc top of the ocean.

(e) The card at the top of a shuffled pack is a King.

(f) The card at the top of a shuffled pack is red.

(a) is likely. The mountain is hard and it will hurt if the mountaineer falls.

(b) is certain. The numbers on an ordinary dice are 1, 2, 3, 4, 5 and 6.

(c) is unlikely. Nobody with any sense cuts the grass when it is snowing.

(d) is impossible. The *Titanic* is made of metal and it will not rise.

(e) is unlikely. There are only 4 Kings in a pack of 52 cards.

(f) is an even chance. The top card will be either red or black.

Exercise 4D

Choose the likelihood which matches the outcome of each event: impossible, unlikely, an even chance, likely or certain.

Give a reason for your answers.

1 It will rain in London at some time during April.

2 The winner of next year's mens finals at Wimbledon will be aged over 30 years.

3 Next year's FA Cup Final will be won by a team from the third division.

4 The next baby to be born will be male.

5 There will be more hours of light during the night than during the day.

6 The record at number 1 in the charts this week will be in the top 10 next week.

7 The Division 1 title will be won by a team from Division 2.

8 Elvis Presley is still alive.

9 You will be involved in a road accident on your way home today.

10 Someone will be involved in a road accident today.

4.5 The likelihood scale

You can mark the chance of an outcome happening on a likelihood scale:

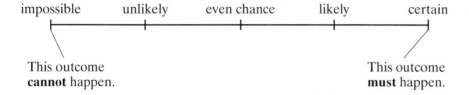

Example 4

Draw a likelihood scale.
Put each of these outcomes in a suitable place on your scale:

(a) It will rain in Ireland next year.
(b) The next baby to be born will be male.
(c) Your dog will live forever.
(d) The next car to pass your school will be P registered.

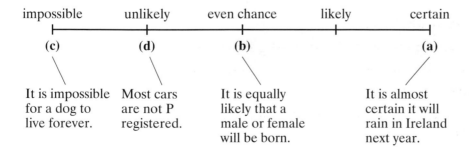

■ **A likelihood scale runs from impossible to certain, with an 'even chance' in the middle.**

Exercise 4E

Draw a likelihood scale.
Mark an estimate of each of these outcomes on your scale.

(a) Sumreen's Budgie will live for ever.

(b) A car travelling on a motorway will be doing 25 miles per hour.

(c) The number on the top face of an ordinary dice will be even.

(d) The day after Christmas Day will be Boxing Day.

(e) It will rain in Manchester during at least one day in March next year.

4.6 Probability

■ **Probability uses numbers to measure the chance of an outcome happening.**

Probability was developed in the 17th Century when Mathematicians tried to work out the likelihood of success and failure in games of chance such as playing with cards or dice.

The probability scale

You can mark the probability of an outcome happening on
a probability scale:

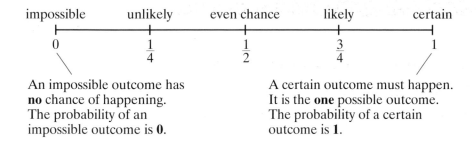

An impossible outcome has
no chance of happening.
The probability of an
impossible outcome is **0**.

A certain outcome must happen.
It is the **one** possible outcome.
The probability of a certain
outcome is **1**.

■ **All probabilities have a value between 0 and 1.**

Example 5

Mark each of these outcomes on a probability scale.
Give reasons for your answers.

(a) It will rain in Scotland on at least one day next year.
(b) The next object you see flying in the sky will be a pink
elephant.
(c) The card on the top of a well shuffled pack will be red.
(d) It will be warm in London next July.
(e) The winner of next year's mens final at Wimbledon will
be aged over 30.

(a) is certain, it is bound to rain at some time.
(b) is impossible.
(c) is an even chance, the card will be either red or black
and both are equally likely.
(d) is likely.
(e) is unlikely, the winner is usually in his twenties.

So on the probability scale the answers look like this:

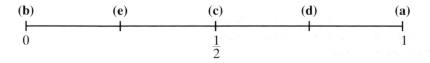

Exercise 4F

1 Draw a probability scale.
Mark each of these outcomes on your scale.
Give reasons for your answers.

(a) The school bus will break down tomorrow.

(b) The next baby to be born will be a girl.

(c) An ice cube will melt when it is left outside on a hot day.

(d) A heavy stone will float when it is dropped in the sea.

(e) The winner of the women's Olympic 100 metres final will be aged under 35 years.

2 An ordinary pack of 52 cards is well shuffled.
The top card is then turned over.
Draw a probability scale and mark on it each of these outcomes:

Give reasons for your answers

(a) The top card will be black.

(b) The top card will not be a picture card.

(c) The top card will be a King.

(d) The top card will be the Queen of Hearts.

(e) The top card will be blank.

(f) The top card will be either a number card or a picture card.

3 Look at this probability scale:

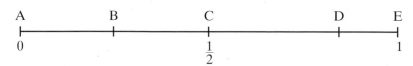

Outcomes A, B, C, D and E have been marked on the scale.
Give at least two possible outcomes for each of these probabilities.

4.7 Events and outcomes

There is a difference between **events** and **outcomes**:

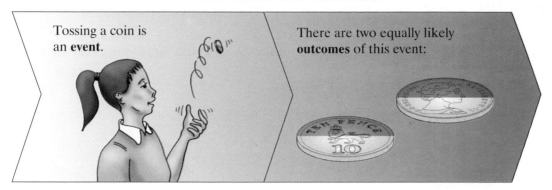

Tossing a coin is an **event**.

There are two equally likely **outcomes** of this event:

Example 6

Amy needs a five to win.
List all the possible outcomes of rolling the dice.

The possible outcomes are:

Each outcome is equally likely.

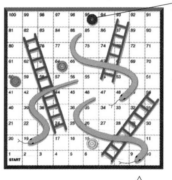

Amy's counter

Example 7

10 people enter this competition.
The winner is chosen by picking a name out of the box without looking.
How many possible outcomes are there?

There are 10 possible outcomes and they are all equally likely.

LUCKY DRAW
Simply write your name on a card & put in the box below

Exercise 4G

1 List all the possible outcomes for the following events:

   (a) Spinning the spinner
   (b) Tossing two coins
   (c) Picking a counter from this box without looking
   (d) Picking 2 beads from this bag without looking

4.8 Calculating probability

Sometimes you can calculate the probability of something happening.

There are 3 equally likely outcomes when you spin this spinner:

Landing on green is just one of the outcomes.

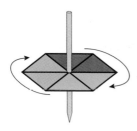

The probability of landing on green is $\frac{1}{3}$

Green is just
1 outcome ——— $\dfrac{1}{3}$
there are **3**
possible outcomes

■ **probability of something happening** $= \dfrac{\textbf{total successful outcomes}}{\textbf{total possible outcomes}}$

Example 8

Grant has a bag containing some red and blue beads:

Grant takes a bead out of the bag without looking. What is the probability that he takes a red bead?

The number of successful outcomes is 3

The total number of possible outcomes is 4

so the probability of picking a red bead is $\frac{3}{4}$

Exercise 4H

1   A box contains 4 bags of herbal tea.
    Lou takes a bag out without looking.
    What is the probability that she picks:

    (a) nettle

    (b) mint?

2   A multi-pack of crisps contains 2 cheese and onion,
    2 ready salted, 3 salt and vinegar and 1 prawn cocktail.

    Morgan takes a bag of crisps without looking. What is
    the probability that he picks:

    (a) ready salted

    (b) salt and vinegar

    (c) cheese and onion

    (d) prawn cocktail?

3   Adrian throws a coin in the air. What is the probability
    it will land on tails?

4   An ordinary pack of 52 cards is well shuffled.
    The top card is then turned over.
    What is the probability that:

    (a) the top card will be either a number card or a
    picture card

    (b) the top card will be blank

    (c) the top card will be red

4.9 The probability of something not happening

The probability of landing on six when you throw a dice is:

   $\dfrac{1}{6}$ one succesful outcome
six possible outcomes

The probability of **not** landing on six is:

 $\dfrac{5}{6}$ five succesful outcomes
six possible outcomes

Notice that:

$$\begin{pmatrix}\text{probability of \textbf{not}}\\\text{landing on 6}\end{pmatrix} = 1 - \begin{pmatrix}\text{probability of}\\\text{landing on 6}\end{pmatrix}$$

■ $\begin{pmatrix}\textbf{probability of an}\\\textbf{event not happening}\end{pmatrix} = \textbf{1} - \begin{pmatrix}\textbf{probability of the}\\\textbf{event happening}\end{pmatrix}$

Example 9

A bag contains only red and green beads.

There are three beads altogether.

The probability of picking a green bead is $\frac{1}{3}$.

What is the probability of picking a red bead?

$$\begin{pmatrix}\text{probability of}\\\text{picking a red bead}\end{pmatrix} = 1 - \begin{pmatrix}\text{probability of}\\\text{picking a green bead}\end{pmatrix}$$

$$= 1 - \frac{1}{3}$$

$$= \frac{2}{3}$$

Notice that the probability of *not* picking a green bead is the same as the probability of picking a red bead.

So the probability of picking a red bead is $\frac{2}{3}$.

Exercise 4I

1 The probability of sunshine on any day in Costa del Ingres is $\frac{3}{4}$.

  What is the probability that it will not be sunny?

2 The probability of landing on an odd number when you roll a dice is $\frac{3}{6}$.

  What is the probability of landing on an even number?

Hint: The probability of landing on an even number is the same as the probability of not landing on an odd number.

3 The probability of picking a red bead from this bag without looking is $\frac{4}{6}$.

What is the probability of:

(a) not picking a red bead

(b) picking a purple bead

(c) not picking a purple bead?

4.10 Experimental probability

Remember that the probability of landing on six when throwing a dice is:

$$\frac{\text{probability of}}{\text{landing on six}} = \frac{1}{6}$$

six is just **1** outcome

out of **6** possible outcomes

You can also estimate the probability of landing on six from an experiment.

The experimental probability may be different from the calculated probability.

■ **experimental probability** $= \dfrac{\textbf{number of successful trials}}{\textbf{total number of trials}}$

Exercise 4J

1 Roll a dice 60 times and record your results in a tally chart.
Work out the experimental probability of landing on six:

$$\frac{\text{experimental probability}}{\text{of landing on six}} = \frac{\text{number of times you landed on six}}{\text{total number of times you rolled the dice}}$$

2 Compare the calculated probability with the experimental probability.
Are they the same or different?

3 If you rolled the dice 600 times, would the experimental probability be the same? Why? Discuss this with your teacher.

To compare the calculated and experimental probabilities change the calculated probability from $\frac{1}{6}$ to $\frac{10}{60}$. There is more about equivalent fractions on p. 161.

Summary of key points

1 When an event has two equally likely outcomes each outcome has an even chance of happening.
For example, when you toss a coin, heads and tails are equally likely. They have an even chance of happening.

2 A likelihood scale runs from impossible to certain, with an 'even chance' in the middle.

3 Probability uses numbers to measure the chance of an outcome happening.

4 All probabilities have a value between 0 and 1.

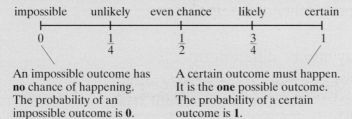

An impossible outcome has **no** chance of happening. The probability of an impossible outcome is **0**.

A certain outcome must happen. It is the **one** possible outcome. The probability of a certain outcome is **1**.

5 probability of something happening $= \dfrac{\text{total successful outcomes}}{\text{total possible outcomes}}$

6 $\left(\begin{array}{c}\text{probability of an}\\\text{event not happening}\end{array}\right) = 1 - \left(\begin{array}{c}\text{probability of the}\\\text{event happening}\end{array}\right)$

7 experimental probability $= \dfrac{\text{number of successful trials}}{\text{total number of trials}}$

5 Multiplication and division

Four hundred years ago most people did not need to multiply and divide.

Today most people do need to multiply and divide.

Calculators can help you, but you also need to be able to multiply and divide without them.

5.1 Multiplication up to 10 × 10

To multiply and divide **quickly** you must learn the multiplication tables up to 10 × 10.

Learning them takes time and practice. Exercise **5A** contains activities to help you practise.

Exercise 5A

1   **Activity**   You need a set of cards numbered 1 to 10, a watch which shows seconds and a copy of the multiplication table you wish to practise, for example the 6 times multiplication table.

  • Shuffle the cards and then turn one over. For each card that is turned over write down its number and multiply it by 6.
  • Time how long it takes you to do all ten cards and then check your answers.
  • Do this several times.

If you can beat 30 seconds you are doing well.

2 **Activity** You need a set of cards numbered 1 to 10.
- Shuffle the cards.
- Turn over the top two cards and multiply the numbers together.
- Turn over the next two cards and multiply the numbers together.
- Continue until you have used all ten cards.
- Add together your five answers to get a total.

Do this several times then try to answer the following questions.

(a) What is the smallest total you could make?

(b) What is the largest total you could make?

$$3 \times 7 = 21$$
$$8 \times 2 = 16$$
$$10 \times 5 = 50$$
$$6 \times 1 = 6$$
$$4 \times 9 = 36$$

Total 129

3 **Activity** This is a game for two players. You need a dice.

Player 1
Roll the dice twice. Multiply the two numbers together.

Player 2
Roll the dice three times. Multiply two of the three numbers together to try to beat Player 1's total.

The player with the higher total gets a point.

Do this five times then change places. The player with the highest number of points, after all ten go's, wins.

You can use your calculator to practise your times tables. Page 369 shows you how.

5.2 Multiples

This is the 3 times multiplication table:

$$1 \times 3 = 3$$
$$2 \times 3 = 6$$
$$3 \times 3 = 9$$
$$4 \times 3 = 12$$
$$5 \times 3 = 15$$
$$\vdots$$
$$28 \times 3 = 84$$
$$29 \times 3 = 87$$

These are the multiples of 3

$28 \times 3 = 84$ so 84 is a multiple of 3

The answers 3, 6, 9, 12, 15, 18, ... are called the **multiples** of 3.
You only need to learn the 3 times multiplication table up to 10×3 but it actually goes on for ever!
That means the multiples of 3 also go on for ever.

Remember:
Multiples of 2 are called even numbers:
2, 4, 6, 8, 10, ...
The numbers
1, 3, 5, 7, ...
are odd

■ **The multiples of 3 are the answers in the 3 times multiplication table.**
You can find the multiples of 3 by multiplying 3 by 1, 2, 3, 4, 5, ...

If you colour the multiples of 3 on a number line you colour every third number.

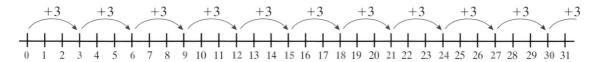

Example 1

What are the multiples of 6 between 50 and 80?

54 is a multiple of 6 because $9 \times 6 = 54$
60 is a multiple of 6 because $6 \times 10 = 60$

Continue to count on in sixes on the number line.

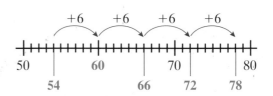

The multiples of 6 between 50 and 80 are 54, 60, 66, 72 and 78.

Example 2

Is 79 a multiple of 4?

$79 \div 4 = 19$ remainder 3, so 79 is not a multiple of 4.

$$\begin{array}{r} 1\ 9 \ \text{remainder 3} \\ 4\overline{)7\ 9} \\ \underline{4} \\ 3\ 9 \end{array}$$

Exercise 5B

1 Which of these numbers is a multiple of 4?
   (a) 15   (b) 16   (c) 32   (d) 31
   (e) 24   (f) 36   (g) 43   (h) 48
   (i) 47   (j) 39   (k) 27   (l) 44

2 Which of these statements is true?
   (a) 45 is a multiple of 5   (b) 56 is a multiple of 8
   (c) 46 is a multiple of 6   (d) 63 is a multiple of 9
   (e) 48 is a multiple of 8   (f) 54 is a multiple of 6
   (g) 38 is a multiple of 8   (h) 26 is a multiple of 7
   (i) 38 is a multiple of 4   (j) 42 is a multiple of 7
   (k) 35 is a multiple of 9   (l) 67 is a multiple of 8

3 What are the multiples of 6 between 60 and 90?

4 What are the multiples of 7 between 80 and 110?

5 What are the first three multiples of 8 after 100?

6 For each statement write true or false.

    (a) 72 is a multiple of 3   **(b)** 138 is a multiple of 5
    (c) 245 is a multiple of 7   **(d)** 236 is a multiple of 6
    (e) 196 is a multiple of 8   **(f)** 332 is a multiple of 4
    (g) 623 is a multiple of 9   **(h)** 392 is a multiple of 7
    (i) 746 is a multiple of 6   **(j)** 882 is a multiple of 9
    (k) 837 is a multiple of 3   **(l)** 414 is a multiple of 7

7 Which is the first number that is a multiple of both:

    (a) 2 and 3   **(b)** 3 and 4   **(c)** 4 and 6
    (d) 6 and 8   **(e)** 6 and 9   **(f)** 3, 4 and 5?

> The first number that is a multiple of both numbers is called the **lowest common multiple**.

8 What is the largest multiple of both 4 and 7 which is less than 100?

5.3 Squares, square roots and cubes

You can arrange 9 square tiles to make a 3 × 3 square.
9 is called a **square number.**

9 is a square number.

$3 \times 3 = 9$

You can't arrange 8 tiles to make a square so 8 is *not* a square number.

 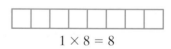

$1 \times 8 = 8$

$2 \times 4 = 8$

■ **When you multiply a whole number by itself you get a square number.**

    $1 \times 1 = 1, \quad 2 \times 2 = 4, \quad 4 \times 4 = 16, \quad 5 \times 5 = 25 \ldots$

    1, 4, 9, 16, 25 ... are square numbers.

■ **Every number has a square root:**
    1 is the square root of 1 because $1 \times 1 = 1$
    2 is the square root of 4 because $2 \times 2 = 4$
    3 is the square root of 9 because $3 \times 3 = 9$

Hint:
Use the $\boxed{\sqrt{}}$ key on your calculator to find square roots:

$\boxed{9}\ \boxed{\sqrt{}}\ \boxed{=}\ 3$

Cube numbers

You can arrange 64 small cubes to make
a 4 by 4 by 4 cube. 64 is called a **cube number**.

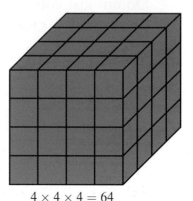

$4 \times 4 \times 4 = 64$

■ **When you multiply a whole number by itself
and by itself again you get a cube number.**
$1 \times 1 \times 1 = 1$, $\quad 2 \times 2 \times 2 = 8$, $\quad 3 \times 3 \times 3 = 27$,
$4 \times 4 \times 4 = 64$, $\quad 5 \times 5 \times 5 = 125$,
$10 \times 10 \times 10 = 1000$
1, 8, 27, 64, 125, ..., 1000, ... are cube numbers.

■ **Every cube number has a cube root:**
2 is the cube root of 8 because $2 \times 2 \times 2 = 8$
5 is the cube root of 125 because $5 \times 5 \times 5 = 125$

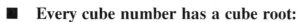

Exercise 5C

1 Find all the square numbers up to 400.

2 What is the square root of:
   (a) 36 **(b)** 64 **(c)** 81 **(d)** 49 **(e)** 169 **(f)** 289
   (g) 196 **(h)** 144 **(i)** 121 **(j)** 400 **(k)** 361 **(l)** 324

3 Find all the cube numbers up to 1000.

4 Which is greater:
   (a) The fifth square number or the third cube number?
   (b) The third square number or the second cube number?
   (c) The seventh square number or the fourth cube number?
   (d) The tenth square number or the fifth cube number?

5 Which square number is nearest to:
   (a) 50 **(b)** 40 **(c)** 20 **(d)** 70 **(e)** 55 **(f)** 75

6 Which cube number is nearest to:
   (a) 10 **(b)** 100 **(c)** 40 **(d)** 50

7 When you add together consecutive odd numbers,
   starting at one, you get the square numbers.
   Explain why.

   Hint: this picture may help.

$$1 = 1$$
$$1 + 3 = 4$$
$$1 + 3 + 5 = 9$$
$$1 + 3 + 5 + 7 = 16$$

8 Use your answer to question **7** to work these out. Do not just add the numbers up.

(b) $1 + 3 + 5 + 7 \ldots + 97 + 99 = ?$

(c) $1 + 3 + 5 + 7 \ldots + 47 + 49 = ?$

(d) $51 + 53 + 55 \ldots + 97 + 99 = ?$

(e) $27 + 29 + 31 \ldots + 47 + 49 = ?$

(f) $17 + 19 + 21 \ldots + 97 + 99 = ?$

(g) $2 + 6 + 10 + 14 \ldots + 94 + 98 = ?$

5.4 Factors

■ **The factors of a number are the numbers that divide into it exactly.**
For example, 1, 2, 3 and 6 are the factors of 6.
A factor is always a whole number.

You can think of factors in several other ways:

1 In the multiplication tables, 6 appears as an answer in the tables for 1, 2, 3 and 6. It does not appear as an answer in any other tables.

The numbers 1, 2, 3 and 6 are called the factors of 6.

$1 \times 1 = 1 \qquad 1 \times 2 = 2 \qquad 1 \times 3 = 3 \qquad 1 \times 6 = ⑥$
$2 \times 1 = 2 \qquad 2 \times 2 = 4 \qquad 2 \times 3 = ⑥$
$3 \times 1 = 3 \qquad 3 \times 2 = ⑥$
$4 \times 1 = 4$
$5 \times 1 = 5$
$6 \times 1 = ⑥$

2 The number 6 is a multiple of 1, 2, 3 and 6.
The numbers 1, 2, 3 and 6 are called the factors of 6.

3 If you take 6 square tiles and put them together to form a rectangle, you can do it in two ways.

$$2 \times 3 = 6 \qquad \text{and} \qquad 1 \times 6 = 6$$

The numbers 1, 2, 3 and 6 are called the factors of 6.

Here are some easy ways to check if numbers divide by 2, 3 or 5:

- Numbers that divide by 2 end in 0, 2, 4, 6 or 8.

- Numbers divisible by 5 end in 0 or 5:

    25, 200, 465, 320, . . .

- To check if a number divides by 3:
    add all the digits together:

    $$396 \rightarrow 3 + 9 + 6 = 18$$

    repeat until you are left with a 1-digit number

    $$18 \rightarrow 1 + 8 = 9$$

    If you are left with 3, 6 or 9 the number is divisible by 3.

Example 3

What are the factors of 12?

Think of pairs of whole numbers which multiply together to give 12.

$$1 \times 12 = 12$$
$$2 \times 6 = 12$$
$$3 \times 4 = 12$$

The factors of 12

The factors of 12 are 1, 2, 3, 4, 6 and 12.

Example 4

Show that 3 is a factor of 48.

$$\begin{array}{r} 1\,6 \\ 3\overline{)4\,8} \\ 3 \\ \hline 18 \end{array}$$ 3 divides into 48 exactly

so 3 is a factor of 48.

Example 5

Which factor of 18 is missing from the cloud?

Put the factors into pairs:
$$1 \times 18 = 18$$
$$2 \times 9 = 18$$
$$3 \times 6 = 18$$

so 6 is the missing factor.

Note that 6×3 is also a factor pair of 18.
This is just another way to write 3×6:

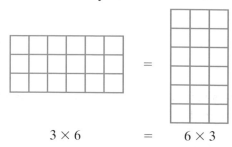

3×6 = 6×3

Because 3×6 means the same as 6×3 you say that multiplication is **commutative**.

Exercise 5D

1 For each number say whether it is divisible by 2, 3 or 5.

    (a) 35   **(b)** 30   **(c)** 98   **(d)** 197   **(e)** 225

    (f) 385   **(g)** 386   **(h)** 387   **(i)** 1215   **(j)** 1782

2 What are the factors of:

    (a) 10   **(b)** 18   **(c)** 7   **(d)** 20   **(e)** 16   **(f)** 48

    (g) 24   **(h)** 36   **(i)** 72   **(j)** 100   **(k)** 84   **(l)** 96?

Hint: Try $1\overline{)48}$

$2\overline{)48}$

$3\overline{)48}$

until you need go no further

3 Which of these are true and which are false?

    (a) 7 is a factor of 196   **(b)** 9 is a factor of 216

    (c) 8 is a factor of 366   **(d)** 6 is a factor of 438

    (e) 7 is a factor of 347   **(f)** 4 is a factor of 356

    (g) 8 is a factor of 746   **(h)** 9 is a factor of 576

    (i) 3 is a factor of 492

4 Find the missing factor by putting the numbers in each cloud into factor pairs:

(a)

3   1
27

Factors of 27

(b)

2   4
5   1   40
10   20

Factors of 40

(c)

8   16
1   32   2

Factors of 32

(d)

12   60
2   4   1   10
30
6   20   3   5

Factors of 60

(e)

1   2
6   42
21   3   14

Factors of 42

(f)

1   9
27   81

Factors of 81

Hint:
81 is a square number so 9 pairs with itself
$9 \times 9 = 81$

5 (a) Which number less than 30 has the greatest number of factors?

    (b) What are its factors?

6 Which number less than 90 has the greatest number of factors and what are its factors? Hint: it is a multiple of the answer to question **5(a)**.

5.5 Prime numbers

■ **A prime number is a whole number greater than 1 with only two factors: itself and 1.**

2, 3, 5, 7, 11, 13, 17, 19, 23, 29, ...
are prime numbers.

1, 4, 6, 8, 9, 10, 12, 14, 15, 16, 18, 20, 21, 22, ...
are not prime numbers.

There is no pattern to the prime numbers and they go on for ever.

2 is the only even prime number.

1×1 1 **is not** a prime number

$1 \times 3 = 3$ 3 **is** a prime number

$1 \times 6 = 6$

$2 \times 3 = 6$ 6 **is not** a prime number

Exercise 5E

1 Activity You need a 100 square for part **(a)**.
You may need a 400 square for part **(b)**.

One way to find prime numbers is to use the sieve of Eratosthenes.

- On your 100 square cross out 1 because it is not a prime number.
- Circle 2 then cross out all other multiples of 2. The next number that is not crossed out is 3.
- Circle 3 then cross out all other multiples of 3. The next number that is not crossed out is 5.
- Circle 5 then cross out all other multiples of 5. Continue like this until you cannot circle any more numbers.
  The circled numbers are the prime numbers less than 100.

Eratosthenes was a Greek mathematician who lived in the third century BC. He was a librarian in Alexandria in Egypt.

(a) Why don't you have to cross off any numbers after you have done the multiples of 7?

(b) Which multiples will you have to check to find all the prime numbers less than 400?

(c) Which numbers will you have to check to find all the prime numbers less than 1000?

2 Can all the square numbers up to 100 be written as the sum of two prime numbers?

For example, 36 can because $17 + 19 = 36$.

3 Here are the rules for growing magic number seeds:
   - the stalk splits if you can find factors like 5×6
   - a leaf grows if the only factors you can find are 1 and the number itself

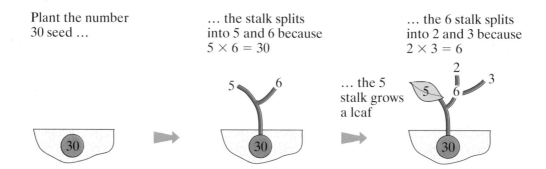

Plant the number 30 seed ...

... the stalk splits into 5 and 6 because $5 \times 6 = 30$

... the 6 stalk splits into 2 and 3 because $2 \times 3 = 6$

... the 5 stalk grows a leaf

(a) Draw the plants that can grow from a number 12 seed.

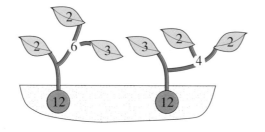

More than one plant can grow from a number 12 seed because $2 \times 6 = 12$ and $3 \times 4 = 12$

(b) Draw the plants that can grow from a number 15 seed.

(c) Which number seeds will not grow?

(d) Which number seeds less than 50 can grow most plants?

(e) Which number seeds less than 50 grow the tallest?

5.6 Multiplying by 10, 100 and 1000

All multiples of 10 have zero units. For example:

10 20 30 40 50 60 70 80 90 100 110 120 130

30 has zero units   120 has zero units

■ **To multiply a whole number by 10 move each digit one column to the left and put 0 in the units column.**

For example: $24 \times 10 = 240$

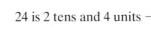

24 is 2 tens and 4 units ————

2 tens × 10 gives 2 hundreds ————

4 units × 10 gives 4 tens ————

There are no units ————
put zero here

There is also a quick way to multiply by 100:

$$100 = 10 \times 10$$
So $24 \times 100 = 24 \times 10 \times 10$
So $24 \times 100 = 2400$

$100 = 10 \times 10$ so you can multiply by 10 and then by 10 again.

■ **To multiply a whole number by 100 move each digit two columns to the left, then put 0 in the tens and units columns.**

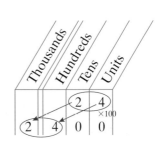

■ **To multiply a whole number by 1000 move each digit three columns to the left, then put 0 in the hundreds, tens and units columns**

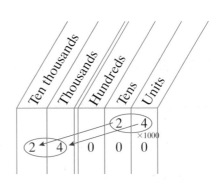

Exercise 5F

1 **(a)** 23×10 **(b)** 76×10 **(c)** 48×100
   (d) 10×97 **(e)** 10×53 **(f)** 100×72 — Remember 100×72 is the same as 72×100.
   (g) 143×10 **(h)** 7×1000 **(i)** 17×1000
   (j) 1000×91 **(k)** 1000×128 **(l)** 4217×1000

2 **(a)** $4 \times 10 \times 100$ **(b)** $10 \times 7 \times 100$
   (c) $10 \times 80 \times 10$ **(d)** $100 \times 6 \times 10$
   (e) $10 \times 37 \times 10$ **(f)** $10 \times 10 \times 21$
   (g) 20×100 **(h)** 10×300

3 Which of these numbers are multiples of 10?
   (a) 270   **(b)** 138   **(c)** 760   **(d)** 1000
   (e) 408   **(f)** 1470   **(g)** 580   **(h)** 706
   (i) 90   **(j)** 6800   **(k)** 1003   **(l)** 2090

4 Which of these numbers are multiples of 100?
   (a) 2460   **(b)** 3200   **(c)** 7040   **(d)** 9000
   (e) 95 000   **(f)** 8000   **(g)** 250   **(h)** 4000
   (i) 9002   **(j)** 1000   **(k)** 4300   **(l)** 1001

5 Which of these numbers are multiples of 1000?
   (a) 1760   **(b)** 9010   **(c)** 4100   **(d)** 6000
   (e) 95 000   **(f)** 1650   **(g)** 11 000   **(h)** 10 000
   (i) 10 010   **(j)** 2000   **(k)** 22 000   **(l)** 17 000

5.7 Dividing by 10, 100 and 1000

■ **To divide a whole number by 10 move each digit one column to the right.**

For example,

$$140 \div 10 = 14$$

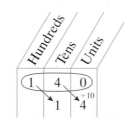

■ **To divide a whole number by 100 move each digit two columns to the right.**

For example,

$$2600 \div 100 = 26$$

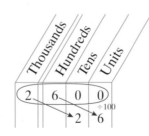

■ **To divide a whole number by 1000 move each digit three columns to the right.**

For example,

$$39\,000 \div 1000 = 39$$

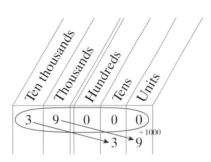

Exercise 5G

1 **(a)** $570 \div 10$ **(b)** $890 \div 10$ **(c)** $2040 \div 10$

 (d) $300 \div 10$ **(e)** $4000 \div 10$ **(f)** $2300 \div 10$

2 **(a)** $4700 \div 100$ **(b)** $3900 \div 100$ **(c)** $4200 \div 100$

 (d) $7000 \div 100$ **(e)** $100 \div 100$ **(f)** $4300 \div 100$

3 **(a)** $4000 \div 1000$ **(b)** $17\,000 \div 1000$

 (c) $171\,000 \div 1000$ **(d)** $90\,000 \div 1000$

 (e) $237\,000 \div 1000$ **(f)** $66\,000 \div 1000$

4 **(a)** $29 \times 100 \div 10$ **(b)** $46 \times 100 \div 10$

 (c) $380 \div 10 \times 100$ **(d)** $780 \div 10 \times 100$

 (e) $960 \times 10 \div 100$ **(f)** $120 \times 10 \div 100$

5.8 Multiplying by multiples of 10, 100 and 1000

What is 23×40?

40 is a multiple of 10: 4×10

Multiply 23 by 4 ...	$23 \times 4 = 92$
... multiply your answer by 10	$92 \times 10 = 920$
So $23 \times 40 = 920$	

On paper you could write this as:

$$\begin{array}{r} 23 \\ \times\ \ 4 \\ \hline 9\,2 \\ \hline \scriptstyle 1 \end{array}$$

■ **To multiply by 40, first multiply by 4 then multiply your answer by 10.**

To multiply by 400, first multiply by 4 then multiply your answer by 100.

To multiply by 4000, first multiply by 4 then multiply your answer by 1000.

To multiply by 200 think of 200 as 2×100

Exercise 5H

1 (a) 32×20 (b) 21×30 (c) 43×40 (d) 63×60
   (e) 28×50 (f) 30×37 (g) 70×18 (h) 50×81
   (i) 40×93 (j) 60×75 (k) 30×47 (l) 86×70

2 (a) 18×200 (b) 4×400 (c) 31×300
   (d) 7×600 (e) 22×300 (f) 21×400

3 (a) 32×80 (b) 9×500 (c) 70×75
   (d) 900×3 (e) 5×700 (f) 90×400

4 (a) 4×9000 (b) 18×2000 (c) 6000×14
   (d) 8000×12 (e) 5000×17 (f) 110×3000

5.9 Multiplication and division problems up to 10 × 10

There are many problems for which you need to multiply or divide to find the answer.

Dividing often produces a remainder and you will need to decide what is a sensible answer.

Example 6

A henkeeper has 50 eggs to put
into boxes.
Each box will hold 6 eggs.
How many boxes can she fill?

$50 \div 6 = 8$ remainder 2

The henkeeper can fill 8 boxes.
She has 2 eggs left over.

Example 7

A group of 23 people are going to a restaurant by taxi.
Each taxi can take 4 people.
How many taxis do they need?

$23 \div 4 = 5$ remainder 3

If they order 5 taxis there will not be room for 3 people so
they must order 6 taxis.

Exercise 5I

In this exercise you must decide whether to multiply or
divide. If you divide and there is a remainder you will need
to decide what is a sensible answer.

1   Sandrine bought 3 packs of fruit juice.
    Each pack cost £4 and contained 9 cartons of fruit
    juice.

    (a) How many cartons of fruit juice did she buy?

    (b) How much did she pay in total?

2   Laurent is organising the food
    for a party.

    He must buy enough sausages
    and bread rolls to make 31 hot
    dogs.

    He buys 4 packs of 8 sausages
    and 5 packs of 6 bread rolls.

    Has he bought enough?

3 Mr Farmer runs a country dance club.
He can put the dancers into groups of 6 or into groups of 8.
One day he has 30 dancers present.
Should he put them into groups of 6 or 8?

4 A fruit grower has 35 apples to put into packets.
Each packet holds 4 apples.
How many packets can he fill?

5 A group of 28 Guides are going camping.
Each tent holds 6 people.
How many tents do they need to take?

6 Minakshi wants to post 68 Christmas cards.
How many books of 10 stamps must she buy?

7 A baker is packing doughnuts in boxes.
She can put them in boxes of 5 or in boxes of 8.
She fills 10 boxes of 5 and 4 boxes of 8 and has 1 doughnut left over.
How could she have packed them to have no doughnuts left over?

5.10 Multiplying or dividing a 3-digit number by a 1-digit number

Today you have calculators to help you with harder problems.

But you still need to be able to do multiplications and divisions using only pencil and paper.

The first pocket calculators appeared in shops in the early 1970s. They were very expensive, about £70.

Example 8

A shop ordered 7 boxes of pencils.
Each box contained 144 pencils.
How many pencils did the shop order?

$$
\begin{array}{r}
144 \\
\times \quad 7 \\
\hline
1008 \\
{\scriptstyle 32}
\end{array}
$$

$144 \times 7 = 1008$ pencils

Example 9

A fruit grower is packing apples.
Each pack holds 4 apples and he has 650 apples.
How many packs can he fill?

$$
\begin{array}{r}
162 \\
4\overline{)650} \\
-4 \\
\hline
25 \\
-24 \\
\hline
10 \\
-\ 8 \\
\hline
2 \text{ (remainder)}
\end{array}
$$

$650 \div 4 = 162$ remainder 2

He can fill 162 packs.

Exercise 5J

1 Ofra gets £7 pocket money a week.
How much does she get in a year?

1 year is 52 weeks
and 1 day
1 year is 365 days

2 A violinist practises for 4 hours every day.
How many hours does he practise in a year?

3 Eight people shared a lottery win of £376.
How much did they each get?

4 160 people are invited to a wedding
reception.
They are each given a glass of
champagne for a toast.
Each bottle of champagne filled 6 glasses.
How many bottles of champagne were
needed?

5 Vasbert ran 7 laps of a running track.
Each lap of the track was 440 metres.
How many metres did he run in total?

6 A racing cyclist does 300 miles of training a week.
He does the same number of miles each day.
How many miles does he cycle each day?

7 Gayle made 9 photocopies of a 24 page booklet.
Each photocopy cost 4p to make.
What was the total cost?

8 In a tombola the tickets which are multiples of 6 win a prize.
Which of the tickets shown would win prizes?

| 94 | 504 | 364 | 824 | 744 | 924 |

9 **Investigation** Choose any three different digits.
Arrange them as a 2 digit number multiplied by a 1 digit number and do the multiplication.
Try other arrangements of the same digits.

7, 4, 6

$67 \times 4 = 268$

$76 \times 4 =$ $46 \times 7 =$

(a) How many different arrangements are there?

(b) Which arrangement gives the largest answer?

(c) Which arrangement gives the smallest answer?

(d) Try other sets of digits.

(e) Can you spot any rules to help you answer parts (b) and (c)?

5.11 Half way between

Ray wants to stop halfway between York and Hull. How far is that?

Think of a number line:

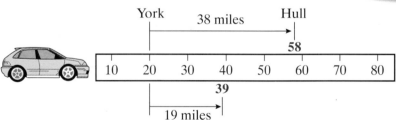

From York to Hull is $58 - 20 = 38$ miles
Half of 38 is $38 \div 2 = 19$ miles

It is 20 miles to York so Ray will stop after:

$20 + 19 = 39$ miles.

There is an easier way to find the number half way between 20 and 58:

Add 20 and 58: $20 + 58 = 78$

Find half of the total: $78 \div 2 \ = 39$

To find half of a number you divide by 2

■ **To find the number half way between two others add the two numbers together and divide by 2.**

Example 10

Find the number half way between 27 and 54

$$27 + 54 = 81$$

$$81 \div 2 = 40\frac{1}{2}$$

so $40\frac{1}{2}$ is half way between 27 and 54.

$$\begin{array}{r} 40 \text{ remainder } 1 \\ 2\overline{)81} \end{array}$$

$$1 \div 2 = \frac{1}{2}$$

so $81 \div 2 = 40\frac{1}{2}$

Exercise 5K

1 Find the number half way between:

(a) 24 and 42   (b) 57 and 31   (c) 16 and 48   (d) 65 and 17
(e) 352 and 126   (f) 613 and 345   (g) 748 and 24   (h) 635 and 257

2 Find the number half way between:

(a) 43 and 26   (b) 33 and 54   (c) 49 and 36   (d) 19 and 66
(e) 427 and 252   (f) 644 and 315   (g) 249 and 726   (h) 938 and 855

5.12 Multiplying a 3-digit number by a 2-digit number

This section shows you how to do multiplications such as 473×64

Think of 64 as $60 + 4$

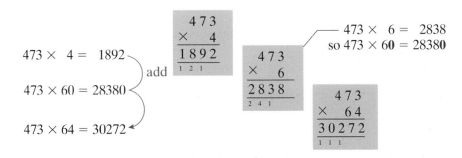

$$473 \times 4 = 1892$$
$$473 \times 60 = 28380$$
$$473 \times 64 = 30272$$

add

$473 \times 6 = 2838$
so $473 \times 60 = 28380$

You can set out 473×64 like this:

$$\begin{array}{r} 473 \\ \times\ 64 \\ \hline 1\,8_29_12 \\ 2\,8_43_18\,0 \\ \hline 3\,0\,2\,7\,2 \\ \hline {\scriptstyle 1\ \ 1\ \ 1} \end{array}$$

473×4

Put a 0 in the units column then multiply 473×6.
This is the same as 473×60.

Add 1892 and 28380 to get 374×64.

Exercise 5L

1 (a) 212×31 (b) 123×23 (c) 234×32
 (d) 436×26 (e) 364×43 (f) 275×34
 (g) 107×27 (h) 461×42 (i) 418×64
 (j) 602×58 (k) 540×76 (l) 183×92

2 Choose any five digits, for example 2, 3, 6, 8, 9.
Write them as a 3 digit $\times$ 2 digit multiplication
and work out the answer.
Try other arrangements of your five digits.
Which arrangement gives the largest answer?
Which arrangement gives the smallest answer?

```
        6 2 8
×         3 9
      5 6₂5₇2
      1 8 8₂4 0
      2 4 4 9 2
        1   1
```

5.13 Dividing a 3-digit number by a 2-digit number

This section shows you how to do divisions such as
$875 \div 24$.

First, here is a simpler example: $947 \div 4$

Divide the 9 hundreds by 4
$9 \div 4 = 2$ remainder 1 ⎯⎯⎯

$$4\overline{)9\ ^14\ 7} \quad \begin{smallmatrix}2\end{smallmatrix}$$

Divide the 14 tens by 4
$14 \div 4 = 3$ remainder 2 ⎯⎯⎯

$$4\overline{)9\ ^14\ ^27} \quad \begin{smallmatrix}2\ 3\end{smallmatrix}$$

Divide the 27 units by 4
$27 \div 4 = 6$ remainder 3 ⎯⎯⎯

$$4\overline{)9\ ^14\ ^27} \quad \begin{smallmatrix}2\ 3\ 6\ \text{rem. }3\end{smallmatrix}$$

You are dividing by 4 and the remainder is 3 so you can write the answer as $236\frac{3}{4}$ or 236.75.
You will learn more about fractions and decimals later.

You could also set it out like this:

Divide the 9 hundreds by 4
$9 \div 4 = 2$ remainder 1 ⎯⎯⎯

```
    2
4)9 4 7
 −8
  1
```

Divide the 14 tens by 4
$14 \div 4 = 3$ remainder 2 ⎯⎯⎯

```
   2 3
4)9 4 7
 −8
  1 4
 −1 2
    2
```

Divide the 27 units by 4
$27 \div 4 = 6$ remainder 3 ⎯⎯⎯

```
   2 3 6 rem. 3
4)9 4 7
 −8
  1 4
 −1 2
    2 7
 −  2 4
      3
```

The second method looks complicated but it is a good way
to set out a division such as $875 \div 24$

You can set out $875 \div 24$ like this:

You cannot divide the 8 hundreds by 24. ————
Divide the 87 tens by 24.
$87 \div 24 = 3$ remainder 15

$$
\begin{array}{r}
3 \\
24\overline{)8\ 7\ 5} \\
-7\ 2 \\
\hline
1\ 5
\end{array}
\qquad
\begin{array}{r}
2\ 4 \\
\times\ \ 3 \\
\hline
7\ 2
\end{array}
$$

Divide the 155 units by 24. ————
$155 \div 24 = 6$ remainder 11

$$
\begin{array}{r}
3\ 6\ \text{rem. }11 \\
24\overline{)8\ 7\ 5} \\
-7\ 2 \\
\hline
1\ 5\ 5 \\
-1\ 4\ 4 \\
\hline
1\ 1
\end{array}
\qquad
\begin{array}{r}
2\ 4 \\
\times\ \ 6 \\
\hline
1\ 4\ 4
\end{array}
$$

Exercise 5M

1 (a) $346 \div 13$ (b) $367 \div 17$ (c) $294 \div 15$
   (d) $691 \div 14$ (e) $719 \div 19$ (f) $849 \div 18$
   (g) $699 \div 13$ (h) $842 \div 16$

2 (a) $879 \div 23$ (b) $963 \div 34$ (c) $854 \div 26$
   (d) $987 \div 42$ (e) $992 \div 47$ (f) $763 \div 21$
   (g) $792 \div 39$ (h) $948 \div 45$

3 (a) $847 \div 76$ (b) $993 \div 82$ (c) $974 \div 91$
   (d) $895 \div 63$ (e) $764 \div 58$ (f) $947 \div 71$
   (g) $863 \div 85$ (h) $683 \div 52$

Exercise 5N

In these questions you will need to either multiply or divide
a 3-digit number by a 2-digit number. If you divide and
there is a remainder you will need to decide what is a
sensible answer.

1 Jack works in a supermarket. He earns £186 a week.
How much does he earn in a 52 week year?

2 A group of 36 children went on a school journey for a
week to the Isle of Wight. Each child paid £213.
What was the total cost of the trip?

3 A garage charges £24 an hour for labour. The garage charges Nigel £336 labour to replace the engine in his car. For how many hours of labour was he charged?

4 A department store ordered 34 television sets at a cost of £357 each. What was the total cost of the television sets?

5 Every year on sports day a school gives a can of cola to each pupil. There are 950 pupils in the school and the cola comes in packs of 24. How many packs does the school need to order?

6 A car uses a gallon of petrol for every 58 miles it travels. How many gallons of petrol will the car use for a journey of 860 miles?

5.14 Powers of whole numbers

Large numbers such as 100, 1000 and 1 000 000 (1 million) can be written as powers of ten.

	How you write it:	How you say it:
$10 = 10$	10^1	10 to the power 1
$100 = 10 \times 10$	10^2	10 to the power 2
$1\,000 = 10 \times 10 \times 10$	10^3	10 to the power 3
$10\,000 = 10 \times 10 \times 10 \times 10$	10^4	10 to the power 4
$100\,000 = 10 \times 10 \times 10 \times 10 \times 10$	10^5	10 to the power 5
$1000\,000 = 10 \times 10 \times 10 \times 10 \times 10 \times 10$	10^6	10 to the power 6

Other numbers can also be written as powers; for example:

■ **3^5 is '3 to the power 5'**
 $3^5 = 3 \times 3 \times 3 \times 3 \times 3 = 243$

A power is also called an **index**.

4×4

4^2 is also called 4 squared because it is the number of small tiles in a 4×4 square.

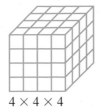

$4 \times 4 \times 4$

4^3 is also called 4 cubed because it is the number of small cubes in a $4 \times 4 \times 4$ cube.

$4 \times 4 = 16$

16 is a **square number**.

There is more about square numbers on page 94.

■ **4^2 or '4 to the power 2' is also called '4 squared'.**
4^3 or '4 to the power 3' is also called '4 cubed'.

Example 11

Write $5 \times 5 \times 5 \times 5$ as a power of 5.

$5 \times 5 \times 5 \times 5 = 5^4$

Example 12

Write 216 as a power of 6.

$216 = 6 \times 6 \times 6 = 6^3$

Example 13

Write 1 000 000 000 as a power of 10. There are nine zeros after the 1 so

$1\,000\,000\,000 = 10^9$

Example 14

Work out 7^3.

$7^3 = 7 \times 7 \times 7 = 343$

Exercise 5O

1 Write:

(a) $3 \times 3 \times 3 \times 3$ as a power of 3

(b) $8 \times 8 \times 8$ as a power of 8

(c) $2 \times 2 \times 2 \times 2 \times 2$ as a power of 2

(d) $10 \times 10 \times 10 \times 10 \times 10 \times 10$ as a power of 10

(e) 7×7 as a power of 7

(f) $9 \times 9 \times 9 \times 9$ as a power of 9

2 Work out:

(a) 4^2 (b) 2^5 (c) 3^4 (d) 7^3 (e) 10^3 (f) 3^2

(g) 1^4 (h) 0^5 (i) 3^5 (j) 8^3 (k) 4^4 (l) 9^4

3 Write:
  (a) 8 as a power of 2
  (b) 9 as a power of 3
  (c) 81 as a power of 9
  (d) 125 as a power of 5
  (e) 100 000 as a power of 10
  (f) 64 as a power of 4
  (g) 16 as a power of 2
  (h) 1 000 000 as a power of 10
  (i) 27 as a power of 3

4 Which is larger:
  (a) 2^3 or 3^2
  (b) 3^4 or 4^3
  (c) 3^3 or 5^2
  (d) 4^3 or 8^2?

5 Work out:
  (a) 6 squared
  (b) 2 cubed
  (c) 5 squared
  (d) 9 squared
  (e) 4 cubed
  (f) 10 cubed
  (g) 10 squared
  (h) 100 squared
  (i) 1 squared
  (j) 3 squared
  (k) 3 cubed
  (l) 5 cubed

Summary of key points

1 The multiples of 3 are the answers in the 3 times multiplication table.
   You can find the multiples of 3 by multiplying 3 by 1, 2, 3, 4, 5, . . .
   They go on for ever: 3, 6, 9, 12, 15, . . . , 84, 87, . . .

2 When you multiply a whole number by itself you get a square number.
   $1 \times 1 = 1$, $2 \times 2 = 4$, $3 \times 3 = 9$, $4 \times 4 = 16$, . . .
   1, 4, 9, 16, . . . are square numbers.

3 Every number has a square root:
   1 is the square root of 1 because $1 \times 1 = 1$
   2 is the square root of 4 because $2 \times 2 = 4$
   3 is the square root of 9 because $3 \times 3 = 9$

4 When you multiply a whole number by itself
   and by itself again you get a cube number.
   $1 \times 1 \times 1 = 1$, $2 \times 2 \times 2 = 8$, $3 \times 3 \times 3 = 27$,
   $4 \times 4 \times 4 = 64$, $5 \times 5 \times 5 = 125$,
   $10 \times 10 \times 10 = 1000$
   1, 8, 27, 64, 125, 1000, . . . are cube numbers.

5 Every cube number has a cube root:
   2 is the cube root of 8 because $2 \times 2 \times 2 = 8$
   5 is the cube root of 125 because $5 \times 5 \times 5 = 125$

6 The factors of a number are the numbers that divide into it exactly.
   For example 1, 2, 3 and 6 are the factors of 6.
   A factor is always a whole number.

7 A prime number is a whole number greater than 1 with only two factors: itself and 1.

 2, 3, 5, 7, 11, 13, 17, 19, 23,...

are prime numbers.

 1, 4, 6, 8, 9, 10, 12, 14, 15, 16, 18, 20, 21, 22,...

are not prime numbers.

8 To multiply a whole number by 10, 100, 1000...
move each digit to the left by the number of zeros.

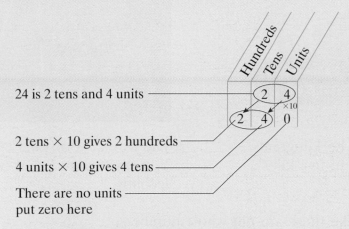

24 is 2 tens and 4 units

2 tens × 10 gives 2 hundreds

4 units × 10 gives 4 tens

There are no units
put zero here

9 To divide a whole number by 10, 100, 1000...
move each digit to the right by the number of zeros.

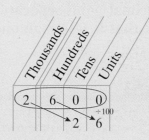

10 To multiply by 40, multiply by 4 then multiply your answer by 10.

11 To find the number half way between two others add the two numbers together and divide by 2.

12 3^5 is called '3 to the power 5
$3^5 = 3 \times 3 \times 3 \times 3 \times 3 = 243$

13 4^2 or '4 to the power 2' is also called '4 squared'.
4^3 or '4 to the power 3' is also called '4 cubed'.

6 Decimals

6.1 Understanding decimals

When you count things you get whole number values:

There are 12 clementines in this bag:

8 runners ran this race:

This bag weighs 1.5 kilograms.
You say 'one point five kilos'.

The winner took 20.51 seconds.
You say 'twenty point five one'
seconds.

Measurements like these are **not** whole numbers.
1.5 and 20.51 are **decimal numbers**.

■ **In a decimal number the decimal point separates the**
whole number from the part that is less than one:

decimal point

20.51

20 is the whole
number

.51 is the part
less than one

This place value diagram will help you
understand what 20.51 means:

The whole number part is 20.
There are 2 tens and zero units.

The decimal part is .51
There are 5 tenths and
1 hundredth.

Hundreds	Tens	Units	•	Tenths	Hundredths	Thousandths
	2	0	•	5	1	

2 tens
0 units

5 tenths
1 hundredth

Example 1

This calculator display shows the decimal number 325.078

(a) Show this number on a decimal place value diagram.

(b) Write down the value of each digit.

(a)

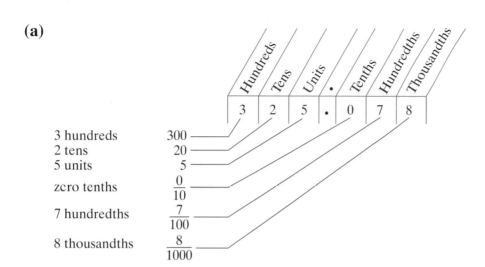

	3 hundreds	300
	2 tens	20
	5 units	5
	zero tenths	$\frac{0}{10}$
	7 hundredths	$\frac{7}{100}$
	8 thousandths	$\frac{8}{1000}$

Even though there are zero *tenths* the 0 has to be recorded.
This keeps the 7 and the 8 in their correct place value positions.

(b) The values of the digits are
3 hundreds, 2 tens, 5 units, 0 tenths, 7 hundredths and 8 thousandths.

Example 2

Write down the value of the digit underlined in each decimal number.

Write .276 as 0.276
The zero draws attention to the decimal point.

(a) 8$\underline{2}$.3   (b) 3.6$\underline{8}$ (c) 4.$\underline{0}$5   (d) 0.27$\underline{6}$

(a) 2 units   (b) 8 hundredths   (c) 0 tenths   (d) 6 thousandths

Exercise 6A

1 Draw a decimal place value diagram like the one in Example 1 and write in these numbers.

   (a) 12.3   **(b)** 4.31   **(c)** 0.56   **(d)** 3.05

   (e) 0.082   **(f)** 930.08   **(g)** 18.62   **(h)** 0.03

2 Write down the value of the digit underlined in each decimal number.

   (a) 3̲7.8   **(b)** 46̲.3   **(c)** 17.6̲5   **(d)** 3.8̲1

   (e) 11.93̲   **(f)** 8.1̲4   **(g)** 6̲27.8   **(h)** 46̲2.9

   (i) 9.127̲   **(j)** 3.5̲24   **(k)** 9.273̲   **(l)** 0.09̲2

6.2 Adding and subtracting decimals

You can add and subtract decimals in the same way you add and subtract money in pounds and pence.

■ **When adding or subtracting decimal numbers always line up the decimal points.**

Example 3

Senga has £43.87 in her savings account and Joshua has £28.30 in his. **Without a calculator** work out the total amount that Senga and Joshua have saved. Show all your working.

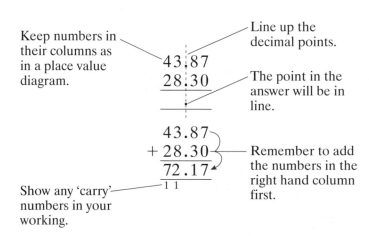

Keep numbers in their columns as in a place value diagram.

Line up the decimal points.

$$\begin{array}{r} 43.87 \\ 28.30 \\ \hline \end{array}$$

The point in the answer will be in line.

$$\begin{array}{r} 43.87 \\ + 28.30 \\ \hline 72.17 \\ \small 1\ 1 \end{array}$$

Remember to add the numbers in the right hand column first.

Show any 'carry' numbers in your working.

The answer is £72.17

Example 4

Work out $6.2 + 14.36 + 22.24$ without using a calculator.

$$
\begin{array}{r}
6.2 \\
14.36 \\
+\ 22.24 \\
\hline
42.80 \\
\scriptstyle 1\ \ \ 1
\end{array}
$$

42.80 and 42.8 have the same value. The answer is not an amount of money, so the zero in the hundredths place **can** be left out.

The answer is 42.8

Example 5

On Thursday evening Liam's temperature was 39.2 °C. The following morning his temperature was 36.7 °C. By how much had Liam's temperature fallen overnight?

$39.2\,°C - 36.7\,°C$

Line up the points

$$
\begin{array}{r}
39.2 \\
-\ 36.7 \\
\hline
\end{array}
$$

Put the point in the answer

$$
\begin{array}{r}
\\
. \\
\end{array}
$$

Hint: There is more about subtraction on page 51.

Now subtract

$$
\begin{array}{r}
\scriptstyle 8\ \ 1 \\
3\not{9}.2 \\
-\ 36.7 \\
\hline
2.5
\end{array}
$$

Liam's temperature fell by 2.5 °C.

Exercise 6B

Show all your working.

1 (a) £21.42 + £35.16   (b) £4.30 + £15.48
   (c) £3.40 + £6.50   (d) £8.97 + £6.35
   (e) £68.47 + £19.33   (f) £16.39 + £97.74

2 (a) 4.2 + 1.8   (b) 6 + 1.47
   (c) 163.7 + 0.45   (d) 9.9 + 9.9
   (e) 4.3 + 16.5 + 7.46   (f) 8.09 + 15 + 0.52

3 (a) £4.83 − £2.71   (b) £3.21 − £1.86

  (c) £15.65 − £9.28   (d) £14.72 − £8.25

4 (a) 0.95 − 0.52   (b) 16.02 − 4.35

  (c) 200.8 − 3.4   (d) 9.237 − 4.7

  (e) 1 − 0.6   (f) 1 − 0.38 ——————— Hint: write 1 as 1.00

5 Katie ran 1.25 km from The Bourne to Millbridge, 2.8 km from Millbridge to Rowledge and 3.24 km from Rowledge to The Bourne.
Work out the total distance that Katie ran.

6 The temperature in Larne at midnight was 4.8 °C.
By noon the temperature had gone up by 4.5 °C.
What was the temperature in Larne at noon?

7 Eleanor sawed a length of 0.26 metres from a one metre piece of wood.
Work out the length of wood left over.

8 The temperature in Oxford at noon was 17.3 °C.
By midnight the temperature had fallen by 7.9 °C.
What was the temperature in Oxford at midnight?

9 A cake weighed 1.42 kg.
What was the weight of the cake after Sean had eaten a slice that weighed 0.17 kg?

10 Asif's empty bag weighs 0.92 kg.
One day Asif had two text books in his bag, weighing 1.05 kg and 0.96 kg, two exercise books each weighing 0.2 kg and a pencil case weighing 0.33 kg.
What was the total weight of Asif's bag and its contents?

11 Winford's packed rucksack weighed 21.2 kg.
Winford removed a radio weighing 0.5 kg, a sweater weighing 0.7 kg and a pair of shoes weighing 1.6 kg.
Work out the new weight of Winford's rucksack.

6.3 Writing decimal numbers in size order

Sometimes you need to sort measurements and decimal numbers in order of size.

Example 6

Write the decimal numbers 2.05, 2.4, 3.7, 2.069, 8 in order of size starting with the largest.

Look at the whole number part of each number

Put the largest whole number first ...

| 2.05 | 2.4 | 3.7 | 2.069 | 8 |

| 8 | 3.7 | 2.05 | 2.4 | 2.069 |

2.05, 2.4, 2.069 all have the same whole number so look at the tenths place.

Put the largest 'tenth' first ...

| 8 | 3.7 | 2.05 | 2.4 | 2.069 |

| 8 | 3.7 | 2.4 | 2.05 | 2.069 |

2.05, and 2.069 have the same tenths so look at the hundredths.

Put the largest 'hundredth' first ...

| 8 | 3.7 | 2.4 | 2.05 | 2.069 |

| 8 | 3.7 | 2.4 | 2.069 | 2.05 |

■ **You can sort decimal numbers in order of size by comparing first the whole numbers, then the tenths, then the hundredths, and so on.**

Exercise 6C

Rearrange these decimal numbers in order of size, starting with the largest:

1 2.4, 3.2, 5.1, 2.8   **2** 4.6, 4.8, 5.9, 5.3

3 3.8, 6.5, 7.2, 3.4, 6.3   **4** 2.91, 3.85, 2.78, 3.96, 4.21

5 5.94, 6.04, 6.43, 8.12, 5.29

Put these numbers in order of size, smallest first:

6 2.92, 4.16, 3.05, 3.74, 3.61   **7** 2.3, 5.1, 4.06, 5.09, 4.71

8 4, 6.8, 4.08, 6.354, 5.02   **9** 17, 9.84, 24.19, 24.3, 9.09

10 12.5, 17.1, 9.074, 17.08, 9.2

You can use these symbols:

< means **less than**
$2.4 < 3.7$

> means **greater than**
$2.4 > 2.05$

6.4 Multiplying decimals by 10, 100 and 1000

To multiply a decimal number by 10 move the digits one place to the left.

For example, $5.6 \times 10 = ?$

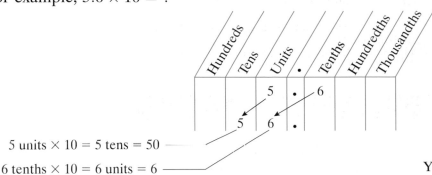

5 units × 10 = 5 tens = 50

6 tenths × 10 = 6 units = 6

So $5.6 \times 10 = 56$

You can use a similar method to show the rules for multiplying decimal numbers by 100 and 1000.

You can write 6 tenths as a
- decimal 0.6
- fraction $\frac{6}{10}$

There is more about fractions on page 166.

■ **To multiply a decimal number by 10 move each digit one place to the left.**

$25.68 \times 10 = 256.8$

■ **To multiply a decimal number by 100 move the digits two places to the left.**

$36.97 \times 100 = 3697$

■ **To multiply a decimal number by 1000 move the digits three places to the left.**

$0.23 \times 1000 = 230$

Example 7

Work out

(a) 2.348×100

(b) 3.67×1000

(a) Move the digits **two** places left.

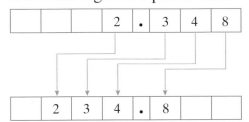

So $2.348 \times 100 = 234.8$

(b) Move the digits **three** places left.

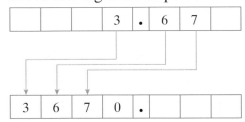

So $3.67 \times 1000 = 3670$

Example 8

Without using a calculator find:

(a) 52.47×10　　(b) 4.83×100　　(c) 2.5×1000

(a) $52.47 \times 10 = 524.7$　　Move the digits 1 place to the left.

(b) $4.83 \times 100 = 483$　　Move the digits 2 places to the left.

(c) $2.5 \times 1000 = 2500$　　Move the digits 3 places to the left.

Exercise 6D

Write down the answers to these calculations:

Hint: draw a place value diagram to help you.

1 (a) 3.63×10 　　(b) 12.4×10 　　(c) 0.402×10
　　(d) 0.068×10 　(e) 56.28×10 　(f) 0.03×10

2 (a) 4.72×100 　(b) 21.48×100 　(c) 2.568×1000
　　(d) 5.38×1000 　(e) 4.7×100 　　(f) 0.06×1000

3 (a) 0.065×100 　(b) 5.307×10 　(c) 0.0202×100
　　(d) 6.88×1000 　(e) 9.36×10 　　(f) 0.0045×1000

4 (a) 98.2×100 　(b) 5.27×1000 　(c) 0.09×10
　　(d) 0.023×100 　(e) 72.54×10 　(f) 18.2×1000

6.5 Dividing decimal numbers by 10, 100 and 1000

To divide a decimal number by 10 move each digit one place to the right.

For example, $83.2 \div 10 = ?$

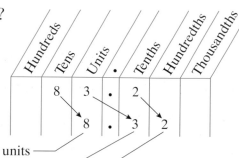

8 tens $\div 10 = 8$ units

3 units $\div 10 = \dfrac{3}{10} = 3$ tenths

2 tenths $\div 10 = \dfrac{2}{100} = 2$ hundredths

So $83.2 \div 10 = 8.32$

You can write 2 hundredths as a

- decimal 0.02
- fraction $\frac{2}{100}$

You can use a similar method to show the rules for dividing decimal numbers by 100 and 1000.

■ **To divide a decimal number by 10 move each digit one place to the right.**

$98.72 \div 10 = 9.872$

■ **To divide a decimal number by 100 move each digit two places to the right.**

$26.5 \div 100 = 0.265$

■ **To divide a decimal number by 1000 move each digit three places to the right.**

$536.8 \div 1000 = 0.5368$

$629.5 \div 100$

Move the digits **two** places right.

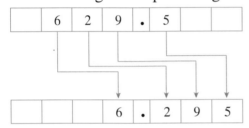

So $629.5 \div 100 = 6.295$

$4382.7 \div 1000$

Move the digits **three** places right.

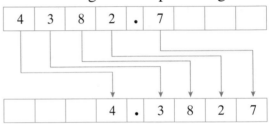

So $4382.7 \div 1000 = 4.3827$

Example 9

Without using a calculator find:

(a) $954.5 \div 10$ (b) $15.26 \div 100$ (c) $92.8 \div 1000$

(a) $954.5 \div 10 = 95.45$ Move the digits 1 place to the right.

(b) $15.26 \div 100 = 0.1526$ Move the digits 2 places to the right.

(c) $92.8 \div 1000 = 0.0928$ Move the digits 3 places to the right.

Exercise 6E

Write down the answers to these calculations.

1 (a) $18.5 \div 10$ (b) $175.4 \div 10$ (c) $2.84 \div 10$
   (d) $563.2 \div 10$ (e) $0.075 \div 10$ (f) $0.06 \div 10$

2 **(a)** $247.2 \div 10$ **(b)** $38.7 \div 10$ **(c)** $1852.4 \div 10$
     (d) $816.7 \div 1000$ **(e)** $4.6 \div 100$ **(f)** $12.5 \div 1000$

3 **(a)** $84.2 \div 10$ **(b)** $153.61 \div 10$ **(c)** $189.2 \div 100$
     (d) $568 \div 1000$ **(e)** $294 \div 100$ **(f)** $36 \div 100$

4 **(a)** $17.5 \div 100$ **(b)** $0.68 \div 10$ **(c)** $2.8 \div 100$
     (d) $5.2 \div 1000$ **(e)** $0.05 \div 100$ **(f)** $42.8 \div 1000$

6.6 Multiplying by 0.1 and 0.01

■ **To multiply a number by 0.1 move the digits one place to the right. Multiplying by 0.1 is the same as dividing by 10.**

■ **To multiply a number by 0.01 move the digits two places to the right. Multiplying by 0.01 is the same as dividing by 100.**

Hint:
4×0.1 is the same as
$4 \times \frac{1}{10} = \frac{4}{10}$
$\frac{4}{10} = 4 \div 10 = 0.4$

Example 10

Work out:

(a) 12×0.1

(b) 309×0.01

(a) Move the digits one place to the right

(b) Move the digits two places to the right

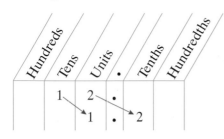

So $12 \times 0.1 = 1.2$

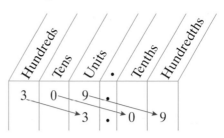

So $309 \times 0.01 = 3.09$

Example 11

Work out:

(a) 14.3×0.1

(b) 32×0.01

(a) $\times 0.1$ is the same as $\div 10$

$14.3 \times 0.1 = 14.3 \div 10 = 1.43$

(b) $\times 0.01$ is the same as $\div 100$

$32 \times 0.01 = 32 \div 100 = 0.32$

Exercise 6F

1 Use a place value diagram to work out:

    (a) 4.7×0.1 **(b)** 26×0.1 **(c)** 370×0.01

    (d) 8×0.01 **(e)** 125×0.01 **(f)** 0.3×0.1

2 Divide by 10 or 100 to work out:

    (a) 88×0.1 **(b)** 13×0.01 **(c)** 1412×0.01

    (d) 9×0.1 **(e)** 409×0.01 **(f)** 640×0.1

6.7 Dividing by 0.1 and 0.01

■ **To divide a number by 0.1 move the digits one place to the left. Dividing by 0.1 is the same as multiplying by 10.**

■ **To divide a number by 0.01 move the digits two places to the left. Dividing by 0.01 is the same as multiplying by 100.**

Hint:
$12 \div 0.1$ is the same as
$12 \div \frac{1}{10}$
$12 \div \frac{1}{10} = 12 \times 10 = 120$
There is more about this on page 169.

Example 12

Work out:

(a) $4.06 \div 0.1$ **(b)** $8.2 \div 0.01$

(a) Move the digits one place to the left

(b) Move the digits two places to the left

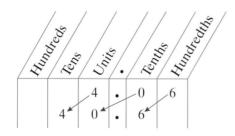

So $4.06 \div 0.1 = 40.6$

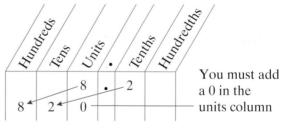

You must add a 0 in the units column

So $8.2 \div 0.01 = 820$

Example 13

Work out:

(a) $41.6 \div 0.1$ **(b)** $0.98 \div 0.01$

(a) $\div 0.1$ is the same as $\times 10$

    $41.6 \div 0.1 = 41.6 \times 10 = 416$

(b) $\div 0.01$ is the same as $\times 100$

    $0.98 \div 0.01 = 0.98 \times 100 = 98$

Exercise 6G

1 Use a place value diagram to work out:

(**a**) $0.3 \div 0.1$ (**b**) $12.4 \div 0.1$ (**c**) $0.77 \div 0.01$

(**d**) $1.03 \div 0.01$ (**e**) $0.07 \div 0.1$ (**f**) $6.8 \div 0.01$

2 Multiply by 10 or 100 to work out:

(**a**) $9 \div 0.1$ (**b**) $0.05 \div 0.01$ (**c**) $25.3 \div 0.1$

(**d**) $83.06 \div 0.1$ (**e**) $4.41 \div 0.01$ (**f**) $63.39 \div 0.01$

6.8 Multiplying decimals by whole numbers

Example 14

Find the cost of 6 books at £5.28 each.

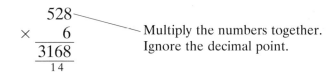

Multiply the numbers together. Ignore the decimal point.

528 is 100 times 5.28

So 3168 is 100 times the actual cost.

To find the cost divide 3168 by 100.

The cost of the books is £31.68

Where to put the decimal point

Look at the original question:

$$5.28 \times 6$$

There are 2 digits after the decimal point.

The answer must also have 2 digits after the decimal point:

$$528 \times 6 = 3168$$

so $5.28 \times 6 = 31.68$

2 digits

Example 15

Without using a calculator work out 7.16×4

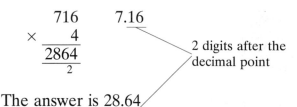

$$
\begin{array}{r}
716 \\
\times \quad 4 \\
\hline
2864 \\
{}_2
\end{array}
\qquad 7.16
$$

2 digits after the decimal point

The answer is 28.64

■ **When you multiply a decimal number by a whole number the answer has the same number of digits after the decimal point as the original decimal number.**

Example 16

Without using a calculator work out 4.36×28

$$
\begin{array}{r}
4\;3\;6 \\
\times \quad 2\;8 \\
\hline
3\;4_2 8_4 8 \\
8\;7_1 2\;0 \\
\hline
1\;2\;2\;0\;8 \\
{}_1\;\;{}_1
\end{array}
$$

Ignore the decimal point

You add a zero when multiplying by the tens

For a reminder on multiplying by a 2-digit number see page 109.

4.36 has two digits after the decimal point.
The answer is 122.08.

Exercise 6H

Show all your working in these questions.

1 Find the cost of:
   (a) 5 books at £4.37 each.
   (b) 4 kg of apples at £0.64 per kg.
   (c) 8 chocolate bars at £0.45 each.
   (d) 6 packets of crisps at £1.38 each.

2 (a) 7.8×2 (b) 5.6×4 (c) 8.4×5
   (d) 2.35×3 (e) 14.6×8 (f) 5.29×6

3 (a) 53.67×9 (b) 7.6×5 (c) 28.63×7
   (d) 8.76×5 (e) 9.25×4 (f) 15.99×8

4 Work out the cost of 9 CDs which cost £12.99 each.

5 Find the total length in metres of seven pieces of wood, each 0.65 metre long.

6 Work out the total length in metres of six pieces of wire, each 0.34 metre long.

7 Find the total cost in pounds (£) of three loaves at £0.82 each and eight cakes at £0.55 each.

8 Calculate the total cost of five cartons of fruit juice which cost £0.70 each and seven packets of biscuits which cost £0.56 each.

9 **(a)** 4.6×12 **(b)** 3.2×21 **(c)** 7.19×15
   (d) 12.46×32 **(e)** 0.36×37 **(f)** 18.02×16

10 Dylan is having a party. He buys

     45 balloons which cost £0.12 each
     12 party hats which cost £1.25 each
     24 party poppers which cost £0.23 each

How much does Dylan spend in total?

6.9 Dividing decimals by whole numbers

Example 17

Four friends share the cost of a meal equally.
The total bill comes to £18.32
How much should they each pay?

You need to work out $18.32 \div 4$

First put the decimal point
in the answer.

Then divide.

$$4)\overline{1\ 8\ .\ 3\ 2}$$

$$4)\overline{1\ 8\ .^2 3^3 2} = 4.58$$

They should each pay £4.58

Example 18

Without a calculator, work out   (a) $36.3 \div 5$ (b) $0.24 \div 8$

(a)
$$
\begin{array}{r}
7.26 \\
5\overline{)36.^13^30}
\end{array}
$$
There is a remainder of 3, so put a zero here.
(36.30 has the same value as 36.3)

The answer is 7.26

(b)
$$
\begin{array}{r}
0.03 \\
8\overline{)0.2^24}
\end{array}
$$
$2 \div 8 = 0$ remainder 2

The answer is 0.03

Example 19

Without using a calculator work out $65.28 \div 17$

Always keep the decimal point in the same place

$$
\begin{array}{r}
3.84 \\
17\overline{)65.28} \\
-51 \\
\hline
14.^{3}{}^{1}28 \\
-13.6 \\
\hline
0.68
\end{array}
$$

$51 = 3 \times 17$

$13.6 = 0.8 \times 17$

2 is less than 6 so you must change 4 into 3 units and 10 tenths

For a reminder on dividing by a 2-digit number see page 110.

The answer is 3.84.

Exercise 61

Work these out **without a calculator**. Show all your working.

1 Find one share if:
   (a) Four people share £5.08 equally.
   (b) Seven people share £215.60 equally.
   (c) Six people share £10.50 equally.
   (d) Eight people share £30.24 equally.

2 (a) $8.6 \div 2$ (b) $5.6 \div 4$ (c) $120.5 \div 5$
   (d) $187.2 \div 3$ (e) $38.82 \div 6$ (f) $17.28 \div 8$

3 (a) $0.612 \div 6$ (b) $0.245 \div 7$ (c) $1.08 \div 4$
   (d) $0.0057 \div 3$ (e) $9.054 \div 9$ (f) $3.75 \div 5$

4 10.8 litres of lemonade are poured equally into six jugs. How much lemonade is in each jug?

5 Four people share equally the cost of hiring a taxi.
The taxi costs £28.60.
How much does each person pay?

6 A box of apples weighing 67.5 kg is packed equally into 9 trays. Work out the weight of apples in each tray.

7 **(a)** $30.24 \div 14$ **(b)** $19.22 \div 31$ **(c)** $143.52 \div 12$
  (d) $58.33 \div 19$ **(e)** $8.17 \div 19$ **(f)** $12.6 \div 15$

8 A lottery win of £351.12 is shared equally amongst 22 people. How much do they each get?

6.10 Numbers half way between

You can use a number line to answer questions about decimals.

Example 20

What number is half way between:

(a) 1 and 2   **(b)** 2.99 and 3.07

(a) Count on from 1 and back from 2 simultaneously:

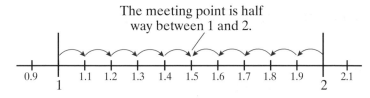

So 1.5 is half way between 1 and 2.

(b) Count on from 2.99 and back from 3.07 simultaneously:

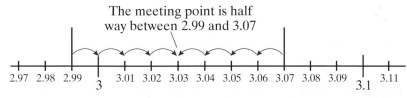

So 3.03 is half way between 2.99 and 3.07.

You can find the answers without using a number line.

Example 21

What number is half way between:

(a) 3.1 and 6.5   **(b)** 4.38 and 7

(a)

Add the numbers together . . .

$$\begin{array}{r} 3.1 \\ +\ 6.5 \\ \hline 9.6 \end{array}$$

. . . then divide the results by 2

$$\begin{array}{r} 4.8 \\ 2\overline{)9.^16} \end{array}$$

The answer is 4.8

(b)

Add the numbers together . . .

$$\begin{array}{r} 4.38 \\ +\ \ 7 \\ \hline 11.38 \end{array}$$

. . . then divide the results by 2

$$\begin{array}{r} 5.69 \\ 2\overline{)11.^13^18} \end{array}$$

The answer is 5.69

■ **To find the number half way between two numbers add them together and divide the result by 2.**

$1 + 2 = 3$ $3 \div 2 = 1.5$

1.5 is half way between 1 and 2.

Exercise 6J

1 Use this number line to find the number which is half way between 6.6 and 6.68

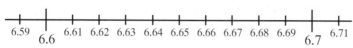

2 Use a number line to find the number half way between:

     (a) 2 and 2.6   **(b)** 7 and 8
     (c) 0.5 and 1.3   **(d)** 6.2 and 6.3
     (e) 0.2 and 1   **(f)** 4.33 and 4.41

3 Write down two pairs of numbers which have 7.1 as their half way point.

4 Without using a number line, find the number half way between:

     (a) 1.6 and 4.2   **(b)** 7 and 12.1
     (c) 2.31 and 6.01   **(d)** 26.1 and 75
     (e) 10.36 and 15.2   **(f)** 9.16 and 103.06

5 What amount of money is half way between £4.99 and £8.25. Give your answer in pounds (£).

6.11 Rounding

It is sometimes useful to round decimals to the nearest whole number, tenth or hundredth.

For a reminder on rounding whole numbers see page 53.

■ **To round to the nearest whole number look at the number in the first decimal place:**
  ● **If it is 5 or more round the units up to the next whole number.**
  ● **If it is less than 5 do not change the units.**

Example 22

Round these decimals to the nearest whole number:

(a) 12.4   (b) 8.53

(a) less than 5 so do not change the units
The answer is 12

(b) 5 or more so round the units up
The answer is 9

The answers must be whole numbers.

■ **To round to the nearest tenth look at the number in the second decimal place:**
  ● **If it is 5 or more round the first decimal place up to the next tenth.**
  ● **If it is less than 5 do not change the first decimal place.**

Rounding to the nearest tenth is sometimes called **rounding to one decimal place**.

Example 23

Round these numbers to one decimal place:

(a) 18.224   (b) 34.65

(a) less than 5 so do not change the first decimal place
The answer is 18.2

(b) 5 or more so round the first decimal place up
The answer is 34.7

The answers must only have one number after the decimal point.

■ **To round to the nearest hundredth look at the number in the third decimal place:**
  ● **If it is 5 or more round the second decimal place up to the next hundredth.**
  ● **If it is less than 5 do not change the second decimal place.**

Rounding to the nearest hundredth is sometimes called **rounding to two decimal places**.

Example 24

Round these numbers to two decimal places:

(a) 6.3244

(b) 14.196

The answers must only have two numbers after the decimal point.

(a) less than 5 so do not change the second decimal place

(b) 5 or more so round the second decimal place up. You have to carry the 1 to the tenths column

The answer is 6.32

The answer is 14.20

You must leave the 0 to show you have rounded to two decimal places.

Exercise 6K

1 Round these decimals to the nearest whole number:

    (a) 4.8   **(b)** 13.14

    (c) 26.5   **(d)** 9.92

    (e) 89.71   **(f)** 0.53

Hint: look at the first decimal place.

2 Round these numbers to one decimal place:

    (a) 14.36   **(b)** 52.05

    (c) 7.492   **(d)** 6.31

    (e) 108.961   **(f)** 3.02

Hint: look at the second decimal place.

3 Round these numbers to two decimal places:

    (a) 2.466   **(b)** 0.1929

    (c) 21.497   **(d)** 9.051

    (e) 3.8595   **(f)** 2.996

Hint: look at the third decimal place.

4 Round 17.483

    (a) to two decimal places
    (b) to one decimal place.

5 **(a)** Round 2.347 to two decimal places.
    (b) Round your answer to part **(a)** to one decimal place.
    (c) Round 2.347 to one decimal place.
    (d) What do you notice about your answers to parts **(b)** and **(c)** ?

6.12 Finding approximate answers

You can use rounding to check answers to calculations.

Example 25

Supraj has calculated 8.3671×1.414. He gets the answer 81.13.

(a) Round the numbers to the nearest whole number and do an approximate calculation.

(b) Could Supraj's answer be correct?

(a) Round to the nearest whole number:
$$8.3671 \times 1.414 \approx 8 \times 1 = 8$$

The answer should be approximately equal to 8

$\approx$ means approximately equal to

(b) Supraj must have made a mistake.

You can also use rounding to estimate answers.

Example 26

Round the first number to one decimal place to estimate these answers:

(a) 6.371×9 (b) $44.4397 \div 12$

(a) Round to one decimal place

$$6.371 \approx 6.4$$

Work out the calculation

$$\begin{array}{r} 64 \\ \times \quad 9 \\ \hline 576 \\ {\scriptstyle 3} \end{array}$$

$$\begin{array}{r} 6.4 \\ 57.6 \end{array}$$

1 digit after decimal point

The answer is approximately equal to 57.6

(b) Round to one decimal place

$$44.4397 \approx 44.4$$

Work out the calculation

$$\begin{array}{r} 3.7 \\ 12 \overline{)44.4} \\ -36 \\ \hline 8.4 \end{array}$$

The answer is approximately equal to 3.7

Exercise 6L

1 Nadia has calculated $41.63 \div 7.19$. She gets the answer 5.79.

    (a) Estimate her answer by rounding to the nearest whole number.

    (b) Do you think she was right?

2 For each calculation
- Estimate the answer by rounding to the nearest whole number.
- Say whether the answer could be correct.

    (a) $29.9 \times 4.2 = 12.56$ **(b)** $3.12 \times 7.73 = 24.12$

    (c) $26.553 \div 2.781 = 5.591$

3 Round the first number to one decimal place to estimate these answers:

    (a) 3.214×7 **(b)** 4.941×18 **(c)** $30.9537 \div 5$

    (d) 7.647×23 **(e)** $4.773 \div 3$ **(f)** $10.4541 \div 25$

4 Repeat question **3** rounding to *two* decimal places to estimate the answers.

5 Work out the exact answers in question **3** using a calculator. Compare your answers.

Summary of key points

1 In a decimal number the decimal point separates the whole number from the part that is less than one:

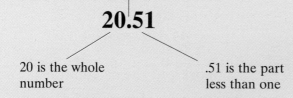

    20.51

    20 is the whole number   .51 is the part less than one

2 When adding or subtracting decimal numbers always line up the decimal points.

3 You can sort decimal numbers in order of size by comparing first the whole numbers, then the tenths, then the hundredths, and so on.

4 To multiply decimal numbers:
- by 0.01 move each digit **two** places to the **right** $12.6 \times 0.01 = 0.126$
- by 0.1 move each digit **one** place to the **right** $22.1 \times 0.1 = 2.21$
- by 10 move each digit **one** place to the **left** $25.68 \times 10 = 256.8$
- by 100 move each digit **two** places to the **left** $36.97 \times 100 = 3697$
- by 1000 move each digit **three** places to the **left** $0.23 \times 1000 = 230$

To divide decimal numbers
- by 0.01 move each digit **two** places to the **left** $0.7 \div 0.01 = 70$
- by 0.1 move each digit **one** place to the **left** $1.3 \div 0.1 = 13$
- by 10 move each digit **one** place to the **right** $98.72 \div 10 = 9.872$
- by 100 move each digit **two** places to the **right** $26.5 \div 100 = 0.265$
- by 1000 move each digit **three** places to the **right** $536.8 \div 1000 = 0.5368$

5 When you multiply a decimal number by a whole number the answer has the same number of digits after the decimal point as the original decimal number.

6 To find the number half way between two numbers add them together and divide the result by 2.

7 To round to the nearest whole number look at the number in the first decimal place:

- If it is 5 or more round the units up to the next whole number.
- If it is less than 5 do not change the units.

8 To round to the nearest tenth look at the number in the second decimal place:

- If it is 5 or more round the first decimal place up to the next tenth.
- If it is less than 5 do not change the first decimal place.

9 To round to the nearest hundredth look at the number in the third decimal place:

- If it is 5 or more round the second decimal place up to the next hundredth.
- If it is less than 5 do not change the second decimal place.

7 Measuring

This unit is about measuring lengths, weights and times.

7.1 Measuring lengths and distances

You can measure:

very short lengths in millimetres (mm)	short lengths in centimetres (cm)	medium lengths in metres (m)	long distances in kilometres (km)

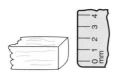
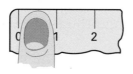
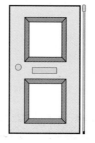

A matchstick is about 2 mm thick. You can use a ruler to measure very short lengths.

A fingernail is about 1 cm wide. You can use a ruler to measure short lengths.

A door is about 2 m high. You can use a tape measure to measure medium lengths.

Three times round a football pitch is about 1 km. You can use a trundle wheel to measure this.

Millimetres, centimetres, metres and kilometres are all **units** of measurement. A unit is a standard amount, the same everywhere in the world.

Exercise 7A

1 Give three examples of things you would measure in:

    (a) mm   **(b)** cm   **(c)** m   **(d)** km

2 What units would you measure these lengths in?

    (a) length of a car   **(b)** length of a hockey pitch

    (c) length of a pencil   **(d)** length of a river

    (e) length of a sheet of paper   **(f)** width of a staple

    (g) height of a building   **(h)** thickness of a piece of glass

    (i) width of a doorway   **(j)** length of the M1 motorway

    (k) thickness of a coin   **(l)** height of a step

7.2 Using a ruler

You can use a ruler to measure in mm and cm.

■   **10 mm = 1 cm**
      1 mm = 0.1 cm

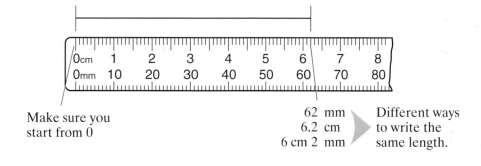

Make sure you start from 0

62 mm
6.2 cm
6 cm 2 mm

Different ways to write the same length.

Exercise 7B

1 Measure these lines:

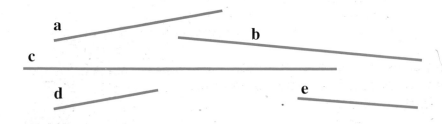

2 Draw these lines:

    (a) 30 mm   (b) 56 mm   (c) 84 mm

    (d) 2.3 cm   (e) 4.9 cm   (f) 6.5 cm

    (g) 2 cm 9 mm   (h) 3 cm 4 mm

3 Write these lengths as centimetres in decimal form:

    (a) 56 mm   (b) 120 mm   (c) 86 mm

    (d) 2 cm 4 mm   (e) 10 cm 2 mm   (f) 93 mm

    (g) 6 cm 7 mm   (h) 7 cm 3 mm

Hint:
    22 mm = 2.2 cm

4 Write these lengths in mm:

    (a) 3.6 cm   (b) 12.8 cm   (c) 7.4 cm

    (d) 14 cm 2 mm   (e) 4.3 cm   (f) 36.9 cm

    (g) 29 cm 7 mm   (h) 0.4 cm

5 Measure these lines as accurately as you can:

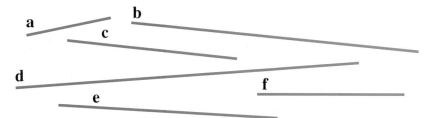

7.3 Longer and longer

■ **1 km = 1000 m**

■
$$\begin{aligned}
1 \text{ m} &= 100 \text{ cm} = 1000 \text{ mm} \\
0.1 \text{ m} &= 10 \text{ cm} = 100 \text{ mm} \\
0.01 \text{ m} &= 1 \text{ cm} = 10 \text{ mm} \\
0.001 \text{ m} &= 0.1 \text{ cm} = 1 \text{ mm}
\end{aligned}$$

You can write the same length in several different ways:

cm	80	90	100	110	120	130
m	0.8	0.9	1.0	1.1	1.2	1.3

0.87 m is in metres   1.23 m is in metres

0 m 87 cm is a mixed length   1 m 23 cm is a mixed length

87 cm is in centimetres   123 cm is in centimetres

870 mm is in millimetres   1230 mm is in millimetres

Example 1

Write 345 cm in as many different ways as you can.

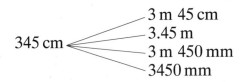

345 cm
- 3 m 45 cm
- 3.45 m
- 3 m 450 mm
- 3450 mm

Exercise 7C

1 Write each of these lengths in as many ways as you can.

   (a) 726 cm   **(b)** 9 m 32 cm   **(c)** 5 m 270 mm

   (d) 8230 mm   **(e)** 3.65 m   **(f)** 89 cm

   (g) 26.9 cm   **(h)** 3765 mm

2 Write in metres:

   (a) 4 km 320 m   **(b)** 32 km 428 m

   (c) 7 km 560 m   **(d)** 81 km 205 m

3 Write in kilometres:

   (a) 1526 m   **(b)** 48 743 m

   (c) 201 591 m   **(d)** 2047 m

4 Activity You need a sheet of A4 paper and a ruler.

   (a) Measure the distance around the edge of an A4 sheet of paper.

   (b) Fold your piece of paper in half. Measure the distance around the half piece of paper.

   (c) Fold the piece of paper in half again. Measure the distance around the quarter piece of paper.

   (d) What do you notice?

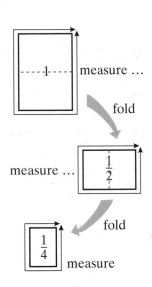

5 Activity You need a metre rule or a tape measure. Find objects in the classroom which are as close as possible to these lengths:

   (a) 78 cm   **(b)** 405 mm   **(c)** 1250 mm

   (d) 7.8 m   **(e)** 0.7 cm   **(f)** 2 m 380 mm

   (g) 19 cm 5 mm   **(h)** 3 m 30 cm

7.4 Ordering lengths

Example 2

Write these lengths in order of size, shortest first:

4 m 53 cm   4 m 48 cm   6 m 38 cm   2 m 31 cm

First sort using the number of metres:

4 m 53 cm   **4** m 48 cm   **6** m 38 cm   **2** m 31 cm

Put the smallest first …

2 m 31 cm   **4** m 53 cm   **4** m 48 cm   **6** m 38 cm

4 m 53 cm and 4 m 48 cm have the same number of metres, so look at the number of centimetres:

2 m 31 cm   4 m **53** cm   4 m **48** cm   6 m 38 cm

Put the smallest first …

2 m 31 cm   4 m 48 cm   4 m 53 cm   6 m 38 cm

Exercise 7D

1   William's six jumps in the long jump final were:

8 m 17 cm   7 m 94 cm   8 m 09 cm   7 m 87 cm
7 m 81 cm   8 m 03 cm

(a) Write these lengths in order of size.

(b) Which was his longest jump?

2   The table shows the six throws of competitors in a discus event.

Name	1st throw	2nd throw	3rd throw	4th throw	5th throw	6th throw
Helena	32.95 m	27.64 m	34.06 m	29.85 m	34.19 m	27.94 m
Fatima	33.14 m	32.94 m	26.85 m	33.98 m	33.94 m	31.94 m
Dionne	35.14 m	35.86 m	32.30 m	32.30 m	24.15 m	36.17 m
Sarah	24.83 m	27.63 m	30.04 m	30.06 m	34.24 m	26.39 m
Elspeth	26.49 m	37.04 m	33.46 m	25.38 m	22.49 m	28.86 m

The competitor who throws the furthest wins the event.

(a) Write down the longest throw for each woman.

(b) Copy and complete the table to find the position of each woman in the event.

Position	Name	Longest throw
1ˢᵗ		
2ⁿᵈ		
3ʳᵈ		
4ᵗʰ		
5ᵗʰ		

3   Put these lengths in order of size:

230 cm   2 m 25 cm   2060 mm   1 m 97 cm   2 m 9 mm

Hint: write each length in the same way then sort them.

7.5 Measuring weights

You can measure weights in:

Milligrams (mg) …   … grams (g)   … kilograms (kg)   … tonnes (t).

A grain of sand weighs about 1 mg

A sheet of A4 paper weighs about 1g

A bag of sugar weighs 1 kg

A small car weighs about 1 t.

Exercise 7E

1   In what units would you measure these objects?
Use mg, g, kg or t.

(a) a sweet   (b) a bicycle   (c) a van

(d) a robin   (e) a goose   (f) a hippopotamus

(g) a grain of sugar   (h) a brick   (i) this textbook

(j) a slipper   (k) a sock   (l) a hair

(m) a jacket   (n) a piano   (o) a spoon

(p) a snowflake   (q) a chair   (r) a cupboard

2   Write down four things you would weigh in each of these units:

(a) milligrams   (b) grams

(c) kilograms   (d) tonnes

7.6 Mixing weights

■   **1000 mg = 1 g**
1000 g   = 1 kg
1000 kg = 1 t

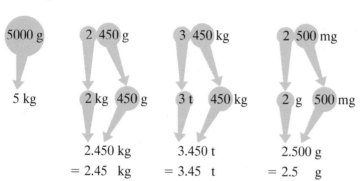

No wonder it's heavy. A tonne is a million grams!

5000 g	2 450 g	3 450 kg	2 500 mg
5 kg	2 kg 450 g	3 t 450 kg	2 g 500 mg
	2.450 kg	3.450 t	2.500 g
	= 2.45 kg	= 3.45 t	= 2.5 g

Example 3

(a) Write 2360 g as a mixed weight.

(b) Write 4028 mg as a mixed weight.

(a)   2 360 g

= 2000 g   360 g

= 2 kg   360 g

(b)   4 028 mg

= 4000 g   28 mg

= 4 g   28 mg

Example 4

Ian bought a chicken weighing 1 kg 315 g, a packet of stuffing weighing 254 g and a $2\frac{1}{2}$ kg bag of potatoes.

What was the total weight of the three items?

Write each weight in kilograms as decimal numbers:

$$1 \text{ kg } 315 \text{ g} \rightarrow 1.315 \text{ kg}$$
$$254 \text{ g} \rightarrow 0.254 \text{ kg}$$
$$2\frac{1}{2} \text{ kg} \rightarrow 2.5 \text{ kg}$$

Add the decimals:

        1.315
        0.254
    + 2.5
    ‾‾‾‾‾‾‾‾
        4.069

The total weight of the three items was 4.069 kg or 4 kg 69 g

Exercise 7F

1 Write down in grams **and** kilograms:

   (a) 3 kg 250 g   **(b)** 6 kg 200 g   **(c)** 9 kg 420 g

   (d) 3 kg 50 g   **(e)** 10 kg 350 g   **(f)** 20 kg 5 g

   (g) 30 000 mg   **(h)** 25 500 mg   **(i)** 14 050 mg

2 Write each of these weights in two different ways:

   (a) 2750 g   **(b)** 3500 g   **(c)** 7570 kg

   (d) 1050 kg   **(e)** 10 024 g   **(f)** 4006 g

   (g) 3.455 kg   **(h)** 7.050 kg   **(i)** 16.45 kg

   (j) 20.02 kg   **(k)** 15.325 g   **(l)** 1.245 t

3 What is the total weight of shopping in each basket?

(a)

(b)

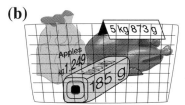

(c)

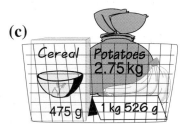

4 A lorry has a maximum weight limit of 5 tonnes.
   Which of these objects can be carried by the lorry in
   one load?

crate	drum	girder	cage	casting
1.75 tonnes	987 kg	2 tonnes 465 kg	1.259 tonnes	2.394 tonnes

Find all the possible combinations.

7.7 Measuring liquids

■ **You can measure liquids in litres, centilitres and millilitres:**

    1000 millilitres (ml) = 1 litre (l)
    100 centilitres (cl) = 1 litre (l)

A standard can of cola contains 330 ml.

Exercise 7G

1 Write these amounts as ml.

(a) 3 litres   (b) 4 litres   (c) 10 litres   (d) $5\frac{1}{2}$ litres

(e) 6.7 litres   (f) 5 cl   (g) 30 cl   (h) 33 cl

(i) 45 cl   (j) $15\frac{1}{2}$ cl

2 Write these amounts in litres.

(a) 6000 ml   (b) 125 000 ml   (c) 3500 ml

(d) 500 ml   (e) 200 cl   (f) 1200 cl

(g) 150 cl   (h) 450 cl

3 A glass holds 25 cl of liquid when full. How many times can it be filled from a $1\frac{1}{2}$ litre bottle?

4 Peter's water boiler holds $22\frac{1}{2}$ litres. He fills it using a 750 ml jug. How many jugfuls does he need to fill the boiler?

7.8 Reading scales

The division marks on a scale may not go up 1 at a time. Sometimes the divisions are 2 units, sometimes 5 units, sometimes 10, 25 or 50 units.

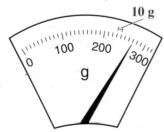

Each division on this scale represents 10 g.
The scale shows 270 g.

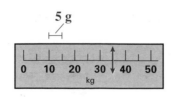

Each division on this scale represents 5 kg.
The scale shows 35 kg.

Exercise 7H

For each scale:
- what does each division represent?
- what weight does the scale show?

(a)

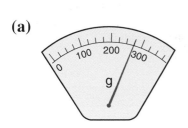

(b)

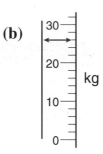

(c)

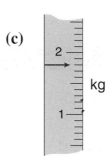

(d)

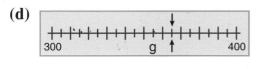

(e)

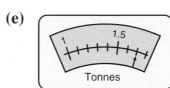

(f)

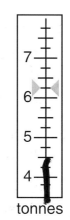

(g)

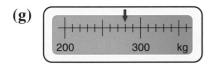

(h)

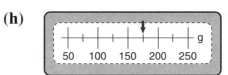

7.9 What time is it?

The 24-hour clock

This clock shows 9 o'clock:

9 o'clock in the morning is 9 am

9 o'clock in the evening is 9 pm

am ante meridiem
before midday

pm post meridiem
after midday

Hint: a comes
before p in the
alphabet.

■ **You use am for times between midnight and midday.**

■ **You use pm for times after midday and up to midnight.**

This video clock uses the 24-hour clock

This shows 9:30 am   This shows 9:30 pm

The 24-hour clock works like this:

12-hour clock times use **am** or **pm** to show whether a time is before or after midday

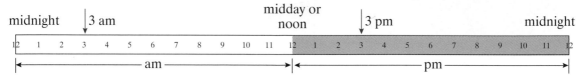

24-hour clock times number the hours from **0** to **23**

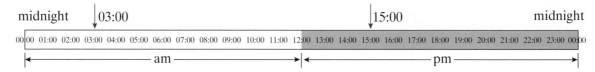

24-hour clock times must have 4 digits.
The first two digits show the hours.
The last two digits show the minutes.

■ **To change 12-hour times to 24-hour times:**

Up to 12 noon the times are the same:

$$8:30 \, am \rightarrow 08:30$$

24-hour time always has 4 digits

After 12 noon add 12 to the hour number:

$$2:57 \, pm \rightarrow 14:57$$

$+\ 12$

except for times from midnight to 1 am. These start with 00

$$12:35 \, am \rightarrow 00:35$$

Exercise 7I

1 Change to 24-hour clock time:

(a) 8:00 am	**(b)** 8:35 pm	**(c)** 11:20 am	**(d)** 1:30 pm
(e) 3:45 pm	**(f)** 4:15 pm	**(g)** 9:15 pm	**(h)** 10:00 pm
(i) 11:15 pm	**(j)** midday	**(k)** 12:20 pm	**(l)** 12:35 am

2 Write these times as 24-hour clock times:
  (a) Quarter past six in the morning. **(b)** Half past two in the afternoon.
  (c) Quarter to ten in the morning. **(d)** Ten to six in the evening.

3 Change to 12-hour clock time:
(a)	11:00	**(b)**	14:45	**(c)**	17:36	**(d)**	03:50
(e)	08:15	**(f)**	21:38	**(g)**	23:17	**(h)**	00:30
(i)	18:23	**(j)**	07:15	**(k)**	12:48	**(l)**	00:47

7.10 How long will it take?

■ **60 minutes = 1 hour**

When you are calculating times remember: there are
60 minutes in an hour **not** 100!

Example 5

Nina takes 10 minutes to walk to the bus stop.
She waits 5 minutes for the bus to arrive.
She is on the bus for 50 minutes.
How long does Nina's journey take altogether?

Add the times together:

   $10 + 5 + 50 = 65$ minutes

It takes 1 hour and 5 minutes altogether.

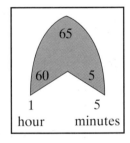

Example 6

Joe started work at 9:15 am and finished at 12:20 pm.
How long was Joe working?

You can work it out like this:

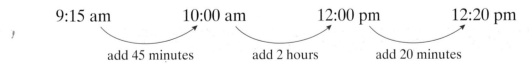

9:15 am   10:00 am   12:00 pm   12:20 pm

   add 45 minutes   add 2 hours   add 20 minutes

45 minutes + 2 hours + 20 minutes
   = 2 hours + 65 minutes
   = 3 hours and 5 minutes

He worked for 3 hours and 5 minutes.

Exercise 7J

1 Sue spends 25 minutes doing French homework, 36 minutes doing maths homework and 20 minutes doing geography homework.
   How long did Sue spend doing her homework?

2 Vijay went on holiday. He travelled on the underground for 35 minutes. He waited in the airport for 55 minutes. The flight took 1 hour 50 minutes. The taxi to the hotel took 20 minutes.
   How long did Vijay's journey take altogether?

3 The train takes 1 hour 31 minutes to travel from London to Eastbourne.
   A train leaves London at 3:48 pm.
   What time does it arrive in Eastbourne?

4 A History lesson is 50 minutes long.
   The lesson starts at 1:25 pm. What time does it finish?

5 It takes Naomi 20 minutes to walk to school.
   What time must she leave home to arrive by five past nine?

6 Here is a list of jobs Gary must do this weekend.

   Gary has $2\frac{1}{4}$ hours free on Saturday to complete some of the jobs.

   (a) Which jobs can he do on Saturday to use up all $2\frac{1}{4}$ hours?

   (b) How much time does he need to spend on Sunday to complete the jobs?

Mow the lawn	35 min
Wash the car	20 min
Hoover the house	40 min
Paint a door	1 hour 10 min
Dust	25 min

7.11 Using timetables

This timetable shows when trains go from Morecambe to Southport in the morning:

Morecambe	0630	0730	0830
Lancaster	0650	0800	0900
Preston	0740	0900	
Southport	0850	0940	1040

The trains leave Morecambe at 0630, 0730 and 0830.

The 0730 train leaves Preston at 0900.

The 0830 train does not stop at Preston.

The trains arrive in Southport at these times.

Example 7

Using the timetable:

(a) What time is the earliest train from Morecambe?

(b) What time does the 0730 train from Morecambe arrive in Lancaster?

(c) How long does the 0830 train from Morecambe take to get to Southport?

(a) The earliest train is at 0630.

(b) The 0730 train arrives in Lancaster at 0800.

(c) The 0830 train gets to Southport at 1040.
The train takes 2 hours 10 minutes.

Exercise 7K

1 Here is part of a bus timetable:

Hertford	0730	0850	0940	1055
Hoddesdon	0746	0906	0956	1111
Nazeing	0759	0919	1009	1124
Harlow	0820	0940	1030	1145

(a) What time does the second bus leave Hertford?

(b) What time does the 0940 bus from Hertford arrive at Harlow?

(c) A bus arrives in Harlow at 1145. When did it leave Hoddesdon?

(d) How long does the journey from Hoddesdon to Nazeing take?

(e) If I *just* miss the 0956 bus from Hoddesdon, how long will I have to wait for the next bus?

2 Here is part of a train timetable:

Derby	----	0729	0802	----	0854
Spondon	----	0734	----	----	----
Long Eaton	----	0741	0811	----	0904
Attenborough	0736	0747	0817	0834	----
Beeston	0740	0751	----	0837	----
Nottingham	0745	0800	0824	0843	0910

(a) Which train takes the least time to travel between Derby and Nottingham?

(b) Which train is the last I could catch from Attenborough to be in Nottingham by 0830?

(c) Which trains from Attenborough stop at Beeston?

(d) I arrive at Derby at 0740. How could I get to Beeston?

3 Here is part of a train timetable:

Kemble	1534	1634	1726	1815
Stroud	1549	1649	1741	1830
Stonehouse	1554	1654	1746	1835
Gloucester	1607	1708	1801	1847
Cheltenham	1620	1719	----	1906

(a) What time does the 1634 train from Kemble arrive at Stonehouse?

(b) I want to arrive in Gloucester before 6 pm. Which trains could I catch from Kemble?

(c) How long does the 1649 from Stroud take to reach Cheltenham?

(d) Which train travels between Stroud and Gloucester in the shortest time?

(e) I leave work in Kemble at 5 pm. What is the earliest I can arrive by train in Cheltenham?

4 Here is part of a railway timetable:

Birmingham	2250	0524	0615	----
Coventry	2310	0546	----	----
Rugby	2324	0600	----	0650
Milton Keynes	0003	0625	----	0714
Watford	0039	0649	0734	0739
London Euston	0105	0710	0754	0800

(a) What time does the 2250 train from Birmingham arrive in London?

(b) How long does the journey take?

(c) Which train from Coventry arrives at Watford at 0649?

(d) The 0615 from Birmingham is running 35 minutes late. What time does it arrive at London Euston?

(e) I get off the 0546 from Coventry at Milton Keynes. How long is it until the next train to London?

Summary of key points

1 10 mm = 1 cm
   1 mm = 0.1 cm

2 1 km = 1000 m

3   1 m = 100 cm = 1000 mm
       0.1 m = 10 cm = 100 mm
      0.01 m =   1 cm =   10 mm
     0.001 m = 0.1 cm =   1 mm

4 1000 mg = 1 g
1000 g   = 1 kg
1000 kg = 1 t

5 You can measure liquids in litres, centilitres and millilitres:
1000 millilitres (ml) = 1 litre (l)
100 centilitres (cl) = 1 litre (l)

6 You use am for times between midnight and midday.

7 You use pm for times after midday and up to midnight.

8 To change 12-hour time to 24-hour time:

8:30 am → 08:30	24-hour time always has 4 digits.
11:25 am → 11:25	The 4 digits stay the same.
2:57 pm → 14:57	For pm times add twelve to the number of hours.
12:35 am → 00:35	Times between midnight and 1 am start with 00.

9 60 minutes = 1 hour

8 Fractions and ratio

All these things are divided into equal parts called **fractions**:

This symbol has two halves.

One part is **one half** or $\frac{1}{2}$ of the symbol.

This swimming pool has four lanes.

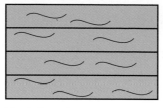

Each lane is **one quarter** or $\frac{1}{4}$ of the pool.

This pie has eight slices.

Each slice is **one eighth** or $\frac{1}{8}$ of the pie.

8.1 Using numbers to represent fractions

Three quarters or $\frac{3}{4}$ of this garden is grass:

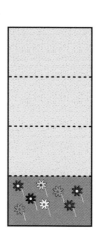

- The top number shows 3 parts are grass.

  The top number is the **numerator**.

  $$\frac{3}{4}$$

  The bottom number shows the garden has 4 equal parts.

  The bottom number is the **denominator**.

When is a fraction not a fraction?

Each slice is the same size. Each slice is $\frac{1}{3}$ or **one third**.

These slices arc unequal. They are **not** thirds.

Example 1

Write down the fraction that is shaded.

(a)

(b)

(a) $\frac{2}{5}$

(b) $\frac{3}{4}$

Exercise 8A

1 Write down the fraction that is shaded.

(a) 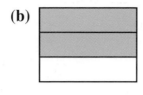 (b) 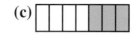 (c) 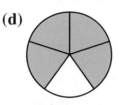 (d)

2 (a) What is the numerator of the fraction $\frac{5}{6}$?
   (b) What is the denominator of the fraction $\frac{3}{10}$?

3 For each shape write down
   • the fraction that is shaded
   • the fraction that is unshaded.

(a) 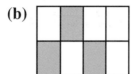 (b) 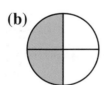 (c)

4 For each circle, write down the fraction that is shaded.

(a) 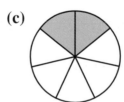 (b) (c) 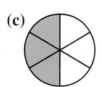 (d)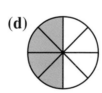

   Notice that all four fractions represent the **same**
   amount of the circle.

5 Each shape is divided into a number of equal parts.
   Copy each shape and shade the fraction marked by it.
   Describe in words what fraction is unshaded.

(a)  $\frac{5}{8}$ (b) $\frac{1}{3}$ (c) $\frac{3}{4}$

6 **(a)** Copy this shape and shade in $\frac{2}{3}$ of it.

(b) On another copy, shade $\frac{3}{5}$ of the shape.

7 This number line shows three fifths. Draw a number line to show seven tenths.

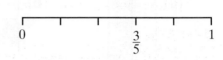

8 Lucy bought a bag of nuts. She kept three eighths of the nuts and gave the rest to her brother. What fraction did she give her brother?

8.2 Mixed numbers and improper fractions

Sometimes whole numbers and fractions are combined.

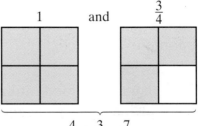

■ **A mixed number has a whole number part and a fraction part,** for example $1\frac{3}{4}$.

A mixed number can be written as a top heavy fraction. For example:

mixed number $1\frac{3}{4} = \frac{7}{4}$ top heavy

$\frac{7}{4}$ is top heavy because 7 is greater than 4

You can convert top heavy fractions back into mixed numbers as well:

$$\frac{13}{5} = \frac{5}{5} + \frac{5}{5} + \frac{3}{5}$$
$$= 1 + 1 + \frac{3}{5} = 2\frac{3}{5}$$

1   and $\frac{3}{4}$

$$\frac{4}{4} + \frac{3}{4} = \frac{7}{4}$$

■ **Top heavy fractions are also called improper fractions. The numerator (top) is greater than the denominator (bottom).** For example $\frac{7}{4}$.

■ **A vulgar fraction's numerator is less than its denominator.** For example $\frac{3}{4}$.

Vulgar fractions are more common than improper fractions.

Vulgar comes from the Latin word *vulgaris* meaning common.

Exercise 8B

1   Write down whether these fractions are:
   - vulgar
   - improper
   - mixed numbers.

   (a) $1\frac{2}{3}$ (b) $\frac{7}{2}$ (c) $3\frac{4}{5}$ (d) $\frac{1}{7}$ (e) $2\frac{1}{4}$ (f) $\frac{6}{4}$

   (g) $\frac{2}{5}$ (h) $\frac{4}{9}$ (i) $\frac{11}{2}$ (j) $5\frac{1}{2}$ (k) $\frac{3}{2}$ (l) $\frac{2}{3}$

2   Notice that $1 = \frac{1}{1} = \frac{2}{2} = \frac{3}{3} = \frac{4}{4}$

   Copy and complete this with three more examples:

   $1 = \frac{8}{8} = \square = \square = \square$

3   Convert these mixed numbers to improper fractions:

   (a) $2\frac{1}{4}$ (b) $1\frac{3}{5}$ (c) $4\frac{1}{8}$ (d) $3\frac{6}{7}$

   (e) $1\frac{1}{11}$ (f) $3\frac{5}{9}$ (g) $2\frac{1}{2}$ (h) $10\frac{11}{16}$

4   Convert these improper fractions to mixed numbers:

   (a) $\frac{6}{5}$ (b) $\frac{9}{4}$ (c) $\frac{7}{5}$ (d) $\frac{13}{9}$

   (e) $\frac{5}{2}$ (f) $\frac{21}{6}$ (g) $\frac{14}{7}$ (h) $\frac{19}{3}$

8.3 Finding a fraction of a quantity

Sometimes you need to find a fraction of a quantity.

■ **You can think of the bottom part of a fraction as a division.** For example:

   to find $\frac{1}{2}$ divide by 2

   to find $\frac{1}{3}$ divide by 3

   to find $\frac{1}{4}$ divide by 4

Example 2

Find $\frac{1}{5}$ of 30.

To find one fifth of 30, divide by 5.

$30 \div 5 = 6$ so $\frac{1}{5}$ of 30 is 6

$30 \div 5$ can also be written as $\frac{30}{5}$

You often have to find fractions of amounts of money, weights, times and lengths.

Example 3

Find $\frac{1}{4}$ of 32p.

To find $\frac{1}{4}$ divide by 4

$32p \div 4 = 8p$ so $\frac{1}{4}$ of 32p is 8p

$32 \div 4$ can also be written as $\frac{32}{4}$

When you find a fraction of a quantity you won't always get a whole number answer.

Example 4

Find $\frac{1}{4}$ of 3 cakes.

$3 \text{ cakes} \div 4 = \frac{3}{4}$ of a cake

Example 5

Divide 4 rolls equally between 3 children.

How many rolls do they get each?

The children each get one whole roll.
The fourth roll is cut into thirds.

$4 \div 3 = \frac{4}{3}$ or $1\frac{1}{3}$.   They each get $1\frac{1}{3}$ rolls.

Exercise 8C

1 Find:

    (a) $\frac{1}{3}$ of 12   **(b)** $\frac{1}{8}$ of 16   **(c)** $\frac{1}{4}$ of 36

    (d) $\frac{1}{5}$ of 8   **(e)** $\frac{1}{6}$ of 5

2 Find:

(a) $\frac{1}{3}$ of 24 records   (b) $\frac{1}{5}$ of £45

(c) $\frac{1}{4}$ of 60 kilograms   (d) $\frac{1}{4}$ of 120 minutes

(e) $\frac{1}{5}$ of 300 cm   (f) $\frac{1}{10}$ of 230p

3 If you divide 5 oranges equally between 3 children how many oranges do they each get?

4 Mrs Shah shares 7 bars of chocolate equally between her 4 children.
How many bars do they each get?

8.4 Finding more than one part

To find three quarters $\left(\frac{3}{4}\right)$ of something first find one quarter, then multiply one quarter by three.

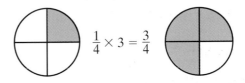

$\frac{1}{4} \times 3 = \frac{3}{4}$

Example 6

Find $\frac{3}{4}$ of 24.

First find $\frac{1}{4}$ of 24.

  $\frac{1}{4}$ of 24   is $24 \div 4 = 6$

If $\frac{1}{4}$ of 24 is 6   then $\frac{3}{4}$ of 24 is $6 \times 3 = 18$

Here is another method:
Find 3 lots of 24
    $3 \times 24 = 72$
Then find one quarter of 72
    $72 \div 4 = 18$

Example 7

Find $\frac{4}{5}$ of £30.

First find $\frac{1}{5}$ of £30.

  $\frac{1}{5}$ of £30   is   £30 $\div 5 =$ £6

If $\frac{1}{5}$ of £30 is £6   then $\frac{4}{5}$ of £30 is   £6 $\times 4 =$ £24

■   **To find $\frac{4}{5}$ of an amount, divide by 5 then multiply by 4.**

Exercise 8D

1 Find:

(a) $\frac{3}{4}$ of 24   (b) $\frac{2}{3}$ of 60   (c) $\frac{2}{5}$ of 35

2 Find:

(a) $\frac{5}{6}$ of 60 minutes   (b) $\frac{3}{4}$ of 200p   (c) $\frac{3}{5}$ of 100 cents

3 $\frac{3}{5}$ of the 250 people at a disco are girls.

(a) How many girls are at the disco?

(b) How many boys are at the disco?

4 Maureen and David are shopping for a picnic. They have £36. They spend $\frac{1}{6}$ of the money on drinks and $\frac{2}{3}$ of the money on snacks.

How much do they spend on:

(a) drinks

(b) snacks?

5 Akila and Andrew both get £5 pocket money each week.

Akila spends $\frac{2}{5}$ of her money on magazines.

Andrew spends $\frac{3}{10}$ of his money on sweets.

(a) How much does Akila spend on magazines?

(b) How much does Andrew spend on sweets?

6 Steven has a dog called K9. He spends $\frac{3}{8}$ of his weekly shopping bill of £32 on food for K9. How much does he spend on K9?

7 Morgan has a company car. His total annual mileage is 12 000 miles. $\frac{5}{8}$ of this mileage is for work.

(a) How many miles does he travel for work?

(b) What fraction of his 12 000 miles is for his personal use?

8.5 Equivalent fractions

Each of these chocolate bars is divided up a different way.
Dominic, Gary, Emma and Anne all eat the same amount.

Dominic eats $\frac{1}{2}$ Gary eats $\frac{2}{4}$ Emma eats $\frac{3}{6}$ Anne eats $\frac{4}{8}$

Notice that $\frac{1}{2}$ a bar is the same as $\frac{2}{4}$, $\frac{3}{6}$ or $\frac{4}{8}$ of a bar.
$\frac{1}{2}$, $\frac{2}{4}$, $\frac{3}{6}$ and $\frac{4}{8}$ all represent the same amount.
They are all **equivalent fractions.**

Equivalent just
means having the
same value.

■ **Equivalent fractions have the same value.**
For example, $\frac{2}{3} = \frac{4}{6} = \frac{6}{9} = \frac{8}{12}$

Example 8

Draw a diagram to show that $\frac{3}{9} = \frac{1}{3}$

$$\frac{3}{9} \quad = \quad \frac{1}{3}$$

You can find equivalent fractions
by multiplying the numerator and
denominator of a fraction by the
same number.

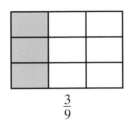

so $\frac{1}{2} = \frac{3}{6}$

You can also find equivalent fractions
by dividing the numerator and
denominator of a fraction by
the same number.

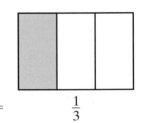

so $\frac{3}{6} = \frac{1}{2}$

$\frac{1}{2}$ is the **simplest form** of the fraction $\frac{3}{6}$.
There is no equivalent fraction with smaller numbers on
the top and bottom.

Example 9

Find an equivalent fraction in sixths for $\frac{2}{3}$

$$\frac{2}{3} = \frac{4}{6}$$

Example 10

Find an equivalent fraction in fifths for $\frac{4}{10}$

$$\frac{4}{10} = \frac{2}{5}$$

Notice that 2 is a factor of 4 and 10. There is more about factors on page 96.

Exercise 8E

1. Draw 4 squares the same size. Use them to show that
   $\frac{1}{2} = \frac{2}{4} = \frac{3}{6} = \frac{4}{8}$
   Label each square with its fraction.

2. Copy and complete these fractions:

   (a) $\frac{1}{2} = \frac{}{4}$ (b) $\frac{1}{3} = \frac{}{12}$ (c) $\frac{1}{} = \frac{3}{6}$ (d) $\frac{3}{8} = \frac{9}{}$

3. Using diagrams (or any other way) find four fractions equivalent to $\frac{1}{3}$

4. John wants to share a chocolate bar between 3 people. What fraction will each person get if:

   (a) it is split into 12 parts

   (b) it is split into 9 parts

   (c) it is split into 15 parts

5. Andrew, Sharon and Rotna each made a cake the same size. Andrew cut his into 12 equal pieces, Sharon cut hers into 8 equal pieces and Rotna cut hers into 4 equal pieces.
   Each offered a friend exactly the same amount. Draw diagrams to show what amount this could be and describe it in words. What other amounts could you have chosen?

6 Mary has $\frac{2}{3}$ of a bar of nougat. Keith has $\frac{4}{6}$ of an identical bar.

Are the following sentences true or false?

(a) Mary has more nougat than Keith.

(b) Keith has more nougat than Mary.

(c) They have the same amount of nougat.

(d) Keith has twice the amount of nougat as Mary.

(e) Keith has smaller pieces of nougat but the same amount as Mary.

7 Pick out three equivalent fractions from this group:

$$\frac{1}{2} \qquad \frac{1}{3} \qquad \frac{3}{4} \qquad \frac{3}{6} \qquad \frac{2}{4} \qquad \frac{4}{10}$$

8.6 Adding and subtracting fractions

It is easy to add and subtract fractions when the denominator (bottom) is the same:

Adding

$$\frac{1}{5} + \frac{2}{5} = \frac{3}{5}$$

Add the numerators (top).

Write them over the same denominator (bottom).

Denominators the same

Subtracting

$$\frac{4}{5} - \frac{2}{5} = \frac{2}{5} \qquad 4 - 2 = 2$$

Keep the same denominator.

■ **To add (or subtract) fractions with the same denominator add (or subtract) the numerators. Write the result over the same denominator.**

Exercise 8F

1 Add these fractions:

(a) $\frac{1}{5} + \frac{2}{5}$ **(b)** $\frac{3}{10} + \frac{1}{10}$ **(c)** $\frac{2}{9} + \frac{5}{9}$ **(d)** $\frac{1}{3} + \frac{2}{3}$

(e) Discuss your answer to part **(d)** with your neighbour.

2   Work out these additions:

(a) $1\frac{3}{4} + \frac{3}{4}$ (b) $\frac{4}{7} + \frac{5}{7}$ (c) $\frac{3}{5} + 2\frac{4}{5}$

3   Work out these subtractions:

(a) $1 - \frac{1}{2}$ (b) $1 - \frac{3}{4}$ (c) $1 - \frac{2}{5}$

(d) $\frac{4}{5} - \frac{1}{5}$ (e) $\frac{5}{6} - \frac{1}{6}$ (f) $\frac{5}{8} - \frac{3}{8}$

> **Remember:**
> You can write 1 as any fraction where the top and bottom are the same:
>
> $1 = \frac{1}{1} = \frac{2}{2} = \frac{3}{3} \cdots$

4   Diana eats $\frac{2}{9}$ of a packet of Yum Yums and Gina eats $\frac{5}{9}$ of the packet.

(a)   What fraction do they eat altogether?

(b)   What fraction is left?

5   Paul's family eats $\frac{5}{8}$ of a pizza and leaves the rest for him. What fraction is this?

8.7 Adding and subtracting fractions with different denominators

$\frac{1}{2}$ and $\frac{1}{4}$ have **different denominators**.

To add them find equivalent fractions with the **same denominators**.

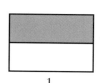
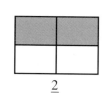

$\frac{1}{2}$ is equivalent to $\frac{2}{4}$

So $\frac{1}{2} + \frac{1}{4} = \frac{2}{4} + \frac{1}{4} = \frac{3}{4}$

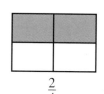
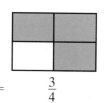

Example 11

Work out $\frac{1}{3} + \frac{1}{5}$

$\frac{1}{3} + \frac{1}{5} = \frac{5}{15} + \frac{3}{15} = \frac{8}{15}$

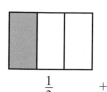

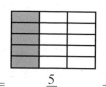

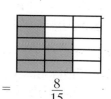

■ **To add (or subtract) fractions with different denominators find equivalent fractions with the same denominators.**

Example 12

Work out $\frac{1}{3} + \frac{1}{4}$

Notice that 3 and 4 are factors of 12.

$\frac{1}{3} = \frac{4}{12}$ and $\frac{1}{4} = \frac{3}{12}$

So $\frac{1}{3} + \frac{1}{4} = \frac{4}{12} + \frac{3}{12} = \frac{7}{12}$

Example 13

Work out $\frac{2}{5} - \frac{1}{4}$

4 and 5 are factors of 20.

$\frac{2}{5} = \frac{8}{20}$ and $\frac{1}{4} = \frac{5}{20}$

So $\frac{2}{5} - \frac{1}{4} = \frac{8}{20} - \frac{5}{20} = \frac{3}{20}$

Exercise 8G

1 Work out:

(a) $\frac{1}{4} + \frac{1}{8}$

(b) $\frac{1}{3} + \frac{1}{6}$

(c) $\frac{2}{5} - \frac{3}{10}$

(d) $\frac{2}{9} + \frac{1}{18}$

(e) $\frac{3}{4} + \frac{1}{20}$

(f) $\frac{1}{5} - \frac{1}{6}$

(g) $\frac{2}{3} - \frac{1}{4}$

(h) $\frac{3}{8} + \frac{1}{2}$

(i) $\frac{1}{6} + \frac{2}{9}$

2 An architect is designing a play area. $\frac{1}{3}$ of the area will be used as a swimming pool and $\frac{1}{5}$ as tennis courts.

(a) How much of the area has the architect used?

(b) How much space does the architect have left? Explain how you worked this out.

3 On Angela and Ian's stall $\frac{1}{4}$ of the space is used for vegetables and $\frac{3}{10}$ is used for fruit.

(a) What fraction of the space has been used up?

(b) The rest is used for flowers. What fraction is this? Show how you worked out your answer.

8.8 Fractions to decimals

Fractions that have a denominator of ten are called tenths:

$\frac{1}{10}$ = one tenth, $\frac{2}{10}$ = two tenths, and so on ...

You can write any tenths fraction as a decimal:

$\frac{1}{10} = 0.1$ = one tenth

$\frac{2}{10} = 0.2$ = two tenths

$\frac{43}{10} = 4.3$ = four and three tenths

Remember:

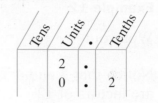

... to divide by ten you move each digit one place to the right.

■ **To change a fraction into a decimal divide the numerator by the denominator:**

$\frac{1}{4} = 1 \div 4 = 0.25$ $\frac{5}{8} = 5 \div 8 = 0.625$

Hint:
You can use your calculator to help:

$\boxed{5} \ \boxed{\div} \ \boxed{8} \ \boxed{=}$

Example 14

(a) Write the fraction $\frac{3}{10}$ in words.   **(b)** Change the fraction $\frac{3}{10}$ to a decimal.

(a) Three tenths   **(b)** $\frac{3}{10} = 3 \div 10 = 0.3$

Example 15

Change the fraction $\frac{3}{4}$ to a decimal.

$\frac{3}{4} = 3 \div 4$ $\begin{array}{r} 0.75 \\ 4\overline{)3.0^20} \end{array}$

So $\frac{3}{4}$ is the same as 0.75.

There is more on dividing with decimals on page 129.

Exercise 8H

1 Write these fractions:
- in words
- as decimals

(a) $\frac{9}{10}$ **(b)** $\frac{7}{10}$ **(c)** $\frac{1}{10}$ **(d)** $2\frac{3}{10}$

2   Change the following decimals into fractions.
Write each fraction in its simplest form.

Hint: Think of the place value of each digit.

(a) 0.4   (b) 0.6   (c) 0.2   (d) 0.5

3   For each fraction:
- find an equivalent fraction in tenths
- write down the decimal equivalent.

(a) $\frac{20}{50}$ (b) $\frac{27}{90}$ (c) $\frac{12}{20}$ (d) $\frac{28}{40}$

4   Write each of the following fractions as a decimal:

(a) $\frac{1}{4}$ (b) $\frac{3}{8}$ (c) $\frac{2}{5}$ (d) $\frac{9}{25}$ (e) $1\frac{3}{5}$

5   Find the matching fractions and decimals in the
diagrams below, (e.g. $0.5 = \frac{1}{2} = \frac{3}{6}$)

```
┌─────────────────┐   ┌──────────────────────────────┐
│  0.2            │   │  1            10         1    │
│                 │   │  2           100         5    │
│  0.1    0.7     │   │                               │
│                 │   │           21           3      │
│                 │   │      1     30          10     │
│  0.3            │   │     10            3           │
│          0.5    │   │          5       6      2     │
│                 │   │         50             10     │
└─────────────────┘   └──────────────────────────────┘
```

8.9 Comparing fractions

You can compare fractions with different denominators to
see which is the largest.

Example 16

Jane and Henry ran in a marathon. Jane ran $\frac{2}{3}$ of the way
and Henry ran $\frac{3}{4}$ of the way.

Who ran the furthest?

Rewrite the fractions so they both have the same denominator.
$\frac{2}{3}$ and $\frac{3}{4}$ can both be rewritten with a denominator of 12.

$$\text{Jane} \quad \frac{2}{3} \overset{\times 4}{\underset{\times 4}{=}} \frac{8}{12} \qquad \text{Henry} \quad \frac{3}{4} \overset{\times 3}{\underset{\times 3}{=}} \frac{9}{12}$$

$\frac{9}{12}$ is larger than $\frac{8}{12}$ so $\frac{3}{4}$ is larger than $\frac{2}{3}$

Henry ran further than Jane.

You can also order fractions by converting them to decimals.

Example 17

Put these fractions in order:

$\frac{3}{5}$, $\quad \frac{7}{8}$, $\quad \frac{4}{10}$, $\quad \frac{3}{4}$

First change them to decimals:

$\frac{3}{5} = 3 \div 5 = 0.6$ $\qquad\qquad$ $\frac{4}{10} = 4 \div 10 = 0.4$

$\frac{7}{8} = 7 \div 8 = 0.875$ $\qquad\qquad$ $\frac{3}{4} = 3 \div 4 = 0.75$

Ordering the decimals gives you the answer:

$$0.4 \; , \; 0.6 \; , \; 0.75 \; , \; 0.875$$
$$\downarrow \qquad \downarrow \qquad \downarrow \qquad \downarrow$$
$$\frac{4}{10} \; , \; \frac{3}{5} \; , \; \frac{3}{4} \; , \; \frac{7}{8}$$

There is more on ordering decimals on page 121.

Exercise 8I

1   Tom feeds both his cats the same tinned food.
    Each day Christobel eats $\frac{3}{8}$ of a tin and Tiny eats $\frac{1}{2}$ a tin.
    Which cat eats more food?

2   Would you prefer $\frac{2}{5}$ of a bag of sweets or $\frac{3}{10}$ of the same
    bag of sweets? Show your working.

3   Are the following statements true or false? Show your
    working.
    (a) $\frac{12}{15}$ is 3 times as big as $\frac{3}{5}$ **(b)** $\frac{3}{5}$ is smaller than $\frac{12}{15}$
    (c) $\frac{12}{15}$ is equivalent to $\frac{3}{5}$ **(d)** $\frac{3}{5}$ is larger than $\frac{12}{15}$

4   Put the following fractions in order of size, smallest first:
    (a) $\frac{2}{3}, \frac{3}{5}, \frac{4}{15}$ $\qquad\qquad$ **(b)** $\frac{3}{10}, \frac{2}{15}, \frac{1}{2}$

5   Put these fractions in order by converting them to decimals.
    (a) $\frac{1}{4}, \frac{5}{8}, \frac{1}{3}, \frac{3}{6}$ $\qquad\qquad$ **(b)** $\frac{3}{4}, \frac{2}{8}, \frac{9}{16}, \frac{3}{15}$
    (c) $\frac{7}{16}, \frac{1}{8}, \frac{11}{25}, \frac{2}{5}$ $\qquad\qquad$ **(d)** $\frac{7}{20}, \frac{9}{30}, \frac{5}{16}$

6   Convert these fraction families into decimals:
    (a) $\frac{1}{7}, \frac{2}{7}, \frac{3}{7}, \ldots$ $\qquad\qquad$ **(b)** $\frac{1}{11}, \frac{2}{11}, \frac{3}{11}, \ldots$
    What do you notice about your answers?

8.10 Dividing a whole number by a fraction

To divide $32 \div 4$ you find how many lots of 4 are in 32.

You can do the same with fractions.

Example 18

Work out:

(a) $5 \div \frac{1}{10}$

(b) $3 \div \frac{1}{7}$

(a) Start with 5:

split into 5 lots of 1:

split each 1 into tenths:

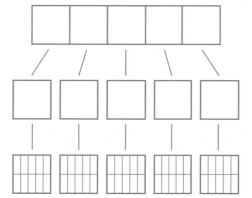

So there are $5 \times 10 = 50$ tenths in 5:

$$5 \div \tfrac{1}{10} = 50$$

Note that the answer is bigger than the original number.

(b) There are 3 lots of 1 in 3.
There are 7 lots of $\frac{1}{7}$ in 1.
So there are $3 \times 7 = 21$ sevenths in 3:

$$3 \div \tfrac{1}{7} = 21$$

Exercise 8J

1 Work out:

(a) $2 \div \frac{1}{3}$ (b) $6 \div \frac{1}{2}$ (c) $9 \div \frac{1}{5}$ (d) $4 \div \frac{1}{11}$

(e) $10 \div \frac{1}{7}$ (f) $2 \div \frac{1}{15}$ (g) $19 \div \frac{1}{4}$ (h) $9 \div \frac{1}{12}$

2 Compare your answers to question **1** with the result of multiplying the number by the denominator of the fraction. What do you notice?

8.11 Using ratios to compare numbers

You can describe this flag:

... using a **fraction**:   ... using a **ratio**:

two thirds of the   the ratio of blue to
flag are blue   red is two to one

$$\frac{2}{3}$$

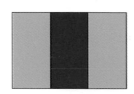

$$2 : \underline{1}$$
                                                                  the colon
                                                                  means 'to'

2 parts out of 3   there are 2 blue parts
are blue   for every 1 red part

Remember: $\frac{2}{3}$ means 2 out of a total of 3.

This is not the same as $2 : 3$ which means 2 for every 3 (or 2 out of a total of 5).

■   **A ratio is a way of comparing numbers or quantities.**

Example 19

What fraction of this cake is green?
What is the ratio of green slices to
yellow slices?

There are 5 slices altogether.
3 slices are green.

  $\frac{3}{5}$ of the slices are green.

The ratio of green slices to yellow slices is: $3 : 2$

**How many parts
altogether?**

In a fraction the
denominator
shows how
many parts
there are
altogether.

$$\frac{2}{3}$$

$2 : 1$
3 parts
$2 + 1$

In a ratio **adding
the numbers** shows
how many parts
there are
altogether.

Exercise 8K

1   For each of these shapes:
    ● What fraction is red?
    ● What is the ratio of red parts to blue parts?

    (a) 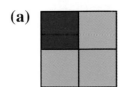   (b)    (c)   (d)

2 This pictogram compares two bus fleets:

Souter Specials	🚌 🚌 🚌 🚌 🚌 🚌 🚌
Hasty Hannah's	🚌 🚌 🚌 🚌 🚌

Each symbol represents one bus.

(a) What fraction of the buses shown are owned by Hasty Hannah?

(b) Write a ratio comparing the two fleets.

3 The ratio of frog juice to bat's blood in a wizard's brew is 2 : 5.
What fraction of the brew is bat's blood?

4 In a survey 7 out of 13 people questioned said they preferred Krespi to Polca Pola.
Which of these statements are true and which false? Explain each answer.

(a) 20 people were questioned altogether.

(b) 7 people preferred Krespi.

(c) The ratio of people who prefer Polca Pola to people who prefer Krespi was 13 to 7

(d) The ratio of people who prefer Krespi to people who prefer Polca Pola was 7 to 6

(e) 6 people in the survey would rather drink Krespi.

5 Write ratios to describe each of these:

(a) One third of the party guests were boys; the rest were girls.

(b) In a penalty shootout two fifths of the shots scored goals.

(c) Nine out of ten mice dislike cats.

(d) In an election $\frac{1}{20}$ of the voting papers were spoiled; the rest were valid.

Spoiled voting papers don't count.

(e) I still have 5 times as far to travel as I have come already.

6 Only $\frac{1}{50}$ of an expensive fragrance is 'ingredient X'.
The rest is tap water. What is the ratio of ingredient X to tap water?

8.12 Equivalent ratios

The ratio of red to blue in these shapes is the same:

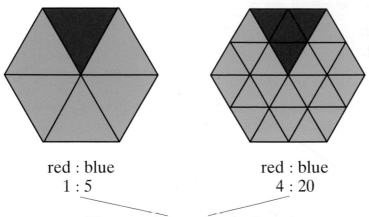

red : blue   red : blue
  1 : 5   4 : 20

These ratios are **equivalent.**
They represent the *same* relationship
between parts coloured red and blue.

Example 20

Kanta mixed 200 ml of orange juice with 600 ml of
lemonade to make a fruit punch.
Write this as a ratio in its simplest form.

The ratio is:

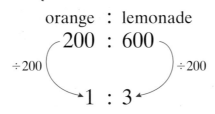

orange : lemonade
÷200 200 : 600 ÷200
1 : 3

Lowest terms

A ratio in its
simplest form is
also said to be in
its lowest terms.

The ratio
4 : 20 is 1 : 5
in lowest terms.

Example 21

Steve mixed 200 ml of orange with 1 litre of water to make
his punch.
Write this as a ratio in its lowest terms.

The ratio is:

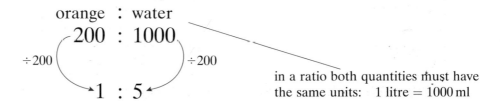

orange : water
÷200 200 : 1000 ÷200
1 : 5

in a ratio both quantities must have
the same units: 1 litre = 1000 ml

Exercise 8L

1 Write these ratios in their simplest form:

(a) 2 : 6   (b) 6 : 2   (c) 6 : 18

(d) 80 : 100   (e) 70 : 130   (f) 220 : 330

(g) 27 : 27   (h) 0.2 : 0.8   (i) 0.25 : 1.5

(j) 5 litres to 30 litres   (k) 1 centimetre to 1 metre

> Remember to change both sides into whole numbers

2 Write ratios in their simplest form to describe each of these:

(a) $\frac{3}{9}$ of the people on the bus were female.

(b) $\frac{24}{27}$ of the iceberg is below the waterline.

(c) $\frac{10}{15}$ of the planet's surface is covered by water.

(d) 6 students in a class of 30 had blonde hair.

3 Write these ratios in their lowest terms:

(a) 15 cm : 150 cm   (b) 40 cm : 1 m

(c) 2 m : 25 cm   (d) 10 p : £1   (e) £4 : 25 p

(f) 1 hour : 15 minutes   (g) 3 minutes : 20 seconds

4 The Great Pyramid of Cheops was built by ancient Egyptians in 4000 BC. Its height is roughly 145 m and the base has sides roughly 230 m long. Write the ratio of the height to the length of one side of the base in its simplest form.

5 These alloys contain different amounts of these metals:

Alloy	Ratio of metals
alpha-bronze	copper : tin 95 : 5
pewter	lead : tin 20 : 80
alpha-brass	copper : zinc 65 : 35
nickel-silver	copper : zinc : nickel 50 : 35 : 15

Write each of these ratios in its lowest terms.

6 These paints contain different amounts of colour.

blue : white   red : white   grey : brown : white
25 : 100   25 : 1775   10 :   25   : 1250

Write these ratios in their simplest form.

7 Work out the ratio of blue to white in these patterns.
Write the ratios in their simplest forms.

(a) 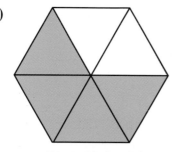   **(b)**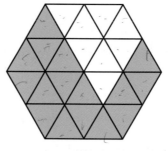

(c) 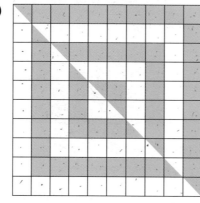   **(d)**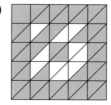

(e)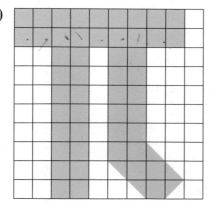

8.13 Calculating with ratios

One way of solving ratio problems is to first reduce one
side of the ratio to one.

Example 22

Anna's chocolate cake uses 1 part milk chocolate to 3 parts
plain chocolate.

If she uses 200 g of milk chocolate, how much plain chocolate
will she need, and how much chocolate will she use altogether?

The ratio of milk to plain
chocolate is:

milk : plain
1 : 3

*Find out how many grammes of plain chocolate are needed for **1 g** of milk chocolate.*

3 g of plain chocolate is needed
for every 1 g of milk chocolate:

milk : plain
1 : 3
×200   ×200
200 : 600

*200 times as much plain chocolate is needed for **200 g** of milk chocolate.*

So 600 g of plain chocolate is needed for 200 g of milk chocolate.

Altogether Anna uses 200 g + 600 g = 800 g of chocolate.

Example 23

Two pandas Chi-chi and Lulu get fed bamboo
at the wildlife park. The length of bamboo
they get depends on the height of the bear.

Chi-chi is 1 m tall and Lulu is 2 m tall.
If Chi-chi is fed 3 m of bamboo, how long will Lulu's bamboo be?

The ratio of the pandas' heights is: Chi-chi : Lulu
1 : 2

*First find out how much Lulu gets if Chi-chi gets **1m** of bamboo.*

Lulu gets 2m of bamboo for every 1 m Chi-chi gets.

Chi-chi : Lulu
1 : 2
×3   ×3
3 : 6

So Lulu gets 3 times as much if Chi-chi gets 3m of bamboo.

So Lulu gets 6 m of bamboo when Chi-chi gets 3 m.

Example 24

Baby polar bears Snowy, Nadine and Blanche get fed fishfingers at the wildlife park. The amount of fishfingers they get depends on how tall they are.

Snowy is 30 cm tall, Nadine is 90 cm tall and Blanche is 1.2 m tall.
If Snowy is fed 50 fishfingers, how many should Nadine and Blanche be fed, and how many fishfingers are eaten altogether?

The ratio of the bears' heights is

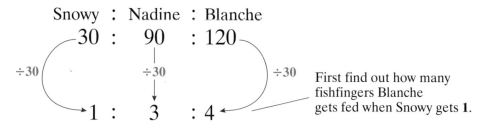

Snowy : Nadine : Blanche
30 : 90 : 120
÷30 ÷30 ÷30 First find out how many fishfingers Blanche gets fed when Snowy gets **1**.
1 : 3 : 4

For every 1 fishfinger Snowy gets fed, Nadine gets 3 and Blanche gets 4.

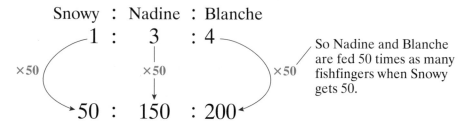

Snowy : Nadine : Blanche
1 : 3 : 4
×50 ×50 ×50 So Nadine and Blanche are fed 50 times as many fishfingers when Snowy gets 50.
50 : 150 : 200

Nadine gets 150 fishfingers and Blanche gets 200 fishfingers when Snowy gets 50.

Altogether $150 + 200 + 50 = 400$ fishfingers are eaten.

Exercise 8M

1 Jake bought 10 packets of seeds for £20.
   How much would he pay for:

   (a) 1 packet   **(b)** 25 packets

2 It takes six workers 12 days to dig up a road.
   How long would it take:

   (a) 1 worker   **(b)** 4 workers

3 Dan is packing lunch for his children Venus, Grace and Flora. For every cookie Venus gets, Grace gets two and Flora gets four. How many cookies should Grace and Flora get if Venus gets 3? How many cookies is that altogether?

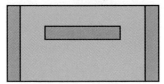

4 Vicky is checking prices for weekend breaks in London, Paris and New York. She writes down the ratio of the prices to help her compare.

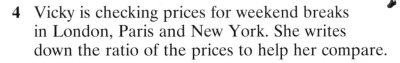

London : Paris : New York
50 : 150 : 250

To stay in a four star hotel in London costs £50. Calculate how much it would cost to stay in a similar hotel:

(a) in Paris   **(b)** in New York

For a five star hotel, it would cost £175 in London. Calculate how much it would cost for a similar hotel:

(c) in Paris   **(d)** in New York

5 Year 8 are designing flags in technology.

Tiffany uses 15 cm² of yellow material for her design.

(a) Use the ratio to calculate how much green material she needs.

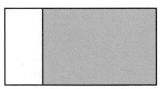

Yellow : Green
3 : 9

Mickey uses 17 cm² of green material for his design.

(b) Calculate how much yellow and red material he needs.

Green : Yellow : Red
2 :   4   : 8

Ruby uses 6 cm² of orange material for her design.

(c) Calculate how much blue material she needs.

Orange : Blue
9 : 27

Summary of key points

1 You can use numbers to represent a fraction:

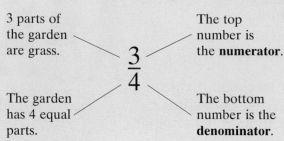

3 parts of the garden are grass.

The top number is the **numerator**.

$$\frac{3}{4}$$

The garden has 4 equal parts.

The bottom number is the **denominator**.

2 A mixed number has a whole number part and a fraction part, for example $1\frac{3}{4}$.

3 Top heavy fractions are also called improper fractions. The numerator (top) is greater than the denominator (bottom), for example $\frac{7}{4}$.

4 A vulgar fraction's numerator is less than its denominator, for example $\frac{3}{4}$.

5 You can think of the bottom part of a fraction as a division. For example:

to find $\frac{1}{2}$ divide by 2

to find $\frac{1}{3}$ divide by 3

to find $\frac{1}{4}$ divide by 4

6 To find $\frac{4}{5}$ of an amount, divide by 5 then multiply by 4.

7 Equivalent fractions have the same value, for example, $\frac{2}{3} = \frac{4}{6} = \frac{6}{9} = \frac{8}{12}$

8 To add (or subtract) fractions with the same denominator, add (or subtract) the numerators. Write the result over the same denominator.

9 To add (or subtract) fractions with different denominators find equivalent fractions with the same denominators.

10 To change a fraction into a decimal divide the numerator by the denominator:

$$\frac{1}{4} = 1 \div 4 = 0.25 \qquad \frac{5}{8} = 5 \div 8 = 0.625$$

11 A ratio is a way of comparing numbers or quantities.

9 Working with algebra

Algebra is a branch of mathematics in which letters are used to represent numbers.

You can use it to solve many mathematical problems.

If phonecalls cost 20p a minute you can find the cost of a call using this algebra:

$$c = 20 \times t$$

cost in pence = 20p × time in minutes

Quite complicated algebra can be used to calculate the speed at which a skydiver falls, and to work out when to open the parachute.

9.1 Using letters to represent numbers

You can use letters to represent numbers even when you don't know what the numbers are yet:

Example 1

Celine has some videos.

You don't know how many videos she has.

Using algebra you could say:

'Celine has x videos.'

Example 2

John has d computer games. Julie has 12 computer games.
How many computer games do they have altogether?

They have $d + 12$ computer games altogether.

Example 3

Fiona has x videos and Marsha has y videos.
How many videos do they have altogether?

They have $x + y$ videos altogether.

Exercise 9A

1   Matthew has a sweets and Bridgit has b sweets.
    How many sweets do they have altogether?

2   Pulin has x pets and Harsha has y pets.
    How many pets do they have altogether?

3   Anthony has a pairs of socks and Phillip has b pairs of
    socks.
    How many pairs of socks do they have altogether?

4   Esther has p posters and Ailsa has 5 posters.
    How many posters do they have altogether?

5   Daniel has 23 marbles and Victoria has m marbles.
    How many marbles do they have altogether?

6   Francoise has x rings and Dylan has 2 rings.
    How many rings do they have altogether?

7   Ben has m pounds. His uncle gives him 3 pounds.
    How many pounds does he have now?

8   Andrea has x pens. Michelle has 2 more pens than
    Andrea.
    How many pens does Michelle have?

9   Pulin has x books, Harsha has y books and Neil has 6
    books. How many books do they have altogether?

10 Sarah earns d pounds. Jane earns 4 pounds less than
    Sarah. How much does Jane earn?

9.2 Collecting up letters

The sugar factory's printer has broken down.
None of the bags have weight labels.

Jim has to find out how many kilograms of sugar there are in stock.

Say there are *l* kilograms of sugar in a large bag.

The large bags contain $l + l + l + l + l$ kilograms altogether.

Jim writes this as 5*l* meaning 5 lots of *l*.

There are *m* kilograms of sugar in a medium bag.

$m + m + m + m = 4m$ kilograms altogether.

4*m* means 4 lots of *m*.

There are *s* kilograms of sugar in a small bag.

He writes this as *s* meaning 1 lot of *s*.

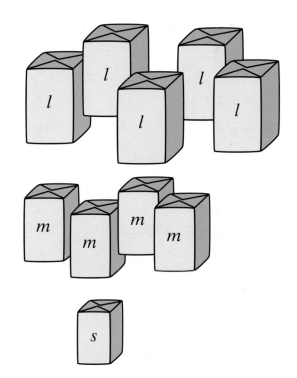

■ **In algebra you write 1 lot of *x* as *x*.**
  ***x* means 1*x*. You don't write 1*x*.**

Altogether Jim has $5l + 4m + s$ kilograms of sugar.

Once he knows how much is in each bag he can give the answer as a number.

Example 4

Write in a shorter form:

(a) $x+x$ **(b)** $y+y+y+y+y$

(a) $x+x$ is 2 lots of x
$\qquad = 2x$
(b) $y+y+y+y+y$ is 5 lots of y
$\qquad\qquad\quad = 5y$

Example 5

Write in a longer form:

(a) $5w$ **(b)** $7t$

(a) $5w$ is 5 lots of w
$\qquad = w+w+w+w+w$
(b) $7t$ is 7 lots of t
$\qquad = t+t+t+t+t+t+t$

Exercise 9B

Write these in a shorter form:

1 $t+t$

2 $s+s$

3 $w+w$

4 $y+y+y$

5 $n+n+n+n$

6 $t+t+t+t+t$

7 $s+s+s$

8 $w+w+w+w$

9 $y+y+y+y+y+y+y$

10 $p+p+p+p+p+p+p$

11 $x+x+x+x+x$

12 $r+r+r+r+r+r+r+r$

13 $t+t+t+t$

14 $n+n+n+n+n+n+n$

Write these in a longer form. The first one has been done for you.

15 $3z = z+z+z$

16 $4p$

17 $2y$

18 $6x$

19 $5n$

20 $7y$

21 $4r$

22 $3t$

23 $5y$

24 $7x$

25 $6t$

26 $4s$

27 Write down the length of each line as simply as possible:

Hint: simply means in as short a form as possible.

9.3 Collecting like terms

Jim had $5l + 4m + s$ kilograms of sugar in his warehouse.

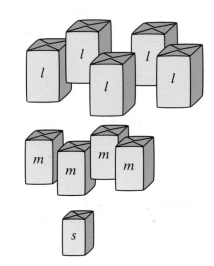

■ **$5l + 4m + s$ is an algebraic expression.**

Each part is called a ***term***.

■ **Terms which use the same letter are called *like terms*.** For example, $2x$ and $8x$ are like terms. They both use the letter x.

Sometimes you can make algebraic expressions simpler by adding or subtracting like terms.

Example 6

Simplify these expressions by adding or subtracting like terms:

(a) $2x + 3x$ **(b)** $6t - 4t$ **(c)** $3y + 4x$ **(d)** $9f - f$

(a) $2x$ and $3x$ are like terms.

2 lots of x + 3 lots of x = 5 lots of x

so $2x + 3x = 5x$

(b) $6t$ and $4t$ are like terms.

6 lots of t − 4 lots of t = 2 lots of t

so $6t - 4t = 2t$

(c) $3y$ and $4x$ use different letters so $3y + 4x$ cannot be simplified.

(d) $9f$ and f are like terms.

9 lots of f − 1 lot of f = 8 lots of f

so $9f - f = 8f$

Exercise 9C

Simplify these expressions by adding or subtracting like terms:

1 $2x + 3x$ **2** $4x - 2x$ **3** $5y + 3y$

4 $5t + 3t$ **5** $6y - 5y$ **6** $y + 7y$

7 $3x + 5x$ **8** $7x - 4x$ **9** $8p + 2p$

10 $9s - 6s$ **11** $2p - p$ **12** $3r + 5r$

13 $2r + 3r$ **14** $7t + 9t$ **15** $2x + 3x + 5x$

16 $5y + 6y - 2y$ **17** $5t + 7t - t$ **18** $21p + 10p - 17p$

19 $6y + 7y - 3y$ **20** $7x - 6x + 4x$ **21** $4t + 6t - 3t$

Simplify if possible:

22 $6a - 2a$ **23** $6a - 2b$ **24** $9b - 2$

25 $x + 2x$ **26** $x + 2$ **27** $s + 6s$

28 $5l + l + 2l$ **29** $5 + l + 2m$ **30** $m + 3m$

9.4 Simplifying more complicated expressions

Sometimes you can simplify expressions by collecting several like terms together.

Example 7

Simplify $2x + 3y + 4x + 5y$

Imagine the x terms are bags containing x coins ...   ... and the y terms are bags containing y coins.

$2x + 3y + 4x + 5y$ looks like this:

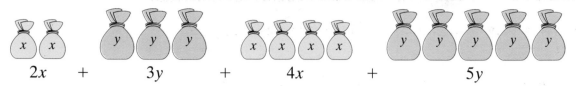

$$2x \quad + \quad 3y \quad + \quad 4x \quad + \quad 5y$$

Collect like terms together:

$$2x \quad + \quad 4x \quad + \quad 3y \quad + \quad 5y$$

Add like terms:

$$6x \quad + \quad 8y$$

So $\quad 2x + 3y + 4x + 5y = 2x + 4x + 3y + 5y = 6x + 8y$

So $\quad 2x + 3y + 4x + 5y = 6x + 8y$

Example 8

Simplify $4p + 3q - 2p + q$

Collect like terms:

$$4p + 3q - 2p + q$$
$$4p - 2p + 3q + q$$
$$2p + 4q$$

Example 9

Simplify $4x + 2y + 3x - y + x$

Collect like terms:

$$4x + 2y + 3x - y + x$$
$$4x + 3x + x + 2y - y$$
$$8x + y$$

Notice that the + or − sign is part of each term.

$-y$ is a term.

Exercise 9D

Simplify these expressions by collecting like terms:

1 $2x + 5y + 2x + 3y$

2 $3p + 2q + 2p + 3q$

3 $3w + 9t + 5w + 6t$

4 $4m + 7n + 3m + 3n$

5 $5x + 9 + 6x + 7$

6 $3a + 4d + 3d + a + d$

7 $5s + 2t - 2s + 3t$

8 $p + 4q + 3p - q$

9 $9x + 4y - 5x + 7y$

10 $9y + 3 - 5y + 8$

11 $3x + 2x + 7x - 5x$

12 $5s + 9t - 4s - 8t$

13 $6s + 5s - 3s + s$

14 $9t - 4t + 5t - t$

15 $5m + 6n + 6m - 3m$

16 $5x + 7y + 2t - 3x + 2y$

17 $8y + 3t + 3y + 2t - y$

18 $7b + 5 + 3b - b + 2$

19 $9x + 3y + 4y + 9y + x$

20 $7t + 6r + 3r - 5t$

21 $4a + 5b - 2b + 6b$

22 $7p + 2p + 1 - 3p + 5$

23 $3a + 4b - 3a + 4b$

24 $11a + 7d - 7a - 5d + 1$

25 $6x + 2 - 3x - 1 + 3x$

26 $11x + 3y - 2x + 4y + 2$

27 $e + 7d + 2c - 6d + c$

28 $11p + 9r - 3p - 4p + 2r$

29 $11x + 7y + 8x - 9x + y - 2x$

30 $3x + 4x - 5x + 6y - 2x - y$

9.5 Multiplying with algebra

Remember $2x$ also means:

$x + x$ or 2 lots of x or $2 \times x$

It's easy to confuse x with $\times$ so in algebra leave out the multiplication sign. Write:

$2 \times x$ as $2x$ and $a \times b$ as ab

Example 10

Write these expressions without multiplication signs:

(a) $3 \times b$ **(b)** $6 \times y$ **(c)** $f \times 4$

(d) $x \times y$ **(e)** $2 \times s \times t$ **(f)** $h \times 3 \times s$

(g) $\frac{1}{2} \times x$ **(h)** $\frac{2}{5} \times a \times b$ **(i)** $d \times \frac{4}{7} \times e$

Always write the number in front of the letters. It's much easier to read $4xy$ than $y4x$

(a) $3 \times b$ is $3b$ **(b)** $6 \times y$ is $6y$ **(c)** $f \times 4$ is $4f$

(d) $x \times y$ is xy **(e)** $2 \times s \times t$ is $2st$ **(f)** $h \times 3 \times s$ is $3hs$

(g) $\frac{1}{2}x$ **(h)** $\frac{2}{5}ab$ **(i)** $\frac{4}{7}de$

Exercise 9E

Write these expressions with multiplication signs.
The first one is done for you.

1 $cd = c \times d$ **2** st **3** wx **4** mn

5 bcd **6** $3a$ **7** $4x$ **8** $5xy$

9 $2st$ **10** $4mnp$ **11** $10abc$ **12** $9xyz$

13 $15abcd$ **14** $11efgh$

Write these expressions without multiplication signs.
The first one is done for you.

15 $b \times c = bc$ **16** $d \times e$ **17** $f \times g \times h$ **18** $2 \times b$

19 $5 \times a$ **20** $3 \times x$ **21** $2 \times x \times y$ **22** $5 \times a \times b$

23 $10 \times s \times t$ **24** $11 \times x \times y \times z$ **25** $v \times 3$ **26** $b \times 3 \times a$

27 $k \times 2 \times j \times l$ **28** $z \times 6 \times y \times w$ **29** $\frac{1}{2} \times y$ **30** $\frac{4}{7} \times b \times c$

31 $9 \times x \times \frac{2}{3} \times y$ **32** $6 \times a \times \frac{1}{2} \times b$

9.6 Multiplying terms together

The area of a rectangle is the length times the width.

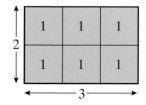

The area of this rectangle
is: $3 \times 2 = 6$ square units.

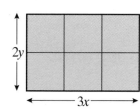

The area of this rectangle
is: $3x \times 2y$ square units.

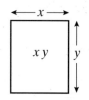

Each part of the
rectangle has
area xy.

There is more
about area
on page 204.

To multiply $3x \times 2y$

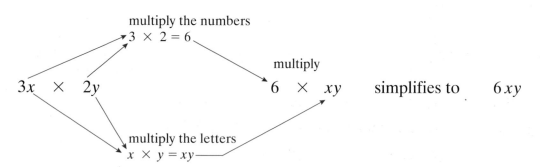

■ **To multiply terms together first multiply the numbers, then multiply the letters. Write the letters in alphabetical order.**

Example 11

Simplify:

(a) $3ab \times 4c$

$\qquad 3 \times 4 = 12$

$\qquad ab \times c = abc$

so $\quad 3ab \times 4c = 12abc$

(b) $2y \times 5xz$

$\qquad 2 \times 5 = 10$

$\qquad y \times xz = yxz = xyz$

so $\quad 2y \times 5xz = 10xyz$

Exercise 9F

Simplify:

1 $3a \times 2b$ 　　　　**2** $3x \times 4y$ 　　　　**3** $2s \times 4t$

4 $3a \times b$ 　　　　**5** $2a \times 6d$ 　　　　**6** $5x \times 6y$

7 $4m \times 7n$ 　　　**81** $5e \times 10f$ 　　　**9** $7g \times 8h$

10 $2ab \times 3c$ 　　**11** $3xy \times 4z$ 　　**12** $5ab \times 2cd$

13 $10ab \times cd$ 　　**14** $3bc \times 2ad$ 　　**15** $5mps \times 5nrt$

9.7 Using brackets in algebra

Brackets are often used in algebra. For example:

$\quad 2 \times (a + b)$ 　means add a to b *before* multiplying by 2

Usually this is written: $2(a + b)$ without the $\times$.
This avoids confusion with the letter x which is
used a lot in algebra.

$\quad 2(a + b)$ 　means 　$2 \times a \;+\; 2 \times b \;=\; 2a + 2b$

Working this out is called **expanding the brackets**.
Actually the brackets disappear!

What could $2(a + b)$
represent?

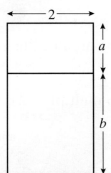

The area of the
whole rectangle is
$2(a + b)$

There is more about
area on page 204.

■ **To expand brackets multiply each term inside the brackets by the term outside.**
For example:

To expand $\quad 3(a + 2b)\ldots$

$3 \times 2b = 6b$

$3(a + 2b) = 3a + 6b$

$3 \times a = 3a$

To expand $\quad a(b + c)\ldots$

$a \times b = ab$

$a(b + c) = ab + ac$

$a \times c = ac$

Example 12

Expand:

(a) $3(2x + 1)$
$= 3 \times 2x + 3 \times 1$
$= 6x + 3$

(b) $4(b - 3c)$
$= 4 \times b - 4 \times 3c$
$= 4b - 12c$

(c) $a(b - c)$
$= a \times b - a \times c$
$= ab - ac$

Exercise 9G

Expand these brackets:

1 $2(a + b)$

2 $4(x + y)$

3 $3(s - t)$

4 $2(c - d)$

5 $4(2x + 5y)$

6 $3(3p + q)$

7 $2(4x + 3y)$

8 $8(2p + 3s)$

9 $7(2p - 7q)$

10 $5(3m - 7n)$

11 $4(3r - 2s)$

12 $2(a + b + c)$

13 $3(2p + 4q - 3r)$

14 $2(2x + 3y - 2z)$

15 $3(2a - 3b + 5c)$

16 $4(2x - y - 5z)$

17 $b(c + a)$

18 $p(q - r)$

19 $a(2b + 3c)$

20 $2l(m + n)$

21 $2p(q + 2r)$

22 $x(y + z + a)$

23 $3r(s + t - u)$

24 $z(a - b - 2c)$

9.8 Factorizing simple expressions

■ **Factorizing is the reverse process to removing brackets.**

To factorize an expression you look for common factors:

$$2x + 4$$

$$2 \times x + 2 \times 2 \qquad \text{2 is a common factor} \dots$$

$$2(x + 2) \qquad \dots \text{so you can take it}$$
outside a bracket.

Example 13

Factorize:

(a) $9x + 3$

(b) $6a - 3b$

(a) $\quad 9x + 3$
$\quad 3 \times 3x + 3 \times 1$
$\quad 3(3x + 1)$

(b) $\quad 6a - 3b$
$\quad 3 \times 2a - 3 \times b$
$\quad 3(2a - b)$

Exercise 9H

Factorize:

1 $3a + 6$

2 $2b + 4$

3 $3d + 9$

4 $4x + 8$

5 $6y + 9$

6 $9a + 12b$

7 $2x + 4y$

8 $6a + 15b$

9 $8x + 12y$

10 $3c - 6d$

11 $12x - 15y$

12 $12a - 60$

13 $3a - 3b$

14 $15a + 20b$

15 $5a - 25b$

16 $10x - 50y$

9.9 Powers in algebra

Page 112 shows you a short way of writing numbers like
1 000 000

$$1\,000\,000 = 10 \times 10 \times 10 \times 10 \times 10 \times 10$$
$$= 10^6$$

How you say it: "10 to the power 6"

$$10^6$$
This number is
the **power** or **index**.

The power tells you how many times something is
multiplied by itself.

■ x^6 **means** $x \times x \times x \times x \times x \times x$.
  You say "x to the power of 6".

Example 14

Write, using powers:

(a) $x \times x$ **(b)** $y \times y \times y \times y$ **(c)** $3 \times p \times p \times p \times p \times p$

(a) x is multiplied by itself 2 times

  $x \times x = x^2$

(b) y is multiplied by itself 4 times

  $y \times y \times y \times y = y^4$

(c) p is multiplied by itself 5 times

  $3 \times p \times p \times p \times p \times p = 3 \times p^5 = 3p^5$

Example 15

Simplify these algebraic expressions using powers:

(a) $2x \times 3x \times y \times x$

(b) $f \times 3f \times g \times 2f \times 2g$

(a) $2x \times 3x \times y \times x$

$= 2 \times x \times 3 \times x \times y \times x$

$= 2 \times 3 \times x \times x \times x \times y$

$= 6 \times x^3 \times y$

$= 6x^3y$

(b) You may find it is quicker to do it this way:

multiply the numbers: $3 \times 2 \times 2 = 12$

multiply the f terms: $f \times f \times f = f^3$

multiply the g terms: $g \times g = g^2$

so $f \times 3f \times g \times 2f \times 2g = 12 \times f^3 \times g^2$

$= 12f^3g^2$

Exercise 9I

1 Write using powers:

(a) 2×2

(b) $4 \times 4 \times 4 \times 4 \times 4 \times 4$

(c) $3 \times 3 \times 3 \times 3$

(d) $5 \times 5 \times 5$

(e) $2 \times 2 \times 2 \times 2 \times 2$

(f) $3 \times 3 \times 3 \times 3 \times 3 \times 3 \times 3$

For a reminder on using powers with numbers see page 112.

2 Write using powers:

(a) $a \times a$

(b) $b \times b \times b$

(c) $c \times c \times c \times c$

(d) $x \times x \times x$

(e) $y \times y \times y \times y \times y$

(f) $s \times s \times s \times s \times s \times s$

(g) $w \times w \times w$

(h) $z \times z$

(i) $p \times p \times p \times p \times p \times p$

(j) $m \times m \times m \times m$

(k) $t \times t \times t \times t \times t$

(l) $c \times c \times c$

(m) $a \times a \times a \times a$

(n) $d \times d \times d \times d \times d \times d$

3 Write without powers:

(a) x^2

(b) y^3

(c) s^2

(d) t^4

(e) m^3

(f) n^5

(g) a^7

(h) b^5

(i) c^4

(j) d^8

(k) r^5

(l) p^4

(m) q^9

(n) z^5

4 Simplify these algebraic expressions:

(a) $2x \times 3x$
(b) $3y \times 4y$
(c) $y \times 2y \times 3y$
(d) $2b \times b \times 3b \times b$
(e) $6t \times t \times 3t \times 2t$
(f) $2p \times p^2$
(g) $x \times 2y \times 3x \times y$
(h) $2f \times 3g \times f \times 2g$
(i) $5m \times n \times 2n \times m$
(j) $2a \times 3a \times b \times a \times 2b$
(k) $3y \times y \times x \times y \times 2x$
(l) $p \times 2q \times 3p \times q \times p$

Summary of key points

1 In algebra you write 1 lot of x as x.
x means $1x$. You don't write $1x$.

2 $5l + 4m + s$ is an algebraic expression.

Each part is called a *term*.

3 Terms which use the same letter are called *like terms*.

4 To multiply terms together first multiply the numbers, then multiply the letters.
Write the letters in alphabetical order.

5 To expand brackets, multiply each term inside the brackets by the term outside. For example:

$$3(a + 2b) = 3a + 6b$$

6 Factorizing is the reverse process to removing brackets.

7 x^6 means $x \times x \times x \times x \times x \times x$.
You say "x to the power of 6".

10 Perimeter, area and volume

10.1 What is a perimeter?

Naomi wants to frame her new picture.
She measures the distance around the
edge in centimetres.
Now she knows how much wood to buy.

■ **The distance around the edge of a
   shape is called the perimeter.**

Remember: you can measure distances
using mm, cm, m or km.

You would measure the perimeter
of this garden in metres.

You would measure the perimeter
of this lake in kilometres.

Example 1

Find the perimeters of these shapes:

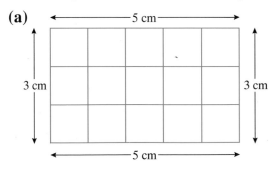

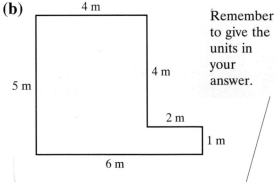

Remember
to give the
units in
your
answer.

(a) Add the lengths of the edges:
    $5 + 3 + 5 + 3 = 16\,\text{cm}$

(b) Add the lengths of the edges:
    $5 + 4 + 4 + 2 + 1 + 6 = 22\,\text{m}$

Exercise 10A

1 What is the most sensible unit to use to measure the
perimeter of:

mm, cm, m and km
are all units of
length.

There is more about
these on page 138.

   (a) a page of this book   **(b)** the room you are in
   (c) the coastline of Ireland   **(d)** an envelope
   (e) the hem of a dress   **(f)** a leaf?

2 These shapes are drawn on centimetre squared paper.
Find the perimeter of each shape.

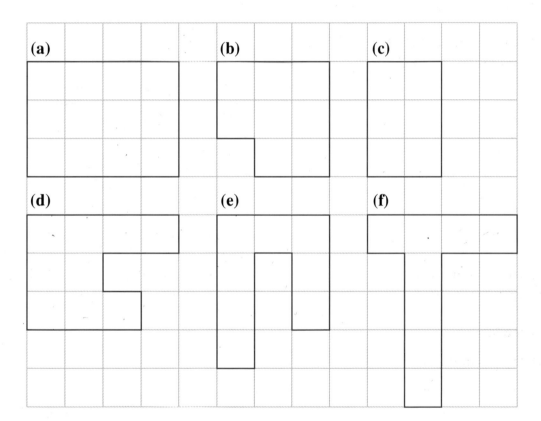

3 Find the perimeter of this rectangle.
Remember to give the units in your answer.

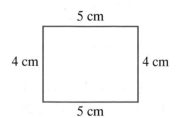

5 cm

4 cm   4 cm

5 cm

4 Find the perimeters of these shapes. Remember to give the units in your answers.

(a)

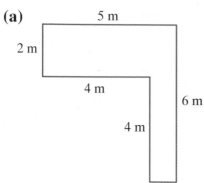

(b)

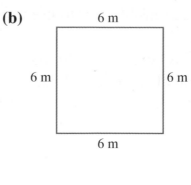

(c)

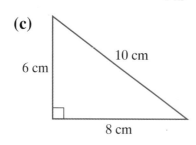

(d)

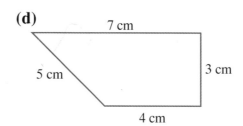

5 A rectangular carpet measures 3 m by 5 m.
Find the perimeter of the carpet.

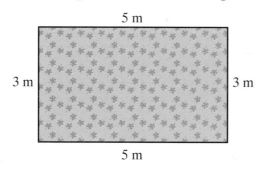

6 Find the perimeters of these triangles:

(a)

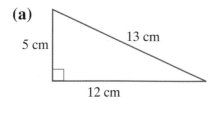

(b)

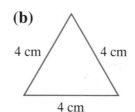

(c)

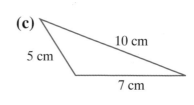

7 A rectangular field is 120 m long and 50 m wide.
Find the perimeter of the field.

8 Find the perimeter of the following shapes.

(a)

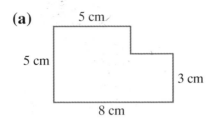

(b)

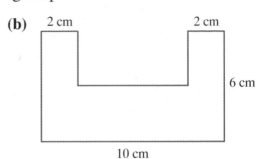

(c)

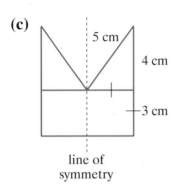

(d)

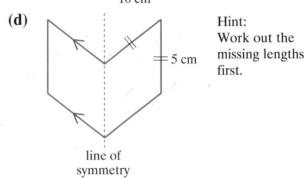

Hint:
Work out the
missing lengths
first.

9 All the triangles are the same size.
Find the perimeter.

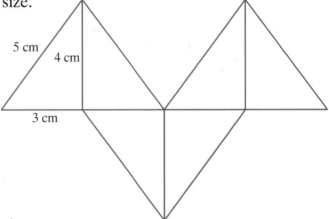

10 All the triangles are the same size.
Find the perimeter of **(a)** and **(b)**.

(a)

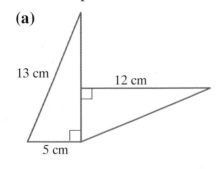

(b)

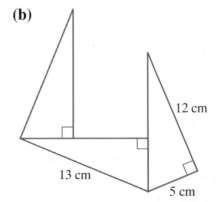

10.2 Perimeter of a rectangle

The opposite sides of a rectangle are the same length.
This makes it easy to work out the perimeter.

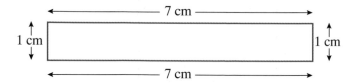

Perimeter $= 1 + 1 + 7 + 7$ or   Perimeter $= 1 + 7 + 1 + 7$
Perimeter $= (2 \times 1) + (2 \times 7)$ or   Perimeter $= 2 \times (1 + 7)$
$\qquad = 2 + 14 = 16\,\text{cm}$ $\qquad\qquad\qquad\qquad = 2 \times 8 = 16\,\text{cm}$

■   **For any rectangle:**

Perimeter $= (2 \times$ length$) + (2 \times$ width$)$
or
Perimeter $= 2 \times ($length $+$ width$)$

Example 2

Find the perimeter of a 4 m by 7 m rectangle.

length $= 7\,\text{m}$ width $= 4\,\text{m}$

Sketch the rectangle:

```
            7 m
        ┌─────────────┐
  4 m   │             │   4 m
        └─────────────┘
            7 m
```

Perimeter $= (2 \times$ length$) + (2 \times$ width$)$ or   Perimeter $= 2 \times ($length $+$ width$)$
$\qquad = (2 \times 7) + (2 \times 4)$ $\qquad\qquad\qquad\qquad = 2 \times (7 + 4)$
$\qquad = 22\,\text{m}$ $\qquad\qquad\qquad\qquad\qquad\qquad = 2 \times 11$
$\qquad\qquad\qquad\qquad\qquad\qquad\qquad\qquad\qquad = 22\,\text{m}$

Exercise 10B

1 Find the perimeters of these rectangles:

(a)   6 cm

4 cm

(b)   10 cm

7 cm

(c)   9 cm

4 cm

2 Work out the perimeter of:

   (a) a rectangular carpet with sides 6 m and 4 m

   (b) a rectangular field with length 120 m and width 60 m

   (c) a square with of sides 5 cm long

   (d) a rectangular table cloth which measures 70 cm by 80 cm

   (e) a rectangular football pitch with length 110 m and width 65 m

   (f) the front cover of this book. (You will need to make some measurements.)

3 The perimeter of a rectangle is 24 cm.
One side measures 9 cm.
How long is the other side?

4 Find these perimeters:

   (a) Square of side 4 cm

   (b) Square of side 3 cm

   (c) Square of side 6 cm

   (d) Square of side 8 cm

of side 4 cm means
each side is 4 cm
long.

5 Using your answers to question **4**, write down a formula for the perimeter of a square.

10.3 Area

How many tiles will Joe need to cover the walls?

How much carpet will Gina need for her bedroom?

Joe and Gina each need to measure an **area**.

■ **Area is the amount of space covered by a shape.**

You use squares to measure area:

1 square millimetre

is about the area of a pinhead.

1 square centimetre

is about the area of a computer key

1 square metre

is about the area of half a door.

1 square kilometre

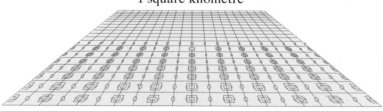

is about the area covered by 200 football pitches.

You will also see measures of area written like this:

1 square millimetre:	1 sq mm	or	$1\,mm^2$
1 square centimetre:	1 sq cm	or	$1\,cm^2$
1 square metre:	1 sq m	or	$1\,m^2$
1 square kilometre:	1 sq km	or	$1\,km^2$

Remember: You write 3×3 as 3^2.

You say '3 squared'.

Example 3

Find the areas of these shapes:

(a)

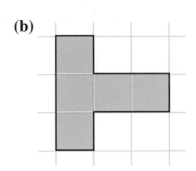

(b)

Remember to
write the units
in your answer.

(a) Count the squares: $12\,cm^2$ **(b)** Count the squares: $5\,cm^2$

Exercise 10C

1 Which units of area would you use to measure the area of:

    mm^2, cm^2, m^2 and km^2 are all units of area.

    (a) a page of this book **(b)** the floor of your classroom
    (c) a leaf   **(d)** a small oil droplet
    (e) the top of a table **(f)** Wales?

2 Write these areas in order of size.
   Start with the smallest.

    $10\,cm^2$ $5\,km^2$ $20\,mm^2$ $6\,m^2$ $100\,m^2$

3 Find the areas of these shapes. They are drawn on centimetre squared paper.

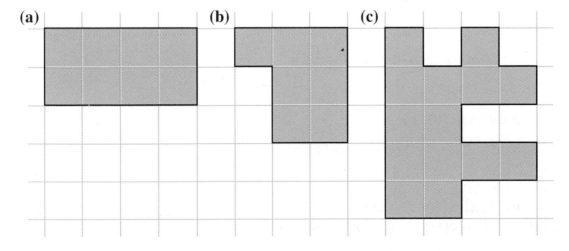

(a)   **(b)**   **(c)**

4 Three possible layouts for a new nature reserve are
drawn on a kilometre squared grid. Find the area of
each layout.

(a)   **(b)**   **(c)**

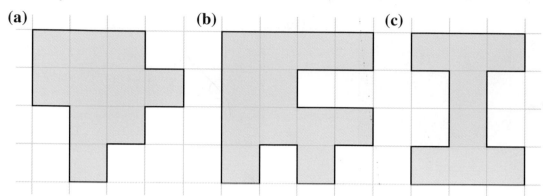

10.4 Estimating areas

To find the area of a curved shape, you need to estimate
the number of squares that it covers.

Example 4

Estimate the area of this leaf:

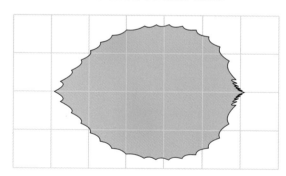

Count the whole squares first:

There are 6 whole squares marked ○

There are 12 part squares marked ✕

A good estimate of the area is:

The whole squares + half the part squares.

    =   6   + half of 12

  = 6 + 6 = 12

The area of the leaf is about 12 cm².

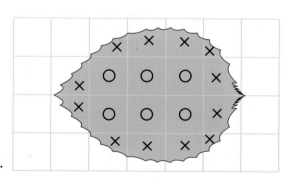

Remember the units!

Exercise 10D

Estimate the areas of these shapes.

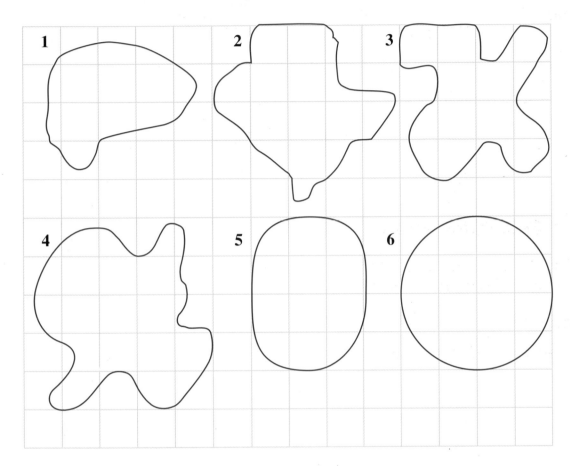

10.5 Areas by multiplying

It can take a long time to count squares.

Sometimes it is quicker to use multiplication:

ONE, TWO, THREE...

This rectangle measures
6 mm by 15 mm

By counting squares:
the area is 90 mm^2

There are 6 rows of 15 mm

By multiplying:
the area is $6 \times 15 = 90$ mm^2

■ **For any rectangle:**
   Area = length × width

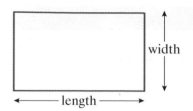

The length and width must be measured in the same units.

Example 5

Find the area of each rectangle:

(a)

4 cm

5 cm

(b)

7 m

3 m

(a) length = 5 cm
width = 4 cm
The units are both cm so use:

area = length × width
    = 5 × 4
    = 20 cm²

(b) length = 7 m
width = 3 m
The units are both m so use:

area = length × width
    = 7 × 3
    = 21 m²

Exercise 10E

1 Find the areas of these rectangles:

(a)   6 cm

4 cm

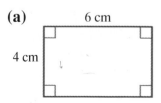

(b)   2 cm

5 cm

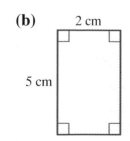

(c)   3 cm

3 cm

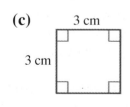

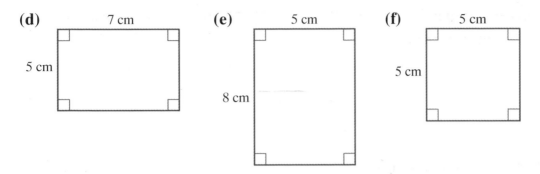

(d) 7 cm 5 cm

(e) 5 cm 8 cm

(f) 5 cm 5 cm

2 A rectangle has a length of 12 cm and a width of 7 cm.
Work out:

   (a) the perimeter of the rectangle

   (b) the area of the rectangle

3 This table shows the lengths and widths of some
rectangles. Copy and complete the table.

Length in cm	Width in cm	Perimeter in cm	Area in cm^2
5	2	14	10
4	3		
5	5		
6	4		
4	4		
7	3		
6	3		
10	2		
5	4		
6	10		
12	5		

4 A rectangular wall measures 4 m by 7 m. Work out:

   (a) the perimeter of the wall

   (b) the area of the wall

5 The width of a rectangle is 8 cm.
The perimeter of the rectangle is 20 cm.
Work out the area of the rectangle.

6 The area of a rectangle is 30 cm^2.
The width of the rectangle is 3 cm.
Find the length of the rectangle.

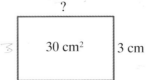

?

30 cm^2 3 cm

7 Investigation You may want to use squared paper.
The diagram shows a rectangle. Its perimeter is 24 cm.

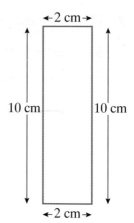

- Draw as many rectangles as you can
  which have a perimeter of 24 cm.

- Write down the length and width of
  each rectangle.

- Work out the area of each rectangle.
  Which of the rectangles has the largest area?

Repeat this investigation for rectangles with a
perimeter of:

(a) 12 cm   **(b)** 20 cm

(c) 36 cm   **(d)** 40 cm

Each time find which rectangle gives the largest area.

8 For each shape write down:

- the length of side x
- the total perimeter

(a)

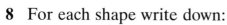

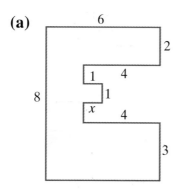

(b)

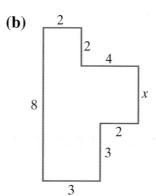

(c)   **(d)**

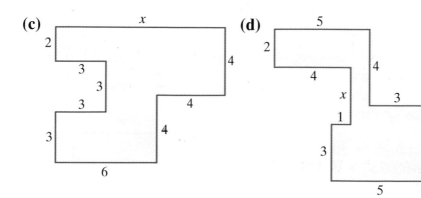

9 For each shape find:

- the lengths of sides x and y
- the total perimeter

(a)

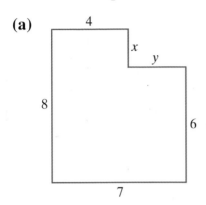

(b)

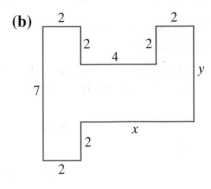

(c)

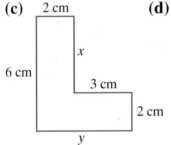

(d)

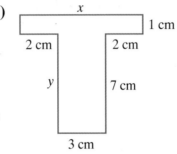

(e)

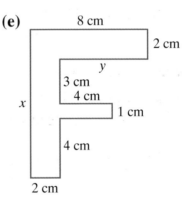

10.6 Area of a right-angled triangle

This triangle has a right angle:

It fits inside a rectangle:

The area of the rectangle is:
base × height

The area of the triangle is:
$\frac{1}{2}$ × base × height

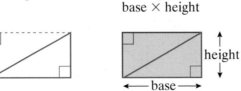

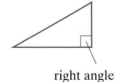

right angle

■   **The area of a right-angled triangle is:**
$\frac{1}{2}$ × **base** × **height**

Example 6

Find the area of this triangle:

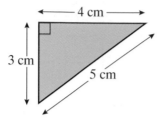

The triangle fits inside a rectangle:

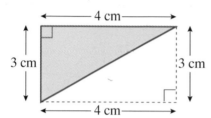

area of rectangle $= 3 \times 4 = 12\,\text{cm}^2$

area of triangle $= \frac{1}{2} \times 3 \times 4 = 6\,\text{cm}^2$

The area of the triangle is $6\,\text{cm}^2$.

Exercise 10F

These triangles are drawn on centimetre squared paper.
For each triangle:

(a) write down the lengths of the perpendicular sides
(b) find the area of the triangle.

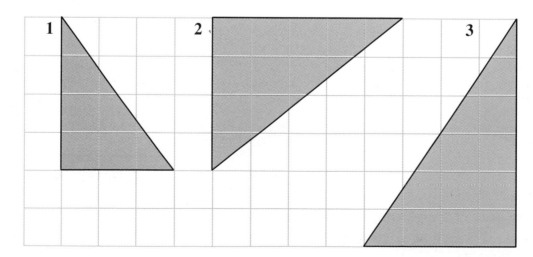

4 Find the area of these triangles. All measurements are in cm.

(a)
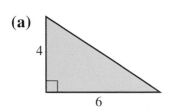
4
6

(b)
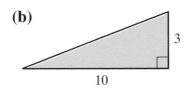
3
10

(c)
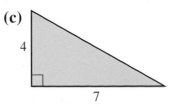
4
7

(d)
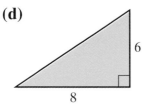
6
8

(e)
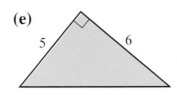
5
6

(f)
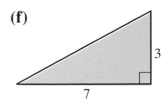
3
7

(g)
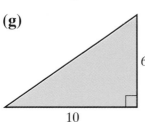
6
10

(h)
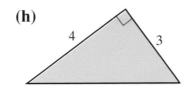
4
3

(i)
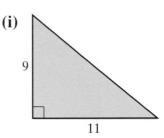
9
11

10.7 Areas of more complex triangles

You can find the area of a triangle like this by splitting it into two right-angled triangles.

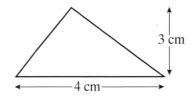
3 cm
4 cm

Split it into two right-angled triangles:

Each triangle fits inside a rectangle:

The area of the large rectangle is:
area = 3 × 4 = 12 cm²

The area of the triangle is:
area = $\frac{1}{2}$ × 3 × 4 = 6 cm²

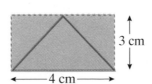

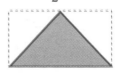
3 cm
4 cm

The area of the triangle is 6 cm².

■ **The area of a triangle is half the area of the surrounding rectangle:**

Area $= \frac{1}{2} \times$ **base** $\times$ **height**

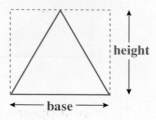

Remember: the base and height must be perpendicular.

Example 7

Find the area of this triangle:

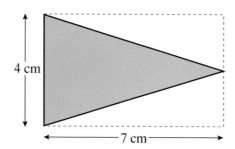

The triangle fits inside a rectangle with sides 4 cm and 7 cm.

The area is $\frac{1}{2} \times 4 \times 7 = 14$ cm^2

Exercise 10G

1 Find the area of each triangle.

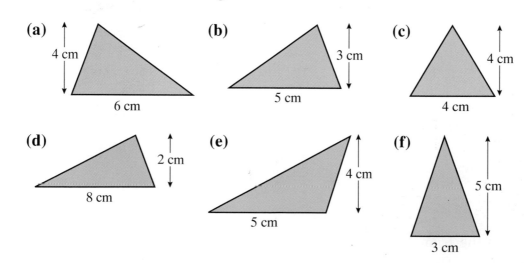

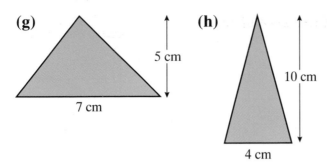

(g) 5 cm / 7 cm

(h) 10 cm / 4 cm

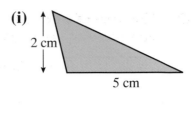

(i) 2 cm / 5 cm

2 Here is another triangle

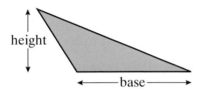

height — base

Use pictures to show why the formula

$$\text{Area} = \tfrac{1}{2} \times \text{base} \times \text{height}$$

still works for this triangle.

10.8 Putting it all together

Nadia is tiling her kitchen floor.
How many tiles should she buy?
She draws a plan of her kitchen to
work out the area:

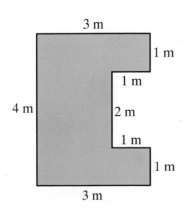

3 m
1 m
1 m
2 m
4 m
1 m
1 m
3 m

Nadia can work out the area of her floor in two ways:

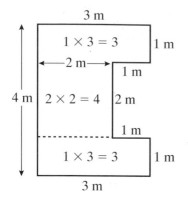

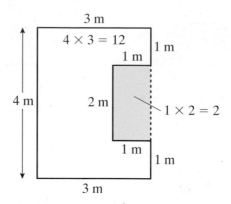

Split it into 3 rectangles.
Then add their areas:

$$3 + 4 + 3 = 10\,m^2$$

Complete the large rectangle.
Take away the shaded area:

$$12 - 2 = 10\,m^2$$

A shape you can break into simpler shapes is called a
composite shape.

■ **To find the area of a composite shape break it into
simpler shapes, for example: rectangles and triangles.**

Exercise 10H

1 Find the area of each shape. All units are in cm.

(a)

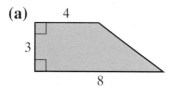

(b)

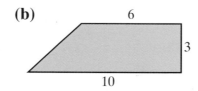

(c)

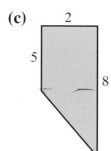

(d)

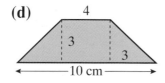

(e)

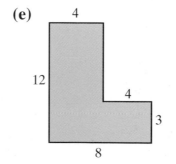

(f)

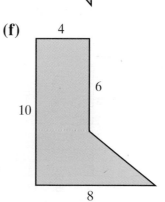

2 Find the shaded area in each shape:

(a)
5 cm

6cm

3 cm

10 cm

(b)
8 cm

6 cm

12 cm

(c)
9 cm

4 cm

4 cm

6 cm

10 cm

(d)
5 cm

2 cm

2 cm 5 cm

Hint: find the whole area.
Subtract the unshaded part.

(e)
4 cm

5 cm

5 cm

12 cm

(f)
8 cm

6 cm

2 cm

4 cm

12 cm

10.9 Volume

How much space will Vic's
CD collection occupy?

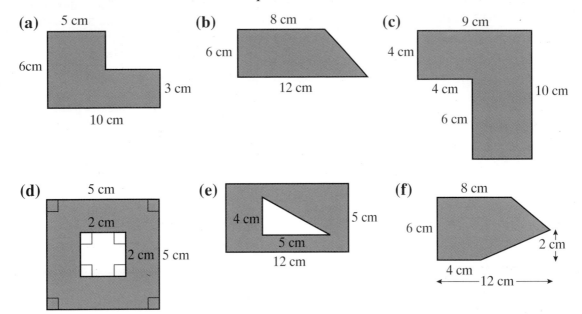

■ **The volume of an object is the
amount of space it occupies.**

You can use cubes to measure volume:

1 millimetre cube	1 centimetre cube	1 metre cube	1 kilometre cube

The size of a grain of sand.	The size of a sugar cube or dice.	The size of a large washing machine.	Bigger than the biggest mountain in Britain.

You will also see measures of volume written like this:

1 millimetre cube: 1 cubic mm or $1\,\text{mm}^3$

1 centimetre cube: 1 cubic cm or $1\,\text{cm}^3$

1 metre cube: 1 cubic m   or $1\,\text{m}^3$

1 kilometre cube: 1 cubic km or $1\,\text{km}^3$

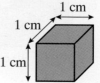

The 3 shows there are 3 dimensions: length, width and height.

Example 8

Find the volume of this box:

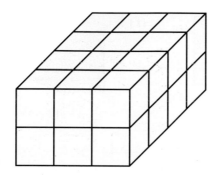

Count the centimetre cubes:
There are 12 cubes in each layer, and 2 layers.

So the volume is $12 \times 2 = 24\,\text{cm}^3$

Remember to use the correct units.

Exercise 10I

1 Which shape has
 (a) the largest volume?
 (b) the smallest volume?

A 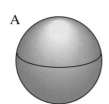   B   C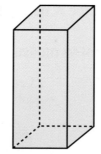

2 Write these objects in order of size.
 Start with the largest volume.

   Brick   Pencil   This book   Loaf of bread   Pin   Orange

3 These objects are made of centimetre cubes.
Find the volume of each object:

(a)

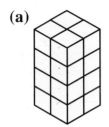

(b)

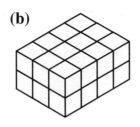

(c)

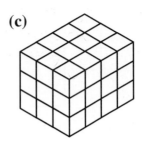

(d)

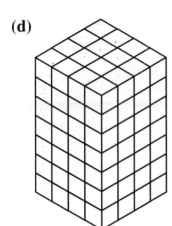

(e)

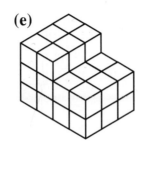

(f)

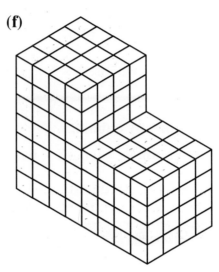

10.10 Volume of a cuboid

A cuboid is a solid shape with rectangular faces:

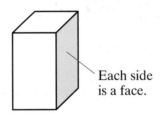

Each side
is a face.

Example 9

Work out the volume of this cuboid:

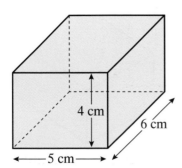

4 cm

6 cm

5 cm

You can fit

5 centimetre cubes in the width	6 centimetre cubes in the length	$6 \times 5 = 30$ centimetre cubes in the base	4 layers like the base

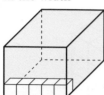 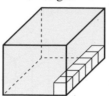 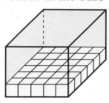 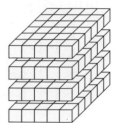

The volume is
$30 \times 4 = 120$ centimetre cubes.

The quick way is: $6 \times 5 \times 4 = 120 \, \text{cm}^3$.

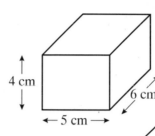

4 cm

6 cm

5 cm

■ **For any cuboid:**

Volume = length × width × height

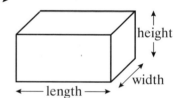

height

width

length

Exercise 10J

Find the volume of each cuboid. All lengths are in cm.

1

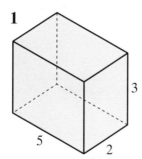

3

5

2

2

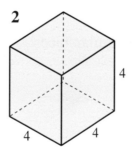

4

4

4

3

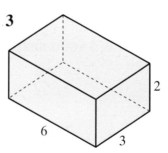

2

6

3

4

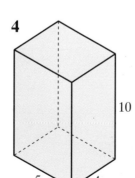

10

5

4

5

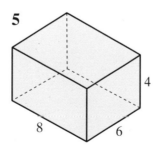

4

8

6

6

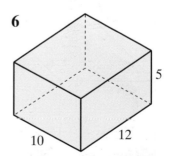

5

10

12

10.11 Capacity

■ **The volume of space inside a hollow object is called its *capacity*.**

You can find the capacity of ...

... an empty box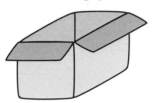

... an empty glass

... a car boot

Imagine the space inside these objects:

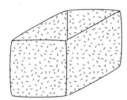

Example 10

Find the capacities of these boxes:

(a)

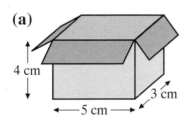

4 cm

5 cm

3 cm

(b)

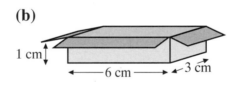

1 cm

6 cm

3 cm

The capacity of an empty box is the volume of space inside it.

The boxes are both cuboids so you can use the formula:

Volume = length × width × height

(a)   Volume = $4 \times 5 \times 3 = 60 \, \text{cm}^3$
  so Capacity = $60 \, \text{cm}^3$

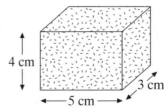

4 cm

5 cm

3 cm

(b)   Volume = $6 \times 3 \times 1 = 18 \, \text{cm}^3$
  so Capacity = $18 \, \text{cm}^3$

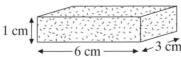

1 cm

6 cm

3 cm

Exercise 10K

1   These objects can all hold liquid.
    Write the objects in order of size.
    Start with the greatest capacity.

    Teacup   Teaspoon   Washing up bowl   Swimming pool

2   All these boxes are empty.
    Find the capacity of each box.

(a)
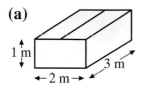

(b)
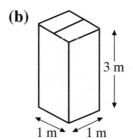

(c)
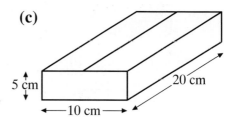

(d)
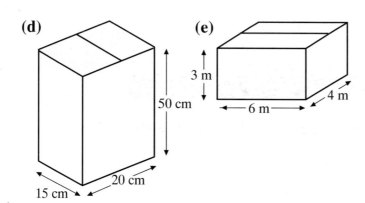

(e)

(c)
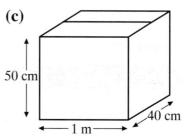

10.12 Surface area

This cuboid has six rectangular faces:

If you add the areas of all six faces together you
get the **surface area** of the cuboid.

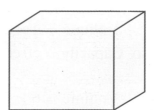

■   **The surface area of a cuboid is the total area
    of all six faces.**

Example 11

Find the surface area of this cuboid:

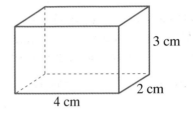

The top and bottom faces are the same:

$$\text{length} \times \text{width} = 4\,\text{cm} \times 2\,\text{cm}$$
$$= 8\,\text{cm}^2$$

The front and back faces are the same:

$$\text{length} \times \text{height} = 4\,\text{cm} \times 3\,\text{cm}$$
$$= 12\,\text{cm}^2$$

The right and left faces are the same:

$$\text{width} \times \text{height} = 3\,\text{cm} \times 2\,\text{cm}$$
$$= 6\,\text{cm}^2$$

So the total surface area is:

$$8 + 8 + 12 + 12 + 6 + 6 = 52\,\text{cm}^2$$

Exercise 10L

1 Work out the surface area of each cuboid in **Exercise 10J**.

2 Write out a word formula for the surface area of a cuboid.

Summary of key points

1 The distance around the edge of a shape is its perimeter.

2 For any rectangle:

$$\text{Perimeter} = (2 \times \text{length}) + (2 \times \text{width})$$

or

$$\text{Perimeter} = 2 \times (\text{length} + \text{width})$$

3 Area is the amount of space covered by a shape.

4 For any rectangle:

Area = length × width

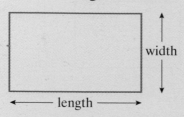

The length and width must be measured in the same units.

5 The area of a right-angled triangle is: $\frac{1}{2}$ × base × height

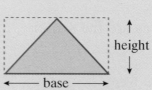

6 Area of a triangle is half the area of the surrounding rectangle:

Area = $\frac{1}{2}$ × base × height

7 You can find the area of a composite shape by breaking it into simpler shapes, for example: rectangles and triangles.

8 The volume of an object is the amount of space it occupies.

9 For any cuboid:

Volume = length × width × height

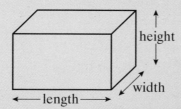

10 The volume of space inside a hollow object is called its **capacity**.

11 The surface area of a cuboid is the total area of all six faces.

11 Formulae and equations

This unit shows you how to use formulae and equations to help solve problems.

11.1 Using word formulae

■ **A formula is a sentence describing a rule or relationship.**
It must contain an equals (=) sign.
For example:

$$\text{speed} = \frac{\text{distance}}{\text{time}}$$

$E = mc^2$ is the famous formula which shows how much energy is released when matter is converted into energy.

Example 1

Helen buys ice creams from a shop. This formula describes the total cost:

    cost of ice creams = cost of one ice cream × number bought

Helen buys 4 ice creams at 80p each.
Put these numbers into the word formula:

    cost of ice creams = cost of one ice cream × number bought
                  =   80p   ×   4
                  = 320p
                  = £3.20

Exercise 11A

1 Andrew buys some pens. He uses the formula:
    cost of pens = cost of one pen × number bought
The cost of one pen is 25p. Andrew buys 2 pens. Find the total cost of the pens.

2 Diana buys some buns. She uses the formula:
    cost of buns = cost of one bun × number bought
The cost of one bun is 55p. Diana buys 4 buns. Find the total cost of the buns.

3 Narinder buys some bags of sweets. She uses the formula:
    cost of sweets = cost of one bag × number bought
The cost of one bag of sweets is 85p. Narinder buys 6 bags. Find the cost of the sweets.

4 Sam buys some choc bars. He uses the formula:

cost of choc bars = cost of one choc bar × number bought

The cost of one choc bar is 25p. Sam buys 3 choc bars.
Work out the cost of the choc bars.

5 Mrs Akeya shares out some money equally among her
family. She uses the formula:

amount each person gets = amount of money ÷ number in family

Work out how much each person gets when Mrs Akeya
shares out £20 among:

(a) 2 people   **(b)** 4 people   **(c)** 5 people

6 The formula to work out the number of people in a
school is:

number of people = number of staff + number of pupils

Work out the number of people in a school which has
47 staff and 1083 pupils.

7 The formula to work out the temperature difference
between Greece and England is:

temperature difference = temperature in − temperature in
                                    Greece   England

Work out the temperature
difference when the
temperatures in Greece
and England are:

	Greece	England
(a)	19°C	7°C
(b)	10°C	0°C
(c)	30°C	16°C

11.2 Using letters to represent numbers

You can fit a
green rod and
a red rod
together ...

... to make the
same length as
a yellow rod.

This mathematical sentence connects the lengths of the rods:

length of yellow = length of red + length of green

You can write this in letters for short:

y   =   r   +   g

You can fit other rods together to match the length of the yellow rod:

length of yellow = length of white + length of white + length of green

In letters this is:

or:

$$y \qquad = \qquad w \qquad + \qquad w \qquad + \qquad g$$

$$y \qquad = \qquad 2w \qquad\qquad + \qquad g$$

2w means 2 × w
or w + w

Exercise 11B

In this exercise either use a set of Cuisenaire rods or trace the rods below.

Use these letters to stand for the lengths of the rods:

w   r   g   p   y

1 Write each of these as a sentence using letters.
(The first one is: $r = 2w$)

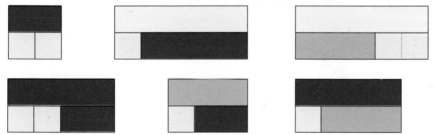

2 Find the three different rod trains equal to the length of the green rod.
Write each one as a sentence using letters.

3 Find all the different rod trains equal to the length of the yellow rod.
Write each one as a sentence using letters.

A **rod train** is any combination of rods in a row.
For example:

11.3 Using letters in formulae

You can shorten formulae by using letters to stand for unknown amounts.

Example 2

The formula for the total distance Joan travels to school is:

total distance = distance travelled by car + distance walked

Write this formula using these letters:

d for total distance travelled
c for distance travelled by car
w for distance walked

The formula is: $d = c + w$

Example 3

Alex works in a sports shop.
He gets £5 for each hour he works.
The formula for his pay is:

pay = 5 × number of hours worked

Write this formula using the letters:

p for pay
n for number of hours worked

The formula is: $p = 5 \times n$ or $p = 5n$

Exercise 11C

1 Write a formula for the cost c of b buns at 35 pence each.

2 Ben has p pens and Bill has q pens. Together Ben and Bill have a total of t pens.
Write a formula for the total number of pens they have.

3 David has s sweets. He divides them equally between his 5 friends. Write down a formula for the number of sweets n each of them receives.

4 The temperature in Greece is g °C.
The temperature in England is e °C.
The difference between the temperatures in Greece
and England is d °C.
Write a formula connecting d, g and e.

5 Savita sells cameras.
She earns a commission of £6 for every sale she makes.
Last month she made s sales and her commission was £c.
Write a formula connecting c and s.

6 (a)

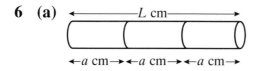

This rod has three equal sections.
Each section is a cm long.
The total length of the rod is L cm.
Write a formula connecting L and a.

(b) A pencil is five times as long as the rod above.
The length of the pencil is P cm

   (i) Write a formula connecting P and L.

   (ii) Write a formula connecting P and a.

7 The perimeter of a flat shape is the total distance
around the edge of the shape. Write formulae for the
perimeters P of these shapes.

Each formula
should begin:

$$P =$$

(i)
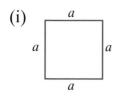

(ii)
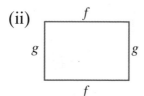

(iii)
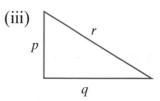

8 Jessica is x years old today.
In 10 years time she will be a years old.
Write a formula connecting x and a.

11.4 Formulae with two operations

One of the rod trains equal to a yellow rod is:

$2 \times \text{white} + \text{green}$

You can think of this in two ways:

Do the addition first:

Do the multiplication first:

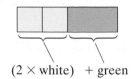

(white + green) $\times 2$ (2 $\times$ white) + green

To see which is right, compare them both with a yellow rod:

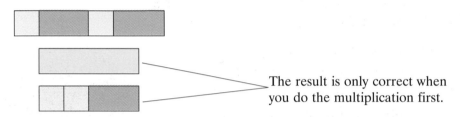

The result is only correct when you do the multiplication first.

The made-up word BIDMAS can help you remember the correct order:

Brackets
Indices
Division
Multiplication
Addition
Subtraction

You do the operation nearest the top of the list first and then work down.

Remember:
Indices are 'to the power of' numbers like 4^3 or 6^7

Example 4

Work out:

(a) $2 + 3 \times 4$ **(b)** $(2 + 3) \times 4$ **(c)** $3 \times (4 + 3^2) - 8$

(a) Do the multiplication first, then the addition:

$2 + 12 = 14$

(b) This time do the brackets first, then the multiplication:

$5 \times 4 = 20$

(c) Do the brackets first:

$(4 + 3^2) = 4 + 9 = 13$

Then do the multiplication, then the subtraction:

$3 \times 13 = 39$
$39 - 8 = 31$

You need to use BIDMAS to work out the bracket as well – work out the indices then add.

Exercise 11D

1 Work out:

(a) $3 + 2 \times 4$ (b) $5 - 2^2 \times 2$ (c) $(2 + 5) \times 2^2$

(d) $3 \times (2 + 6)$ (e) $(3 - 2) \times 5$ (f) $(6 + 8) \div 2$

(g) $(5 + 7) \div 3$ (h) $(10 - 6) \times 4$ (i) $12 \div (9 - 6)$

(j) $6 - 3 \times 2^3$ (k) $10^2 - 5 \times 2$ (l) $15 \div 5 - 3$

2 Jaqui joins a video club.
She has to pay a membership fee and then £2 for each video she hires.

(a) Write this as a formula in words.

(b) Work out the total amount Jaqui will pay if the membership fee is £5 and she hires 15 videos.

3 The instructions for cooking a turkey are 'Allow 45 minutes for each kilogram the turkey weighs, then add another 30 minutes.'

(a) Copy and complete this formula in words:

   time to cook a turkey =

(b) How many minutes will it take to cook a turkey weighing 10 kilograms?

4 The total monthly cost of using a mobile phone is the monthly line rental plus £12 for each hour the phone is used.

(a) Write this as a formula in words.

(b) If line rental is £40, find the total monthly cost of using a mobile phone for:

   (i) 5 hours   (ii) $\frac{1}{2}$ an hour

11.5 Using algebraic formulae

Tony's garage uses this formula to work out how much to charge:

   charge = cost of spare parts + 15 × number of hours worked

It's quicker to write this using letters:

Use c for the charge

   s for the cost of spare parts

   n for the number of hours worked.

The formula becomes:

   $c = s + 15n$

Example 5

Samantha went to the school disco. She paid 50p for her ticket, then 30p for each drink she bought.

Write a formula for the total cost of going to the school disco:

(a) in words   **(b)** using letters

(a) In words the formula is:

cost of going = price of ticket + 30 × number of drinks bought

Or   cost =   50   + 30 × number of drinks bought

(b) Use c for cost
         n for number of drinks bought.

The formula is:

$$c = 50 + 30n$$

Remember:
You can only collect terms with the same letters.

$50 + 30n$ is **not** $80n$

Exercise 11E

1 The instructions for cooking a joint of beef are:

'allow 45 minutes for each kilogram then add a further 30 minutes.'

A joint of beef weighs w kilograms. The total time to cook it is t minutes.
Using letters write a formula connecting w and t.

2 In this diagram, the length of each side is in centimetres:

The perimeter of the triangle is p cm.

Write a formula connecting p and x.

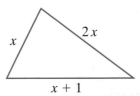

Remember: the perimeter of a flat shape is the total distance around the edge of the shape.

3 A football team gets 3 points for a win and 1 point for a draw.
Last season they got p points.
They won w games and drew d games.
Using letters write a formula connecting p, w and d.

11.6 Substituting into formulae

You can substitute numbers back into formulae to help solve problems.

Example 6

What is the perimeter of a rectangle if $l = 4$ cm and $w = 3$ cm?

There is more about perimeter on page 194.

The formula for the perimeter of a rectangle is:

$$\text{Perimeter} = 2 \times \text{length} + 2 \times \text{width}$$

Using algebra you can write:

$$P = 2l + 2w$$

Now substitute in l and w to find the answer:

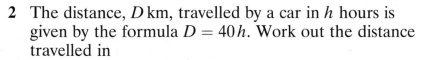

So the perimeter is 14 cm.

Exercise 11F

1 The formula for the perimeter of a square is $P = 4l$. Work out the perimeter P when l is:

    (a) 5 cm   **(b)** 2 cm   **(c)** 3 cm   **(d)** 10 cm

2 The distance, D km, travelled by a car in h hours is given by the formula $D = 40h$. Work out the distance travelled in

    (a) 3 hours   **(b)** 2 hours   **(c)** 5 hours

3 The Perimeter P of a rectangle is given by the formula $P = 2l + 2w$. Work out the perimeter when

    (a) $l = 4$, $w = 3$ **(b)** $l = 10$, $w = 4$ **(c)** $l = 5$, $w = 2$

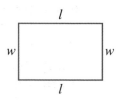

4 When a ball is thrown into the air its speed, s, after t seconds is given by the formula

$$s = 50 - 10t$$

Work out the speed of the ball when t is:

(a) 1 second **(b)** 3 seconds **(c)** 5 seconds

5 The cost c, in pence, of printing w worksheets is given by the formula:

$$c = 40 + 2w$$

Work out the cost of printing:

(a) 50 worksheets **(b)** 200 worksheets
(c) 1000 worksheets

6 Use substitution to check which of these expressions are the same.

(a) $a^2 + a$; $a(a + 1)$; $3a$
(b) $2n + 4$; $2(n + 4)$; $2(n + 2)$
(c) $d^2 + d - 1$; $d(d - 1)$; $d(d + 1) - 1$
(d) $4b^2 + 2a$; $2(2b^2 + a)$; $2b(2b + 1a)$
(e) $12yz - 10y$; $8y(z + 2)$; $2y(6z - 5)$

Hint: Always substitute in a few different values to check your answer.

11.7 Solving equations

■ **Equations and formulae are different:**

Equation	Formula
$2 + m = 8$	$\text{cost} = \text{price} \times \text{number bought}$
This **equation** is **only true** when $m = 6$	$c = p \times n$
6 is a **solution** of the equation. Finding the value of m is called **solving the equation**.	You can put **any values** into these parts of the **formula** and get a result for the cost.

Equations may be true for one value (like $m = 6$) or several values but are not generally true for any value.

Using number machines to solve equations

To solve the equation $p + 3 = 10$
you need to find the value of p.

First write $p + 3 = 10$
as a number machine:

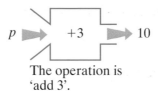

The operation is
'add 3'.

Now find a number machine
to 'undo' the operation 'add 3':

This is an **inverse number machine**.

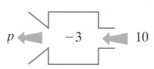

The operation is
'subtract 3'.

Use the inverse number machine
to find the value of p:

$p = 7$ is a solution of the equation
$p + 3 = 10$

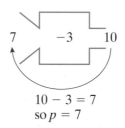

$10 - 3 = 7$
so $p = 7$

Exercise 11G

Solve these equations using inverse number machines:

(a) $a + 4 = 6$ (b) $b + 3 = 7$

(c) $c + 2 = 7$ (d) $d + 3 = 8$

(e) $r + 2 = 12$ (f) $s + 5 = 10$

(g) $t + 8 = 12$ (h) $u + 7 = 8$

(i) $e - 6 = 1$ (j) $f - 5 = 6$

(k) $g - 3 = 1$ (l) $h - 4 = 4$

(m) $7e = 21$ (n) $3f = 18$

(o) $2g = 10$ (p) $5h = 25$

(q) $5i = 0$ (r) $6j = 24$

(s) $8k = 16$ (t) $2l = 20$

(u) $t \div 4 = 0$ (v) $j \div 3 = 4$

(w) $k \div 4 = 6$ (x) $l \div 5 = 20$

(y) $\dfrac{m}{3} = 2$ (z) $\dfrac{n}{4} = 2$

Solving more complex equations

To solve the equation $3x - 2 = 13$
you need a two step number machine.

First write $3x - 2 = 13$
as a number machine:

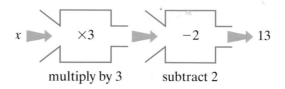

Now find an inverse number
machine to undo the operations
'multiply by 3' and 'subtract 2':

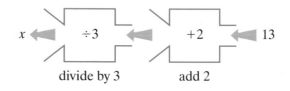

Use the inverse number
machine to find the value
of x:

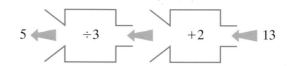

$x = 5$ is a solution of the equation $3x - 2 = 13$

Check:
$3 \times 5 - 2 = 15 - 2$
$= 13$
So $x = 5$ is correct.

Exercise 11H

Solve each of these equations:

(a) $2x - 1 = 9$

(b) $4p - 3 = 5$

(c) $3z + 2 = 17$

(d) $3t + 1 = 19$

(e) $4g - 2 = 22$

(f) $5x - 3 = 32$

(g) $4p - 3 = 7$

(h) $5n - 3 = 2$

(i) $6p - 1 = 20$

(j) $4x - 2 = 20$

(k) $2t - 1 = 0$

(l) $3t - 7 = 11$

(m) $5p + 4 = 19$

(n) $2 + 5x = 22$

(o) $10x - 100 = 0$

Hint:

Operation:	Inverse:
$+$	$-$
$-$	$+$
$\times$	$\div$
$\div$	$\times$

11.8 Using algebra to solve equations

You can think of an equation as a balance:

To solve $3x - 4 = 11$ you need to get x on its own on one side of the scales.

First add 4 to both sides:

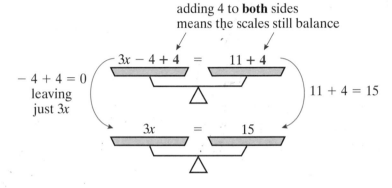

To get x on its own divide both sides by 3:

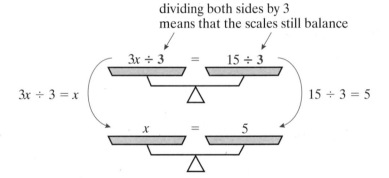

The scales balance when $x = 5$

$x = 5$ is a solution of $3x - 4 = 11$

Exercise 11I

Solve each of these equations:

(a) $3x - 2 = 16$ (b) $2y + 1 = 9$ (c) $5t - 2 = 8$

(d) $4x - 3 = 21$ (e) $5n + 3 = 13$ (f) $7p - 1 = 20$

(g) $8y + 2 = 58$ (h) $4p - 1 = 9$ (i) $6n + 3 = 30$

(j) $5t - 3 = 17$ (k) $8n - 3 = 9$ (l) $4x - 3 = 6$

(m) $6x - 7 = 5$ (n) $5 + 4x = 17$ (o) $7q - 35 = 0$

11.9 Writing equations

Sometimes you will need to write an equation to find an unknown value.

Example 7

The perimeter of this triangle is 12 cm.
(a) Write down an equation for the perimeter.
(b) Solve the equation.
(c) Write down the length of each side of the triangle.

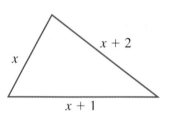

(a) The equation is: $\quad x + x + 1 + x + 2 = 12$

Collect like terms: $\quad\quad 3x + 3 = 12$

(b) Subtract 3 from both sides: $\quad 3x + 3 - 3 = 12 - 3$
$$3x = 9$$

Divide both sides by 3: $\quad\quad 3x \div 3 = 9 \div 3$
$$x = 3$$

Check:
$3 + 4 + 5 = 12$
So $x = 3$ is correct.

(c) The sides are x, $x + 1$ and $x + 2$
so the sides are 3 cm, 4 cm and 5 cm.

Example 8

Complete this number pyramid.
The number in each brick is
the sum of the two bricks above.

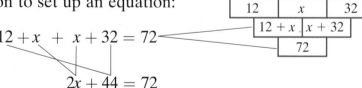

Use the information to set up an equation:

$$12 + x \ + \ x + 32 = 72$$

and solve it:
$$2x + 44 = 72$$
$$2x + 44 - 44 = 72 - 44$$
$$2x \div 2 = 28 \div 2$$

so $\quad\quad\quad\quad\quad\quad\quad x = 14$

Finally, substitute in $x = 14$ and complete the pyramid:

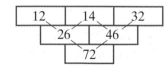

Example 9

Find x, y and n in this arithmogon:

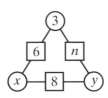

Remember:
The sum of two numbers in a circle goes in the square between them.

First find x:	Then use x to find y:	Then use y to find n:
$3 + x = 6$ so $\qquad x = 3$	$\begin{array}{c} x + y = 8 \\ x = 3 \downarrow \\ 3 + y = 8 \end{array}$ so $\qquad y = 5$	$\begin{array}{c} y + 3 = n \\ y = 5 \downarrow \\ 5 + 3 = n \end{array}$ so $\qquad n = 8$

Exercise 11J

1 The perimeter of this quadrilateral is 33 cm.

(a) Write an equation for the perimeter.

(b) Solve the equation.

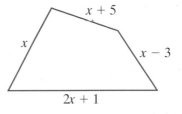

2 Jaqui is a years old.
   Her mum's age is $3 \times$ Jaqui's age plus another 4 years.
   Jaqui's mum is 40 years old.

(a) Write down an equation for Jaqui's age using a.

(b) Find the value of a.

3 The cost of a choc-bar is n pence. Asif buys 4 choc bars.
   He pays for them with a £2 coin and gets 60p change.
   By writing down and solving an equation, find the cost of one choc bar.

4 Ken thinks of a number.
   He multiplies it by 3.
   Then he takes away 5.
   His answer is then 7.
   Write an equation and use it to find the number Ken thought of. Use n for the number Ken thought of originally.

5 Complete these number pyramids:

(a)
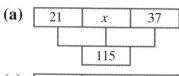
| 21 | *x* | 37 |
| | 115 | |

(b)
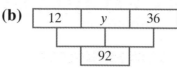
| 12 | *y* | 36 |
| | 92 | |

(c)
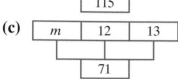
| *m* | 12 | 13 |
| | 71 | |

(d)
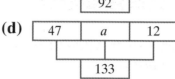
| 47 | *a* | 12 |
| | 133 | |

6 Complete these arithmogons:

(a)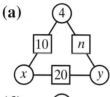

(b)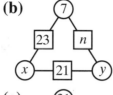

(c)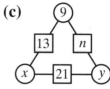

(d)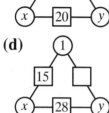

(e)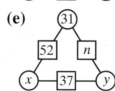

(f)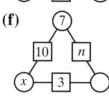

Summary of key points

1 A formula is a sentence describing a rule or relationship. It must contain an equals ($=$) sign.
For example

$$\text{speed} = \frac{\text{distance}}{\text{time}}$$

2 Equations and formulae are different:

Equation	**Formula**
$2 + m = 8$	cost = price × number bought
This **equation** is **only true** when $m = 6$	$c = p \times n$
6 is a **solution** of the equation. Finding the value of m is called **solving the equation**.	You can put **any values** into these parts of the **formula** and get a result for the cost.

Equations may be true for one value (like $m = 6$) or several values but are not generally true for any value.

12 Negative numbers

12.1 Measuring temperatures

This thermometer measures temperatures in degrees
Celsius, written °C for short.

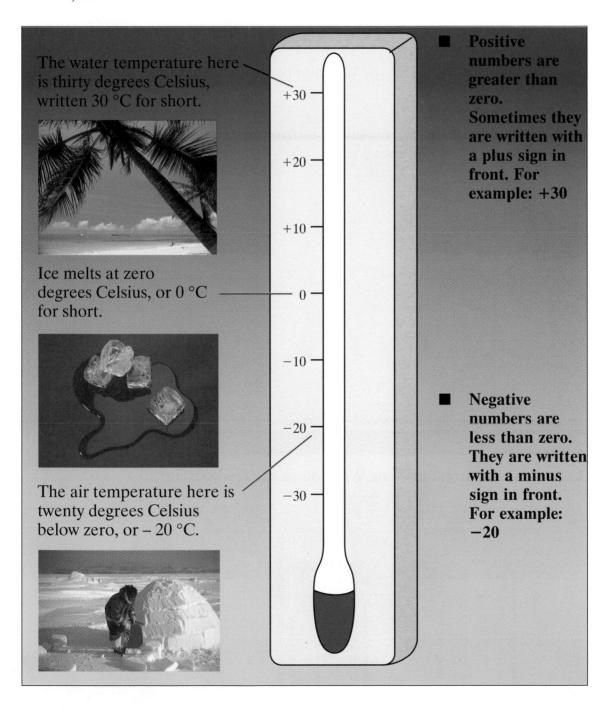

The water temperature here
is thirty degrees Celsius,
written 30 °C for short.

Ice melts at zero
degrees Celsius, or 0 °C
for short.

The air temperature here is
twenty degrees Celsius
below zero, or – 20 °C.

■ **Positive
numbers are
greater than
zero.
Sometimes they
are written with
a plus sign in
front. For
example: +30**

■ **Negative
numbers are
less than zero.
They are written
with a minus
sign in front.
For example:
−20**

Example 1

What temperature does the thermometer show?
Write your answer:

(a) in words

(b) in figures.

(a) negative eight degrees Celsius

(b) $-8\,°C$

Example 2

Mark these temperatures on the thermometer activity sheet:

(a) $+3\,°C$ **(b)** $-4\,°C$

(a) The temperature $+3\,°C$ means three degrees Celsius above zero. This is what it looks like on a thermometer.

(b) The temperature $-4\,°C$ means four degrees Celsius below zero. This is what it looks like on a thermometer.

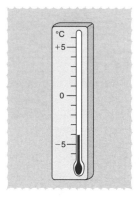

Exercise 12A

1 Look at the thermometers. Write down each temperature:
   (i) in words   **(ii)** in figures.

(a)  **(b)**  **(c)**  **(d)**  **(e)**  **(f)**

2 Mark these temperatures on the thermometers on activity sheet 8.

The symbol ° is short for degrees.

   (**a**) $+5\,°C$ (**b**) $-3\,°C$ (**c**) $-6\,°C$ (**d**) $+9\,°C$

   (**e**) $-2\,°C$ (**f**) $-4\,°C$ (**g**) $+6\,°C$ (**h**) $-7\,°C$

   (**i**) $-1\,°C$ (**j**) $-11\,°C$ (**k**) $+4\,°C$ (**l**) $-8\,°C$

12.2 Writing temperatures in order of size

You need to be able to sort a list of temperatures in order of size.

On this weather map the numbers are temperatures in degrees Celsius.

⑧ means $8\,°C$ or $+8\,°C$.

Ⓐ means $-1\,°C$. You might hear a weather person say 'minus four' instead of 'negative four'.

Example 3

From the weather map write down

(**a**) the highest temperature in $°C$,

(**b**) the lowest temperature in $°C$,

(**c**) all the temperatures in order of size, starting with the highest.

(**a**) The highest temperature is $20\,°C$.

(**b**) The lowest temperature is $-4\,°C$.

(**c**) Sketch a thermometer scale going from $20\,°C$ to $-5\,°C$.
Mark each temperature on the scale. Then write the temperatures in order, starting from the top of the scale:

$20\,°C, 13\,°C, 12\,°C, 10\,°C, 9\,°C, 8\,°C,$
$0\,°C, -1\,°C, -4\,°C.$

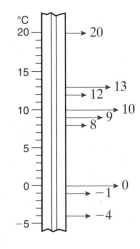

$-4\,°C$ is below $-1\,°C$, $0\,°C, 8\,°C$ and all the other temperatures.

Exercise 12B

On the weather maps in questions **1** and **2** the numbers are
temperatures in degrees Celsius.

1 From the weather map write down:

(a) the hottest place,

(b) the coldest place,

(c) all the temperatures in order of size,
starting with the highest.

2 Look at the weather map and write
down:

(a) the highest temperature,

(b) the lowest temperature,

(c) all the temperatures in order of
size, starting with the lowest.

3 Write down the higher of the two temperatures:

(a) $1\,°C$ and $4\,°C$ (b) $-9\,°C$ and $3\,°C$

(c) $-1\,°C$ and $0\,°C$ (d) $-2\,°C$ and $4\,°C$

(e) $-5\,°C$ and $-3\,°C$ (f) $-2\,°C$ and $-5\,°C$

4 Write down the lower of the two temperatures:

(a) $3\,°C$ and $1\,°C$ (b) $0\,°C$ and $-2\,°C$

(c) $-4\,°C$ and $3\,°C$ (d) $-3\,°C$ and $-4\,°C$

(e) $-6\,°C$ and $-4\,°C$ (f) $-5\,°C$ and $-9\,°C$

5 Write down the highest temperature in each list:
   (a) +2 °C, −3 °C, +3 °C, −7 °C, +9 °C, −6 °C
   (b) +1 °C, +3 °C, −4 °C, −8 °C, −1 °C, +4 °C
   (c) −3 °C, −6 °C, −1 °C, −5 °C, −9 °C, −4 °C

6 Write down the lowest temperature in each list:
   (a) +2 °C, −3 °C, +3 °C, −7 °C, +9 °C, −6 °C
   (b) +1 °C, +3 °C, −4 °C, −8 °C, −1 °C, +4 °C
   (c) −3 °C, −2 °C, −9 °C, −8 °C, 0 °C, −7 °C

7 Write down these temperatures in order of size, starting with the highest.
   (a) −5 °C, −2 °C, 2 °C, −4 °C, −8 °C, 9 °C
   (b) 2 °C, −5 °C, 0 °C, −9 °C, −8 °C, −1 °C
   (c) −5 °C, −2 °C, −3 °C, −8 °C, −7 °C, −1 °C
   (d) −9 °C, −4 °C, −5 °C, −2 °C, −1 °C, −11 °C

8 Write down these temperatures in order of size, starting with the lowest.
   (a) 2 °C, −3 °C, −7 °C, −11 °C, −1 °C, −6 °C
   (b) −7 °C, −12 °C, −1 °C, −4 °C, 5 °C, 2 °C
   (c) −2 °C, −7 °C, 0 °C, −8 °C, 3 °C, −13 °C
   (d) −5 °C, 1 °C, −11 °C, −8 °C, −4 °C, 2 °C

12.3 Positive and negative temperatures

You can use a picture of a thermometer to help you answer questions involving changes in temperature.

Example 4

The temperature in Derby at midnight was −3 °C. By noon the following day the temperature had gone up to 4 °C. How much did the temperature rise?

Start at the −3 °C mark.

To get to the 4 °C mark you go up 7 degrees.

The temperature rise was 7 °C.

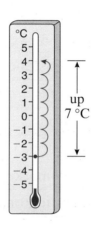

Example 5

The temperature in Leeds at midday was 2 °C.
By midnight the temperature had gone down by 6 °C.
Work out the temperature in Leeds at midnight.

Start at the 2 °C mark and go down 6 °C.

You end up at −4 °C.

The temperature in Leeds at midnight was −4 °C.

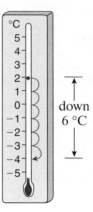

Exercise 12C

1 The temperature in Bangor at midnight was −4 °C.
By noon the next day the temperature had gone up to
5 °C. How much did the temperature rise?

2 The temperature in Watford at noon was 4 °C. By 8 pm
the same day the temperature had gone down to −1 °C.
Work out the fall in temperature.

3 The temperature in Guildford at midnight was −6 °C.
By noon the next day the temperature had gone up by
eight degrees. Work out the temperature in Guildford
at noon.

4 The temperature in Bolton at noon was −2 °C. By midnight the temperature had gone down by seven degrees.
What was the temperature in Bolton at midnight?

Copy and complete the tables for questions **5** and **6**.

5

Town	Temperature at midnight	Temperature at noon the next day	Rise in temperature
Maidstone	−3 °C	5 °C	
Taunton	−1 °C	6 °C	
Luton	−5 °C	−1 °C	
Preston	−2 °C		7 °C
Newmarket	−4 °C		5 °C
Darlington	−6 °C		3 °C

6

Town	Temperature at noon	Temperature at 2 a.m. the next day	Fall in temperature
Hatfield	5 °C	1 °C	
Oldham	4 °C	−3 °C	
Matlock	−3 °C	−9 °C	
Oxford	−2 °C		6 °C
Brighton	1 °C		3 °C
Norwich	−4 °C		2 °C

12.4 Using number lines

■ **You can use a number line to help you answer
questions involving negative numbers.**

Example 6

Find the value of:

(a) $2 + 6$ **(b)** $-2 + 6$ **(c)** $2 - 6$ **(d)** $-2 - 6$

(a) $2 + 6 = 8$

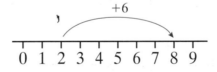

(b) $-2 + 6 = 4$

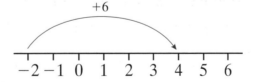

(c) $2 - 6 = -4$

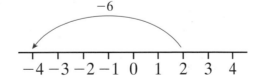

(d) $-2 - 6 = -8$

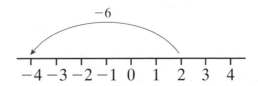

Example 7

Write down all the whole numbers that are larger than −8, smaller than 6 and are even.

You need numbers smaller than 6 so 6 is not included.

You need numbers larger than −8, so −8 is not included.

The numbers you need are −6, −4, −2, 0, 2 and 4.

Exercise 12D

1 Use the number line at the top of the page to find the number that is:

   (a) 6 more than 3   **(b)** 7 more than −2

   (c) 5 less than −5   **(d)** 4 less than −2

   (e) 8 more than −5   **(f)** 5 less than 0

   (g) 7 more than −4   **(h)** 5 more than −3

   (i) 6 more than −6   **(j)** 9 more than −4

   (k) 3 more than −8   **(l)** 6 more than −5

2 Write down all the whole numbers that are larger than −5 and smaller than 4.

3 Write down all the numbers that are larger than −7, smaller than 9 and are odd.

4 Write down all the numbers that are smaller than 8, larger than −5 and are even.

5 Use a number line to find the value of:

   (a) $8 - 3$ **(b)** $3 - 5$ **(c)** $4 - 9$

   (d) $3 - 7$ **(e)** $-5 + 2$ **(f)** $-3 + 9$

   (g) $-2 + 6$ **(h)** $-3 - 6$ **(i)** $-6 - 3$

   (j) $-8 + 5$ **(k)** $2 - 6$ **(l)** $-9 + 5$

6 Find the value of:

   (a) $7 - 2$ **(b)** $3 - 9$ **(c)** $2 - 8$

   (d) $5 - 9$ **(e)** $-6 + 2$ **(f)** $-4 + 9$

   (g) $-2 + 6$ **(h)** $-3 - 7$ **(i)** $-5 - 8$

   (j) $-11 + 4$ **(k)** $1 - 7$ **(l)** $-23 + 6$

7 Liam chose a number that is smaller than −3, larger than −8 and is a multiple of 3. What is the number Liam chose?

8 Write down the next two numbers in each pattern:

(a) 9, 5, 1, −3, ...   (b) 7, 4, 1, −2, ...
(c) 12, 9, 6, 3, ...   (d) 5, 3, 1, −1, ...
(e) 3, −1, −5, −9, ...   (f) −3, −5, −7, −9, ...
(g) −11, −8, −5, −2, ...   (h) −13, −8, −3, 2, ...

9 You need a calculator.

(a) Step 1: Enter the number 10 on the calculator.
Step 2: Use the calculator to subtract 3 and record the result from the calculator display.
Step 3: Continue to subtract 3 and record the results.
Step 4: Write down what you notice about the results.

(b) Repeat part (a), but subtract 4 each time instead of 3.

(c) Compare the results you obtain in parts (a) and (b).

10 You need a calculator.

(a) Step 1: Enter the number −90 on the calculator.
Step 2: Use the calculator to add 4 and record the result from the calculator display.
Step 3: Continue to add 4 and record the results.
Step 4: Write down what you notice about the results.

To enter '−90' on your calculator: Key in 90 then press the ± key.

(b) Repeat part (a), but add 5 each time instead of 4.

(c) Compare the results you obtain in parts (a) and (b).

11 What number is:

(a) 20 more than −50   (b) 30 less than −10
(c) 70 greater than −30   (d) 80 smaller than 20
(e) 120 smaller than −40   (f) 50 greater than 300
(g) 400 greater than −100   (h) 170 greater than −200
(i) 130 more than −20   (j) 300 less than −300
(k) 18 more than −33   (l) 29 more than −16

12.5 Ordering positive and negative numbers

You can use a number line to help you sort numbers in order of size:

Example 8

Write down these numbers in order of size, starting with the smallest:

  5, 2, −3, −8, 0, 1, −2, −6

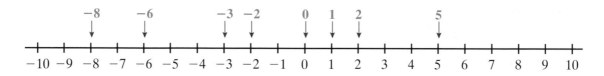

The order is −8, −6, −3, −2, 0, 1, 2, 5

Example 9

Write down the two missing numbers in each sequence:
(a) 7, 5, 3, 1, —, —, −5
(b) −14, −11, −8, −5, —, —, 4

(a) The numbers go down by 2 each time.
The missing numbers are −1 and −3

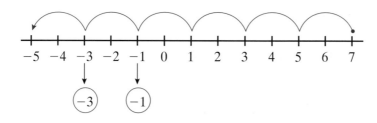

(b) The numbers go up 3 each time.
The missing numbers are −2 and 1

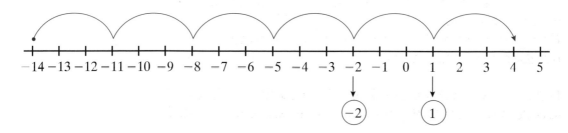

Exercise 12E

1   Write down these numbers in order of size, starting
    with the smallest:
    (a) 3, −9, −1, 0, 6, −5
    (b) 7, −2, 4, −3, 3, −8
    (c) −4, 8, −7, 2, −1, 0
    (d) −1, 5, 10, −8, 2, −3
    (e) 5, −9, 2, 8, −12, −1
    (f) 22, 71, 0, −89, −98, −3
    (g) −68, 43, 2, 101, −19, 72
    (h) −19, 5, 18, −21, −3, −4

2   Write down the two missing numbers in each sequence:
    (a) 13, 10, 7, 4, ——, ——, −5
    (b) −9, −7, −5, −3, ——, ——, 3
    (c) 19, 15, 11, 7, ——, ——, −5
    (d) −13, −9, −5, −1, ——, ——, 11
    (e) 15, 14, 12, 9, ——, ——, −6
    (f) −18, −16, −12, −6, ——, ——, 24

3   Priyah starts with the number −18 and keeps adding 4.
    Write down in order all the numbers she gets that are
    smaller than 40.
    Samir starts with the number −18 and keeps adding 5.
    Write down in order all the numbers he gets that are
    smaller than 40.
    Compare the numbers that Priyah gets with the
    numbers that Samir gets.

4   Jaspal starts with the number 50 and keeps subtracting
    6. Write down in order all the numbers she gets that
    are larger than −50.
    Martin starts with the number 50 and keeps subtracting
    5. Write down in order all the numbers he gets that are
    bigger than −50.
    Compare the numbers that Jaspal gets with the
    numbers that Martin gets.

5   Natalie works out 9 more than −3. Then she works out 7
    less than her result. What number does she end up with?

12.6 Adding and subtracting negative numbers

Adding negative numbers

■ **When you add two negative numbers the result is a negative number.**

$-2 + -3$ is the same as $-2 - 3 = -5$

Subtracting negative numbers

<table>
<tr><td>

Subtracting involves finding the difference between two numbers:

$$5 - 3 = 2$$

0 1 2 3 4 5

The difference between 5 and 3 is 2

</td><td>

Subtracting a negative number also involves finding the difference between two numbers:

$$4 - -2 = 6$$

-3 -2 -1 0 1 2 3 4

The difference between 4 and -2 is 6

</td></tr>
</table>

■ **Subtracting a negative number has the same effect as adding a positive number.**

For example

$4 - -2$ is the same as $4 + 2 = 6$
$-3 - -2$ is the same as $-3 + 2 = -1$

Exercise 12F

1 Copy and complete the subtractions on these number lines. The first one is done for you:

(a) $2 - 3 = -1$ (b) $1 - 6 =$

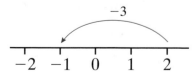

2 Do these subtractions:

(a) $3 - 1$ (b) $1 - 4$ (c) $2 - 3$ (d) $3 - 5$

(e) $-2 - 3$ (f) $-5 - 2$ (g) $-3 - 5$ (h) $-4 - 1$

3 Sketch a number line to help you answer these questions:

(a) $-2 + 5$ (b) $-2 - 5$ (c) $3 + -4$ (d) $3 - 4$

(e) $1 - 5$ (f) $1 + -5$ (g) $-1 - 4$ (h) $-1 + -4$

4 Copy and complete these subtractions. The first one is done for you:

(a) $2 - -3 = 5$

    $2 - -3$ is the same
    as $2 + 3 = 5$

(b) $4 - -4 =$

(c) $3 - -1 =$

(d) $0 - -2 =$

5 Work out:

(a) $7 - -2$ (b) $6 - -1$ (c) $4 - -5$

(d) $5 - -5$ (e) $3 - -4$ (f) $0 - -4$

(g) $4 - -6$ (h) $9 - -8$ (i) $-2 - -3$

6 Work out:

(a) $-3 + 7$ (b) $7 - -3$ (c) $5 - -1$ (d) $4 + -3$

(e) $7 + -3$ (f) $-3 + -7$ (g) $-2 + 5$ (h) $-1 + -1$

(i) $-3 + -5$ (j) $-5 + -7$ (k) $-2 + -3$ (l) $-1 + 7$

(m) $-7 + -3$ (n) $-2 - -5$ (o) $5 - -2$ (p) $-8 - -2$

7 Work out:

(a) $10 - -7$ (b) $100 + -70$ (c) $23 - -17$ (d) $-8 - -16$

(e) $-5 - -11$ (f) $-11 - -5$ (g) $-19 - -9$ (h) $-23 - 23$

(i) $-15 - -8$ (j) $-13 - -19$ (k) $19 - -19$ (l) $47 - -100$

12.7 Working with negative numbers

This section will give you lots of practice in using negative numbers.

Example 10

Fill in the gaps in this number wall:

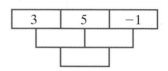

To fill in a blank square, look at the two numbers above and subtract the right hand number from the left:

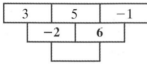

$3 - 5 = -2$

$5 - -1 = 6$

$-2 - 6 = -8$

<hr>

Exercise 12G

1 Use the method in example 10 to fill in the gaps in these number walls:

(a) 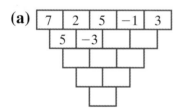 **(b)** 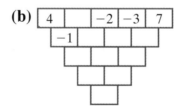 **(c)**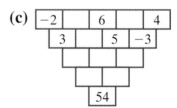

2 Complete these arithmogons. The total of the numbers in the circles goes in the square between them.

You can practice these with positive numbers on p. 32.

(a) 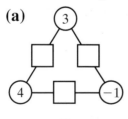 **(b)** 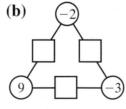 **(c)**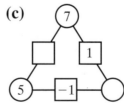

(d) 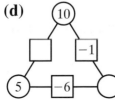 **(e)** 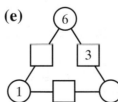 **(f)**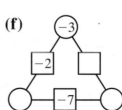

3 Complete these number squares so that each horizontal and vertical line add up to the same number.

(a)

3		−1
1	−4	
2		

(b)

1		
−2		9
7		−6

(c)

	−3	
5	2	−9
		5

Summary of key points

1 Positive numbers are greater than zero. Sometimes they are written with a plus sign in front. For example: +30

The temperature here is thirty degrees Celsius, written 30 °C for short.

Water freezes at zero degrees Celsius, or 0 °C for short.

2 Negative numbers are less than zero. They are written with a minus sign in front. For example: −30

The temperature here is twenty degrees Celsius below zero, or − 20 °C.

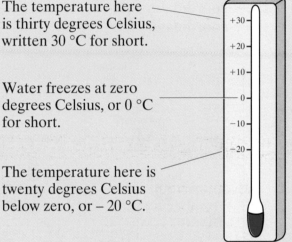

3 You can use a number line to help you answer questions involving negative numbers.

$2 - 6 = -4$

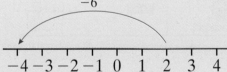

4 When you add two negative numbers the result is a negative number.

$-2 + -3$ is the same as $-2 - 3 = -5$

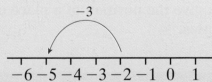

5 Subtracting a negative number has the same effect as adding a positive number:

$4 - -6$ is the same as $4 + 6 = 10$

13 Graphs

13.1 Reading and writing coordinates

This grid shows the positions of places in a theme park.

You can use two numbers to describe where a place is.
For example, the pirate ship is 4 units across and
7 units up, written (4, 7). The numbers (4, 7) are the pirate
ship's coordinates.

4 is the x-coordinate.
7 is the y-coordinate.

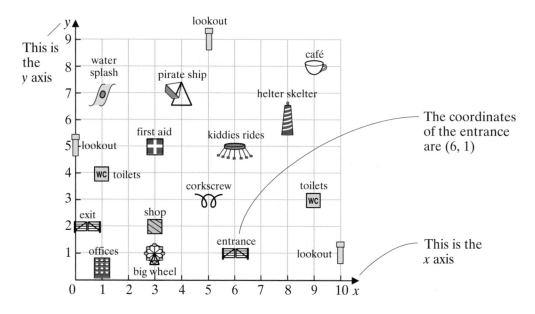

You always give the x-coordinate before the y-coordinate.
x comes before y in the alphabet.

Hint: x is a **cross**

■ **You can give the position of a place on a grid using coordinates.**

Exercise 13A

1 Look at the map of the theme park. What can be found at:
   (a) (10, 1)   **(b)** (8, 6)   **(c)** (5, 3)
   (d) (0, 5)   **(e)** (1, 0)   **(f)** (3, 5)

2 What are the coordinates of these places on the map of the theme park?

(**a**) kiddies rides   (**b**) big wheel

(**c**) pirate ship   (**d**) café

(**e**) water splash   (**f**) each lookout post

(**g**) shop   (**h**) both toilets

3 Look at the map of the zoo. What can be found at:

(**a**) (8, 2)   (**b**) (5, 0)

(**c**) (8, 9)   (**d**) (4, 5)

(**e**) (4, 2)

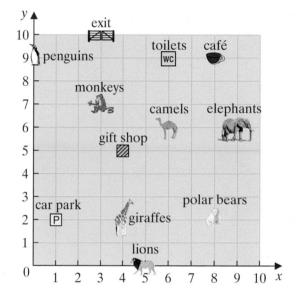

4 What are the coordinates of:

(**a**) the exit

(**b**) the camels

(**c**) the car park

(**d**) the monkeys

(**e**) the penguins

5 A new enclosure is placed half-way between the giraffes and the polar bears.

What are the coordinates of the new enclosure?

6 A lifeboat starts from the position (1, 6).

The map shows the route it takes.

It goes to the wreck then on to the hospital.

Copy and complete these directions:

From (1, 6) to (1, 2)

From (1, 2) to (,)

From (,) to (,)

From (,) to (,)

From (,) to (8, 7).

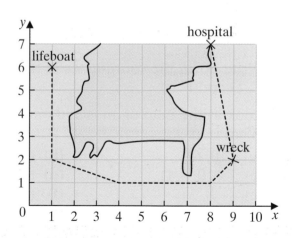

13.2 Extending the coordinate grid

This radar screen shows aircraft positions.

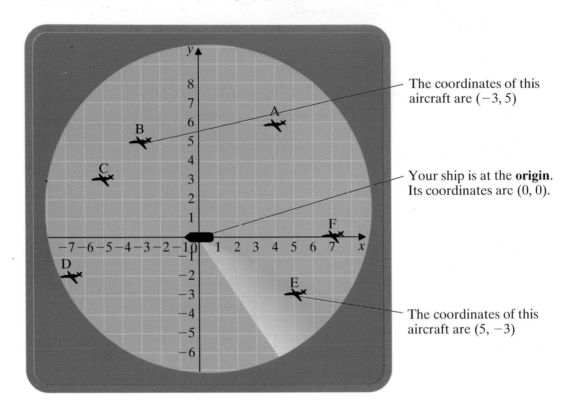

The coordinates of this aircraft are $(-3, 5)$

Your ship is at the **origin**. Its coordinates arc $(0, 0)$.

The coordinates of this aircraft are $(5, -3)$

Exercise 13B

1 Write down the coordinates of the aircraft marked A, C, D and F.

2 Look at the map of an island on page 255.
   What is at:
   (a) $(10, 6)$ (b) $(8, -6)$
   (c) $(-10, -4)$ (d) $(0, 0)$
   (e) $(-8, 5)$ (f) $(7, -1)$
   (g) $(0, 4)$ (h) $(0, -5)$

3 What are the coordinates of the:
   (a) shops (2 answers)   (b) lighthouse
   (c) hospital   (d) radio station
   (e) caves   (f) pier
   (g) harbour   (h) castle

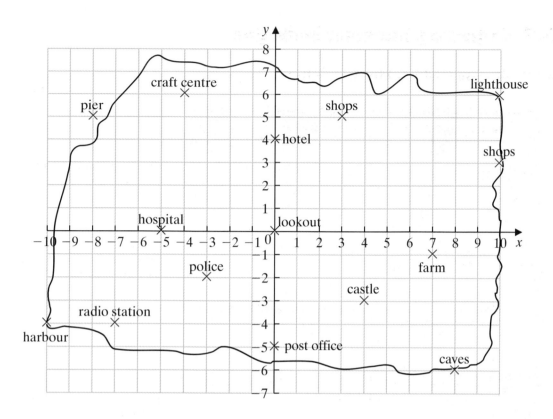

4 This grid shows a game of 'battleships'.

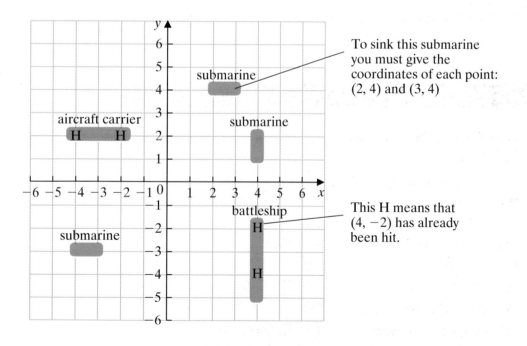

To sink this submarine you must give the coordinates of each point: (2, 4) and (3, 4)

This H means that (4, −2) has already been hit.

What coordinates should be given to sink:
(a) the aircraft carrier **(b)** the battleship **(c)** each submarine?

13.3 Drawing coordinate grids

Sometimes you will need to draw your own coordinate grid.

Draw two perpendicular **axes** long enough for all the points you need to plot.

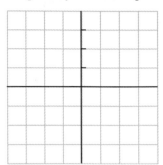

Number the axes. Write 0 where they meet.

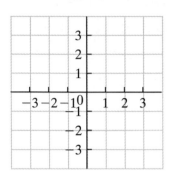

Label the horizontal · axis *x* and the vertical axis *y*.

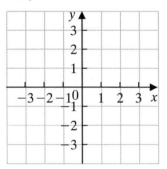

Exercise 13C

1 Draw a −10 to 10 coordinate grid on squared paper. Plot these points and join them up in order.

Marking points on a coordinate grid is called plotting the points.

   (a) (6, 10) (9, 10) (9, 7) (6, 7) (6, 10)

   (b) (1, 0) (1, 3) (6, 3) (6, 0) (1, 0)

   (c) (−8, 8), (−8, 4), (−5, 8), (−8, 8)

   (d) (−2, 3), (−2, 1), (2, −4), (2, 3), (−2, 3)

   (e) (−5, 4), (−4, 7), (2, 7), (1, 4), (−5, 4)

Name as many of these shapes as you can.

2 Draw a coordinate grid on squared paper. Number each axis from −10 to 10.
Plot these points and complete the shapes.
Each shape has one corner missing.
Write down the missing coordinates.

   (a) square: (1, 1), (5, 1), (1, 5), (—, —)

   (b) rectangle: (2, 7), (7, 7), (7, 10), (—, —)

   (c) parallelogram: (−9, 10), (−7, 10), (−6, 7), (—, —)

   (d) square: (4, −2), (7, −5), (4, −8), (—, —)

   (e) rectangle: (2, −1), (9, −1), (9, 2), (—, —)

   (f) octagon: (−6, −1), (−4, −3), (−2, −3), (0, −1),
          (0, 1), (−2, 3), (−4, 3), (—, —)

3 Mid points

Draw a coordinate grid from −10 to 10 in both directions.

On your grid, draw the square with corners: A(8, 8), B(8, −8), C(−8, −8) and D(−8, 8).

Mark the mid points of each of the sides.

Write down the coordinates of the mid points.

Join these 4 points together to make a new shape.

Find the mid points of each side of the new shape.

Join them and make a second new shape.

Repeat.

What do you notice?

Remember:

├───✗───┤

The mid point of a line is the halfway point.

13.4 Line them up

Example 1: four in a row

Two people take turns to put a counter on the grid.

To win the game, get four of your counters in a straight line.
The line can be horizontal, vertical or diagonal.

This game has been started. It is blue's turn.
Can blue win the game with the next counter?
Write down the coordinates of the points that make a winning line.

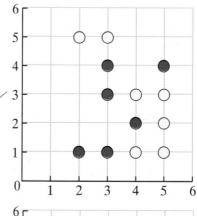

Yes. If they put a counter at (3, 2) they can win the game.

(3, 1), (3, 2), (3, 3) and (3, 4) make a vertical line.

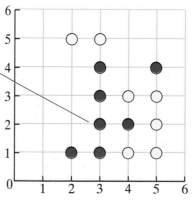

Exercise 13D

1 Look at this game of four in a row. Where could yellow go to win the game? Write down the coordinates of the points that make a winning line.

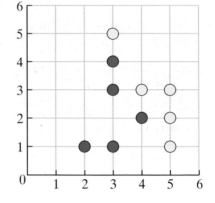

2 Copy the grid and play your own game of four in a row. Write down the coordinates of the points that make a winning line. Write down whether the line is horizontal, vertical or slanted. Play the game 10 times.

3 Write down what you notice about the coordinates of:

(a) a horizontal winning line

(b) a vertical winning line

(c) a slanted winning line

13.5 Naming straight lines

These points are all on a straight line.

Their coordinates show a pattern:

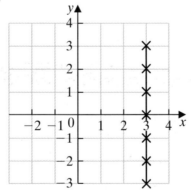

$(3, -3)$ $(3, -2)$ $(3, -1)$ $(3, 0)$ $(3, 1)$ $(3, 2)$ $(3, 3)$

The x coordinate of each points is always 3.

The line is called $x = 3$.

$x = 3$ is the **equation of the line.**

Example 2

From the grid, write down:

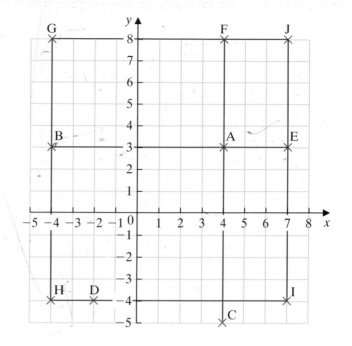

(a) the coordinates of the
points A, C and F

(b) the equation of the line
joining A, C and F

(c) the coordinates of the
points G, F and J

(d) the equation of the line
joining G, F and J

(a) A = (4, 3)   F = (4, 8)
C = (4, −5)

(b) All the x-coordinates are 4.
The equation of the line
is $x = 4$.

(c) G = (−4, 8)   F = (4, 8)
J = (7, 8)

(d) All the y-coordinates are 8.
The equation of the line is $y = 8$.

■ **You can use an equation to describe a straight line.**
For example:

$$x = 3$$

Exercise 13E

1 Look at the grid at the top of this page.
Find the equation of the line joining the points:

Hint:
List the coordinates
of each point.

(a) G B H   (b) H D I

(c) B A E   (d) J E I

2 Find the equation of the line connecting these points:

(a) (3, 0), (5, 0), (−6, 0)   (b) (0, 5), (0, 8), (0, −6), (0, −1)

(c) (2, 3), (2, −1), (2, 6)   (d) (5, 4), (5, 5), (5, 7)

(e) (3, 6), (4, 6), (−1, 6)   (f) (0, 7), (1, 7), (7, 7)

(g) (4, −1), (5, −1), (7, −1)   (h) (−3, 4), (−3, 6), (−3, 8)

3 Look at the coordinate grid below. Find the equations of each of the lines shown. (Each will start with $x =$ or $y =$)

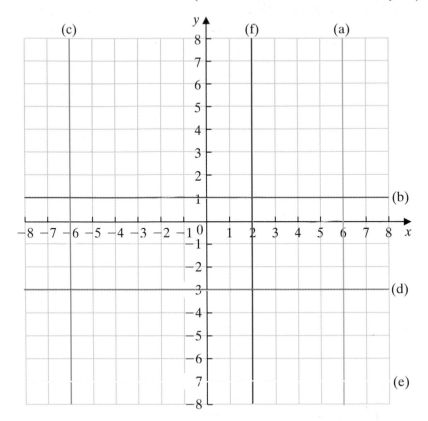

13.6 Naming sloping lines

The points A, B and C on this grid are on a straight line. They have coordinates (1, 1), (3, 3) and (6, 6).

The y-coordinate is the same as the x-coordinate.
So y-coordinate $= x$-coordinate.
The equation of the line is $y = x$.

The points D, E, F and G have coordinates (0, 2), (1, 3), (3, 5) and (5, 7).

To name the line, find a rule connecting the x-coordinate and the y-coordinate:

$$(0, 2) \quad (1, 3) \quad (3, 5) \quad (5, 7)$$
$$+2 \qquad +2 \qquad +2 \qquad +2$$

The rule is 'add 2 to the x-coordinate'
The equation is $y = x + 2$.

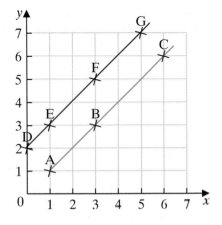

y-coordinate is
x-coordinate $+2$

Example 3

Find the equations of the lines on this grid.

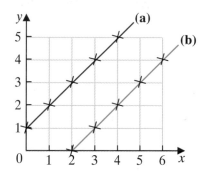

(a) Write down the coordinates of the points on the line:

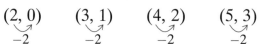

$(0, 1)$ $(1, 2)$ $(2, 3)$ $(3, 4)$
  $+1$ $+1$ $+1$ $+1$

The rule is 'add 1 to the x-coordinate'
The equation is $y = x + 1$.

(b) The coordinates are:

$(2, 0)$ $(3, 1)$ $(4, 2)$ $(5, 3)$
  -2 -2 -2 -2

The rule is 'subtract 2 from the x-coordinate'.
The equation is $y = x - 2$.

Notice that these lines are parallel.

■ **The equation of a vertical line is x = a number.
The equation of a horizontal line is y = a number.**

■ **To find the equation of a sloping line find a rule connecting the x-coordinate and the y-coordinate.**

1 Find the equations of the lines on this grid:

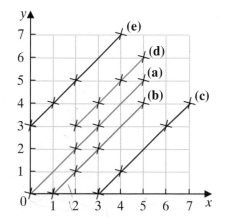

2 Find the equations of these lines:

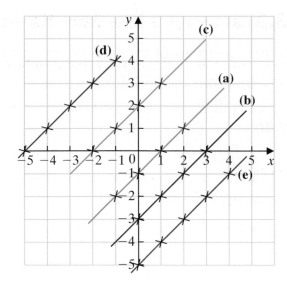

3 Find the equations of these lines:

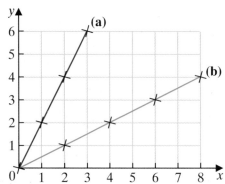

4 These lines all have equations of the form:

$$y = 2x + \boxed{}$$

For each line, write down the number you think should go in the box.

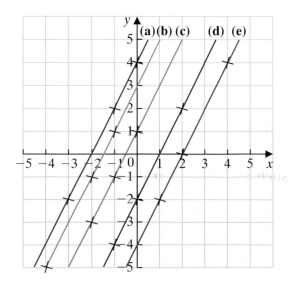

Hint:
Think about when $x = 0$.

A group of parallel lines are sometimes called **a family**.

13.7 Drawing a line from its equation

Sometimes you will be given the equation of a line and asked to draw it.

You use the equation to find the coordinates of points on the line.

Example 4

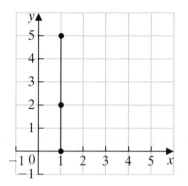

(a) Draw the line with equation $x = 1$.

You need the coordinates of any three points on the line. These will do:

$(1, 0)$ $(1, 2)$ $(1, 5)$

Plot these points and join them up with a straight line.

(b) Draw the line with equation $y = x + 3$.

You need the coordinates of any three points on the line.

To find these points, give x three different values:

When $x = 0$ $y = 0 + 3$ $y = 3$
When $x = 1$ $y = 1 + 3$ $y = 4$
When $x = 3$ $y = 3 + 3$ $y = 6$

So the three points are:

$(0, 3)$ $(1, 4)$ $(3, 6)$

Plot these points and join them up with a straight line.

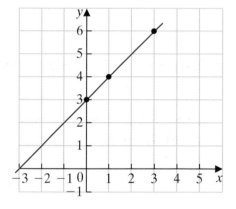

Using a table of values

When you need to draw a sloping line like $y = x - 1$ use a table of values.

Choose some values for x, such as 1, 2, 3, 4 and 5.
Draw a table like this:

x	1	2	3	4	5
y					

Work out $x - 1$ for each x value. For example:

When $x = 1$, $y = 1 - 1 = 0$

Put the answers in the table:

x	1	2	3	4	5
y	0	1	2	3	4

The coordinates are:

(1, 0) (2, 1) (3, 2) (4, 3) (5, 4)

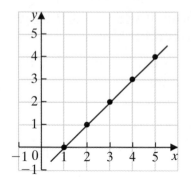

Exercise 13G

1 Draw a coordinate grid labelling the axes from -8 to 8 in each direction.

Plot each of these lines on the grid and label them:

(a) $x = 2$ **(b)** $x = 6$ **(c)** $x = 4$ **(d)** $y = 3$

(e) $y = 4$ **(f)** $x = -5$ **(g)** $y = -6$ **(h)** $x = 0$

2 Draw a -10 to 10 grid and plot the straight line for each of these equations.

(a) $y = x + 1$ **(b)** $y = x - 2$ **(c)** $y = x + 4$

(d) $y = 2x$ **(e)** $y = 5 + x$

Remember:
$2x$ means $2 \times x$

3 For each equation:
- Copy and complete the table of values.
- Plot the points on a coordinate grid and draw the line.

(a) $y = x + 6$

x	-3	-2	-1	0	1	2	3	4
y		4		6				10

(b) $y = x + 3$

x	-3	-2	-1	0	1	2	3	4
y	0			3		5		

(c) $y = x - 1$

x	-3	-2	-1	0	1	2	3	4
y		-3		-1		1		

(d) $y = x - 3$

x	-3	-2	-1	0	1	2	3	4
y		-5			-2			1

(e) $y = 2 + x$

x	-3	-2	-1	0	1	2	3	4
y	-1			2				6

4 (a) For **(a)** to **(e)** in question **3** write down the coordinate where the line crosses the y-axis.

(b) Compare the point where a line crosses the y-axis with the equation of that line.
What do you notice?

5 For each of these equations, write down where the line will cross the y-axis.

Hint: The line crosses the y-axis when x is equal to 0.

(a) $y = x + 3$ **(b)** $y = x - 1$

(c) $y = 2x - 3$ **(d)** $y = 3x + 1$

(e) $y = \frac{1}{2}x + 2$ **(f)** $y = 4x$

6 Draw a coordinate grid and label the axes from 0 to 10 in each direction. Draw each of these lines on the grid.

(a) $y = 2x$ **(b)** $y = 3x$

(c) $y = \frac{1}{2}x$ **(d)** $y = x$

7 For **(a)** to **(d)** in question **6** compare the steepness of the line with its equation.
What do you notice?

Remember:
$y = x$ is the same as $y = 1x$.

8 Without drawing the lines, put these equations in order according to the steepness of their lines, steepest first.

$$y = 6x, \quad y = \tfrac{1}{4}x, \quad y = 42x, \quad y = x, \quad y = 4x$$

13.8 Conversion graphs

When you draw the line $y = x + 3$ on a coordinate grid, it is called the **graph** of $y = x + 3$.

■ **A graph shows a relationship on a coordinate grid.**

This graph shows the relationship between miles and kilometres:

On this scale:
  10 squares represent   20 kilometres
so 1 square represents 20 ÷ 10
                     = 2 kilometres

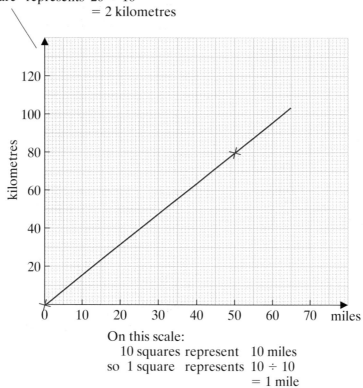

On this scale:
    10 squares represent   10 miles
  so 1 square represents 10 ÷ 10
                       = 1 mile

You can use the graph to convert from one measurement to another.

Example 5

Use the graph to convert:

(a) 50 miles to kilometres

(b) 100 kilometres to miles

(a)

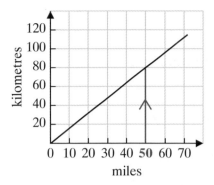

Find 50 on the miles axis.
Draw a line up to the graph.

Draw a line from the graph
to the kilometres axis.

Read off the value:
50 miles = 80 kilometres

(b)

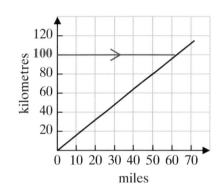

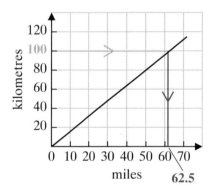

Find 100 on the kilometres axis.
Draw a line up to the graph.

Draw a line from the graph
to the miles axis.

Read off the value:
100 kilometres = 62.5 miles

Using scales

The scales on these axes are different.

On the *y*-axis:
   10 small squares represent 50 units
so 1 small square represents $50 \div 10$
                              = 5 units

On the *x*-axis,
   10 small squares represent 5 units
so 1 small square represents $5 \div 10$
                             = 0.5 units

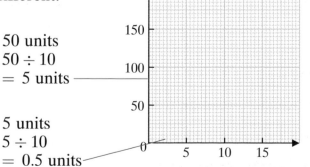

The most common scales to use are the factors of 10: 1, 2, 5, 10 and multiples of 10: 10, 20, 50, 100

For example, if you use 10 small squares for 5 units, count in 5s: 5, 10, 15,...

If you use 10 small squares for 50 units, count in 50s: 50, 100, 150, 200,...

Exercise 13H

1 You can use this graph to convert weights between kilograms and pounds.

(a) Work out the scale on each axis. (What does 1 small square represent?)

Use the graph to convert:

(b) 50 kilograms to pounds

(c) 30 kilograms to pounds

(d) 66 pounds to kilograms

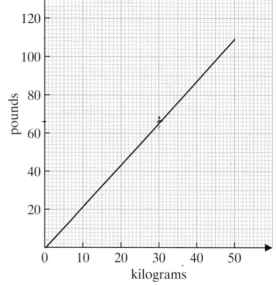

2 This graph converts between inches and centimetres.

(a) Work out the scale on each axis.
(What does 1 small square represent?)

Use the graph to convert:

(b) 6 inches to centimetres

(c) 20 centimetres to inches

(d) 1 inch to centimetres

(e) 1 centimetre to inches

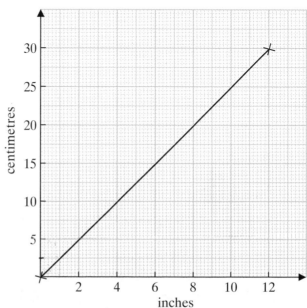

3 Draw two axes.
Label the *x*-axis litres and the *y*-axis pints.

Use 10 small squares to represent 5 litres
on the *x*-axis and 10 small squares to represent
10 pints on the *y*-axis.

Plot two points: (0, 0) and (20, 35).
Join them up.

You can use this graph to convert between litres and
pints.

> 20 litres = 35 pints
> so you can plot the
> point (20, 35) on
> your graph.

Use the graph to convert:

(a) 10 litres to pints   **(b)** 20 pints to litres

(c) 1 pint to litres   **(d)** 1 litre to pints

4 Draw two axes on a large piece of graph paper.
Label the *x*-axis °C and the *y*-axis °F.

Use 10 small squares to represent 10 °C on the *x*-axis and
10 small squares to represent 20 °F on the *y*-axis.

Plot the points (0, 32) and (80, 176) and join them up.

This graph converts between degrees Celsius (°C) and
degrees Fahrenheit (°F).

Use your graph to convert, roughly:

(a) 10 °C to °F   **(b)** 100 °F to °C

(c) 35 °C to °F   **(d)** 40 °F to °C

5 Draw a graph to convert between old pence (d) and
new pence (p).

Use these facts:

    0p = 0d   (plot (0, 0))
100p = 240d   (plot (100, 240))

Plot new pence (p) on the *x*-axis and old pence (d) on
the *y*-axis.
Choose your own scales.
Use your graph to convert:

(a) 30p to d   **(b)** 100d to p

13.9 Using graphs

Graphs are often used to represent real-life events.

Example 6

The sailfish can swim at 110 kilometres per hour. A sailfish starts 500 metres from a fishing boat and swims away from it. This graph shows the relationship between the distance from the boat and the time taken.

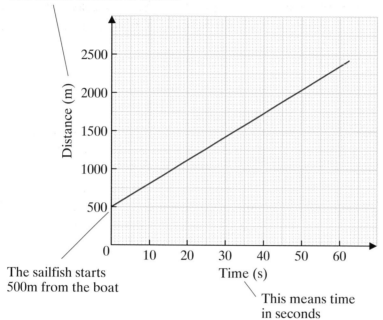

This means distance in metres

The sailfish starts 500m from the boat

This means time in seconds

This is called a **distance-time** graph.

You should give answers to the nearest half square on the graph.

(a) How far was the sailfish from the boat after 40 s?

(b) How long did it take the sailfish to get 1 km from the boat? (1 km = 1000 m)

(a)

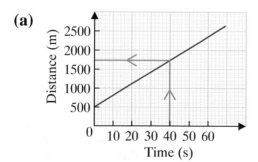

The answer is 1725 m.

(b)

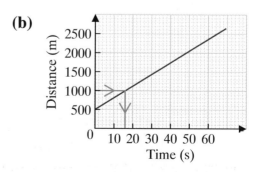

The answer is 16.5 s.

Sometimes you need to draw your own graphs.

Example 7

A Porsche 911 Turbo accelerates from
0 to 60 miles per hour in 4.2 seconds.

(a) Draw a straight-line graph showing the
relationship between the speed of the
car and the time taken.

(b) Use your graph to find out how fast
the car is travelling after 3 seconds.

(a)
Draw the axes:

After 0 seconds the car
is travelling at 0 mph.

After 4.2 seconds the car
is travelling at 60 mph.

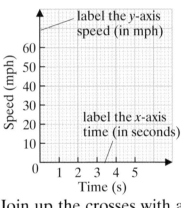

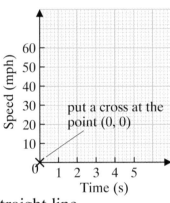

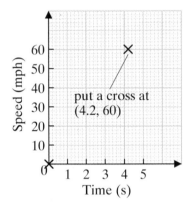

Join up the crosses with a straight line.

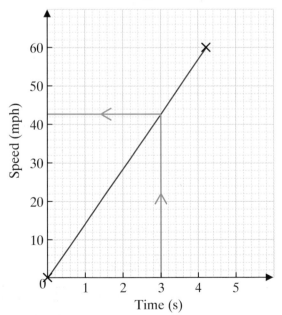

This is called a
speed-time graph.

(b) You can now read the answer from your graph.
After 3 seconds the car is travelling at 43 mph.

Remember:
Read up from 3 s on
the horizontal axis,
then across to the
vertical axis.

Exercise 13I

1 Kieron plants a tree in his garden. This graph shows the relationship between the height of the tree and the time since he planted it.

(a) How tall was the tree when Kieron planted it?

(b) How tall was the tree after a year (12 months)?

(c) After how long was the tree 2 m tall?

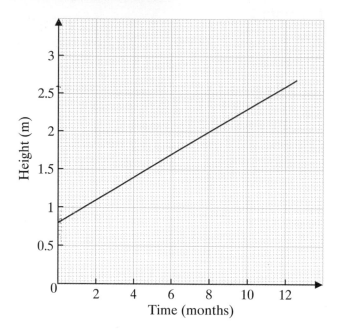

2 A cookery book gives instructions for roasting a chicken.

Cook for 25 minutes per 500 grams of weight plus 25 minutes.

(a) Copy and complete this table.

Weight of chicken (kg)	0.5	1	1.5	2	2.5	3
Cooking time (minutes)	50	75				

(b) Draw two axes. Label the horizontal axis 'Weight' and mark it from 0 to 4 kg. Label the vertical axis 'time' and mark it from 0 to 200 minutes.
Plot the points from your table and join them up with a straight line.

(c) Use your graph to estimate the cooking time of a chicken weighing 1.8 kg.

3 A train starts at Euston Station and travels away at a constant speed. After $2\frac{1}{2}$ hours it is 310 miles away.

(a) Draw a distance-time graph for the train's journey.

Constant speed means the distance-time graph will be a straight line.

Hint: at time 0 the train is in the station. You can plot (0, 0).

(b) Use your graph to find out how long the train took to travel 200 miles.

(c) How fast was the train travelling? Give your answer in miles per hour.

Hint: How far did the train travel in 1 hour?

4 This graph shows a car journey.

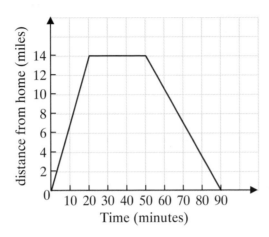

(a) How far from home was the car after:

(i)   10 minutes

(ii) 50 minutes

(iii) 90 minutes

(b) What do you think the car was doing between 20 minutes and 50 minutes?

(c) How fast was the car travelling for the first 20 minutes of the journey? Give your answer in miles per hour.

5 Beth cycles to the cinema, which is 16 miles from her home. It takes her 50 minutes. She watches a film which is 120 minutes long, and then cycles back in 80 minutes.

(a) How long was Beth away from home?

(b) Draw a distance-time graph for Beth's journey.

(c) How far from home was Beth after 3 hours?

(d) There is a shop 10 miles from Beth's house on the road to the cinema. When does she pass the shop?

Hint: There will be two answers.

Summary of key points

1 You can give the position of a place on a grid using coordinates.

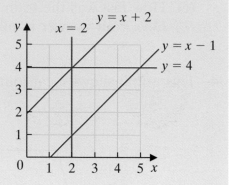

2 You can use an equation to describe a straight line. For example: $x = 3$

3 The equation of a vertical line is $x =$ a number.

The equation of a horizontal line is $y =$ a number.

4 To find the equation of a sloping line find a rule connecting the x-coordinate and the y-coordinate.

5 A graph shows a relationship on a coordinate grid.

14 Angles

The disco light is turning:

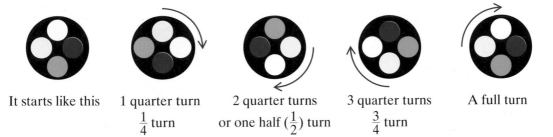

It starts like this — 1 quarter turn $\frac{1}{4}$ turn — 2 quarter turns or one half ($\frac{1}{2}$) turn — 3 quarter turns $\frac{3}{4}$ turn — A full turn

This unit shows you how to measure turns.

14.1 Turning shapes

You can turn a shape clockwise or anticlockwise.

Example 1

Draw this flag when it has turned:

(a) $\frac{1}{4}$ turn clockwise

(b) $\frac{1}{4}$ turn anticlockwise

(c) $1\frac{1}{2}$ turns.

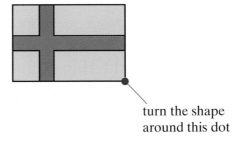

turn the shape around this dot

Trace the shape.

Turn it:

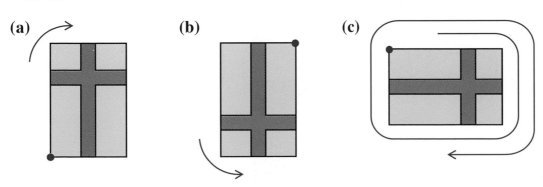

(a)   **(b)**   **(c)**

Exercise 14A

1 Trace each of these shapes.
Draw each shape when it has turned clockwise through:
- $\frac{1}{4}$ turn
- $\frac{1}{2}$ turn
- $\frac{3}{4}$ turn

(a)

(b)

(c)

(d)

(e)

(f)

2 Write down the letter the arrow will point to after each of these turns:
- **(a)** $\frac{1}{4}$ turn clockwise from F
- **(b)** $\frac{1}{2}$ turn from C
- **(c)** $\frac{1}{4}$ turn clockwise from B
- **(d)** $\frac{1}{4}$ turn anticlockwise from A
- **(e)** $\frac{1}{4}$ turn anticlockwise from E

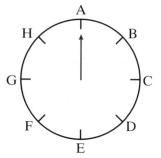

3 Using the diagram from question **2**, describe the turn needed to move from:
- **(a)** B to D
- **(b)** H to D
- **(c)** D to B
- **(d)** G to A
- **(e)** E to G

14.2 Rotational symmetry

This shape is **rotating** – another word for turning:

| Start | $\frac{1}{4}$ turn | $\frac{1}{2}$ turn | $\frac{3}{4}$ turn | Full turn |

In a full turn these **two** positions look exactly the same.
This shape has rotational symmetry of order 2.

■ **A shape has rotational symmetry if it looks exactly the same <u>two or more times</u> in a full turn.**

■ **The order of rotational symmetry is the number of times it looks exactly the same in a full turn.**

Any irregular shape – like this – must have rotational symmetry of order 1. It looks the same if you rotate it a full turn. But we usually say that such a shape does *not* have rotational symmetry.

Example 2

For each shape:

● Does it have rotational symmetry?

● If it does, what is the order of rotational symmetry?

(a)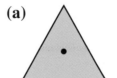

(b)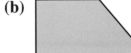

(a) Trace the shape. Make a mark in one corner. Rotate the shape this way ⟲ around the dot ●

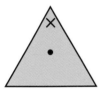 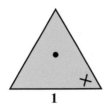 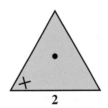 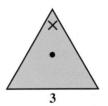

It looks exactly the same in 3 positions so it has rotational symmetry of order 3.

Remember not to count the full turn as different. It's the same as the start!

(b) Trace the shape and rotate it:

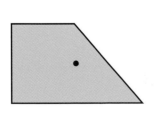 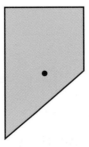 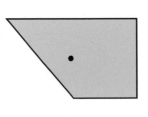 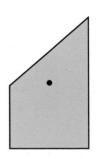

This shape does **not** have rotational symmetry.

Exercise 14B

For each of these shapes

● Does the shape have rotational symmetry?

● If it does, what is the order of rotational symmetry?

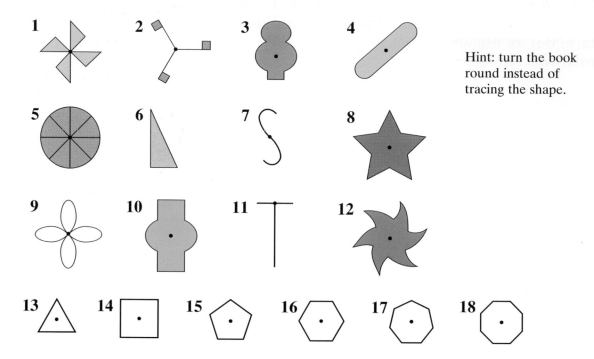

Hint: turn the book round instead of tracing the shape.

19 The shapes in questions **13** to **18** are all regular polygons: the sizes of each of their angles and the lengths of each of their sides is the same. Write down a rule about the rotational symmetry of a regular polygon.

14.3 Angles

Most rotations are not simple fractions of a turn:

This is about $\frac{1}{10}$ of a turn.

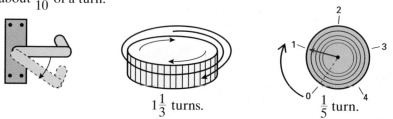

$1\frac{1}{3}$ turns.

$\frac{1}{5}$ turn.

Instead of fractions you can use **angles** to describe the rotation.

■   **An angle is a measure of turn.**
     An angle is usually measured in degrees, ° for short.

■   **There are 360° in a full turn.**

You can use a protractor to measure angles in degrees:

Angle measurer
You can use an angle measurer instead of a protractor.

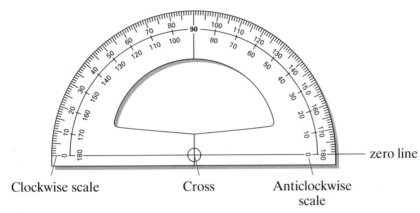

Clockwise scale   Cross   Anticlockwise scale   zero line

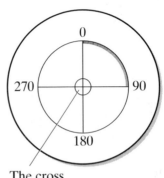

The cross is at the centre.

Example 3

Measure the angle between these lines:

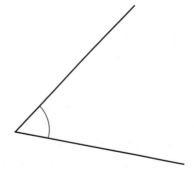

Place the protractor over one line like this:

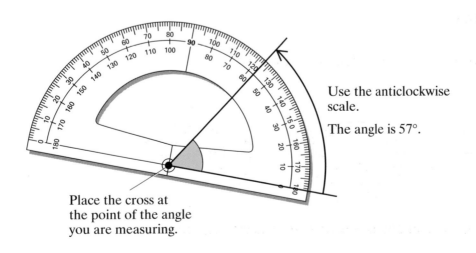

Place the cross at the point of the angle you are measuring.

Use the anticlockwise scale.

The angle is 57°.

Exercise 14C

1 Use a protractor to measure these angles:

(a)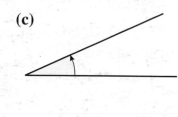
anticlockwise
scale

(b)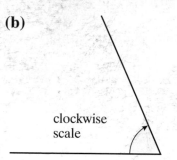
clockwise
scale

(c)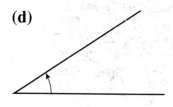

(d)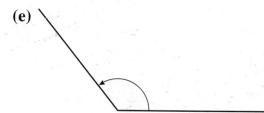

(e)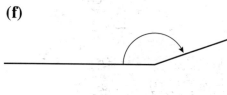

(f)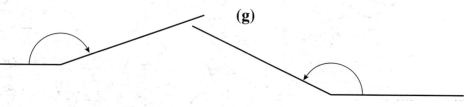

(g)

(h)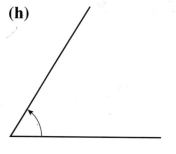

(i)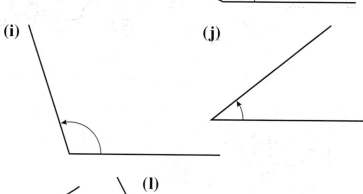

(j)

(k)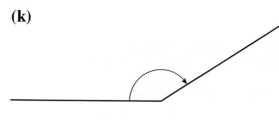

(l)

2 How many degrees are there in:
 (a) $\frac{1}{4}$ turn **(b)** $\frac{1}{2}$ turn **(c)** $\frac{3}{4}$ turn

14.4 Types of angles

The angle between these lines is 90°.

The angle between these lines is 180°.

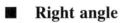
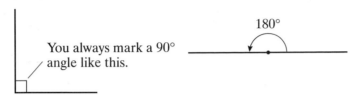

You always mark a 90° angle like this.

A $\frac{1}{4}$ turn is 90°   A $\frac{1}{2}$ turn is 180°

You name an angle depending on its size:

■ **Right angle**   **Acute angle**   **Obtuse angle**   **Reflex angle**

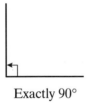   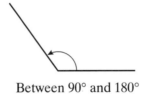   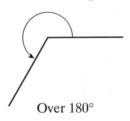

Exactly 90°   Less then 90°   Between 90° and 180°   Over 180°

Example 4

For each of these angles choose the correct description from the list:

(a) 35°   **(b)** 72°   **(c)** 108°   **(d)** 184°   **(e)** 220°

acute angle   obtuse angle   reflex angle   right angle

Hint: compare each angle with 90° and 180°.

(a) acute angle   **(b)** acute angle   **(c)** obtuse angle
(d) reflex angle   **(e)** reflex angle

Exercise 14D

Write down the correct description for each angle:

1    2 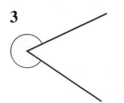   3 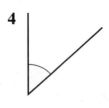   4

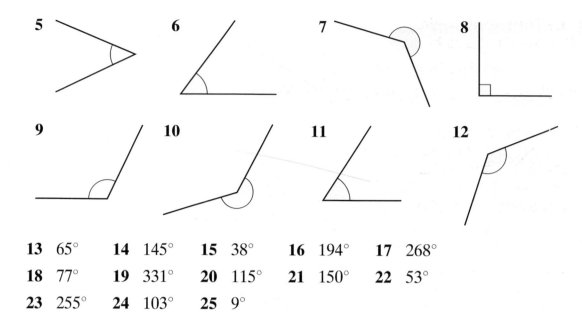

13 65°   **14** 145°   **15** 38°   **16** 194°   **17** 268°

18 77°   **19** 331°   **20** 115°   **21** 150°   **22** 53°

23 255°   **24** 103°   **25** 9°

14.5 Estimating angles

You can estimate the size of an angle by comparing it with a right angle.

Example 5

For each angle:

*   What type of angle is it?
*   Estimate the size of the angle.

(a) 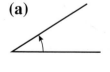   **(b)** 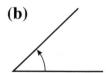   **(c)** 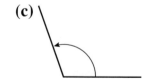   **(d)**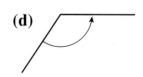

(a) Compare this angle with a right angle (like the corner of this page). It is roughly $\frac{1}{3}$ of the right angle.

$$\frac{1}{3} \text{ of } 90° \text{ is } 30°$$

The angle is acute. It is about 30°

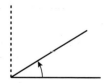

(b) This is an acute angle.
It is roughly $\frac{1}{2}$ a right angle.

$\qquad \frac{1}{2}$ of $90°$ is $45°$

The angle is acute. It is about $45°$

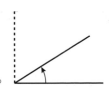

(c) This angle is obtuse.
You need to estimate the
part that is over $90°$.
It is about $\frac{1}{5}$ of $90° = 18°$
So the angle is roughly

$\qquad 90 + 18 = 108°$

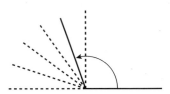

(d) This angle is obtuse.
The part greater than $90°$ is
approximately $\frac{1}{3}$ of $90° = 30°$
So the angle is

$\qquad 90 + 30 = 120°$

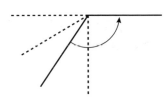

Exercise 14E

Estimate the sizes of these angles and write down whether
they are acute or obtuse:

1   **2**   **3**

4   **5**   **6**

7   **8** 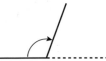   **9**

10    **11** 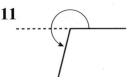   **12**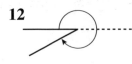

14.6 It all adds up

You can put 2 or more angles
together to make a right angle:

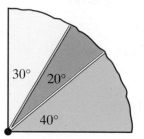

The angles must add up to 90°

You can also put 2 or more angles together to make a
straight line:

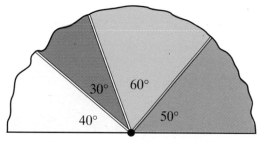

The angles must add up to 180°

Hint: Compare this
with a protractor.

- **Angles in a right angle add up to 90°.**

- **Angles on a straight line add up to 180°.**

Example 6

In these diagrams what angles do the letters represent?

There is more about
using letters to
represent numbers
on page 179.

(a)

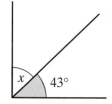

(b)

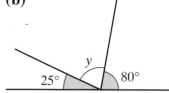

(a) Angles add up to 90°
so $x + 43 = 90$
$x = 90 - 43$
$x = 47°$

(b) Angles add up to 180°
$y + 25 + 80 = 180$
$y + 105 = 180$
$y = 180 - 105$
$y = 75°$

Exercise 14F

What angles do the letters represent?

1
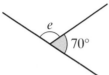
130°
a

2
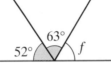
45° *b*

3
c
158°

4

d
45° 40°

5
e
70°

6

63°
52° *f*

7
53° *g*

8
35° *h*
73°

9
42°
i

10
j
27° 32°

14.7 Angles at a point

You can put 2 or more angles together to make a full turn.

These 4 angles add up to 360°:

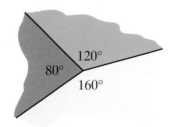

120°
80°
160°

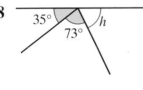

c
a *b*
d

The point where the lines cross is called the **intersection**.

a and *b* are opposite each other: $a = b$
c and *d* are opposite each other: $c = d$

■ **Angles at a point add up to 360°.**

■ **When two straight lines cross, the opposite angles are equal.**

Example 7

What angles do the letters represent? Explain your working.

(a)

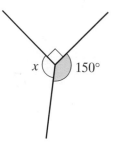

(b)

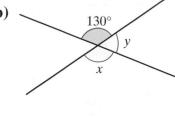

(a) Angles at a point
add up to 360°

$x + 150 + 90 = 360$
$x + 240 = 360$
$x = 360 - 240$
$x = 120°$

(b) Opposite angles are
equal

$x = 130°$
$y + 130 = 180$ (angles on a straight line)
$y = 180 - 130$
$y = 50°$

Exercise 14G

What angles do the letters represent? Explain your working:

1

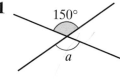

150°

a

2

75°

b

3

c
105°
135°

4

30°
d

5

e
75°

6

50°
f

7

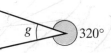

g
320°

8

130°
h

9

j
65°
230°

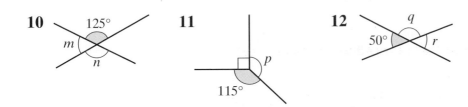

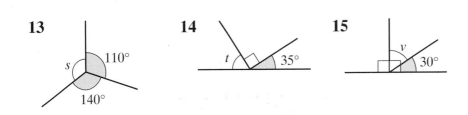

16 Using a pencil and ruler draw
   a triangle on a piece of paper.
   Cut out the triangle.
   Colour the three angles.
   Cut out the angles.
   Fit them together.
   What do you notice?

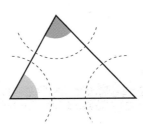

14.8 Angles in shapes

If you cut out the corners of a triangle and put them
together like this they make a straight line:

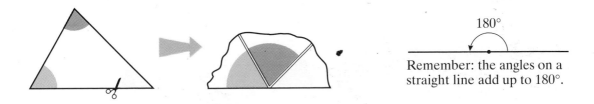

Remember: the angles on a
straight line add up to 180°.

■ **The angles of a triangle add up to 180°.**

Example 8

What angles do these letters represent?

(a)

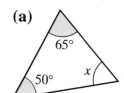

(b)

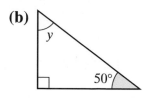

(c)

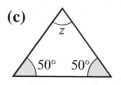

(a)

Angles add to 180°

$x + 50 + 65 = 180$

$x + 115 = 180$

$x = 180 - 115$

$x = 65°$

(b)

Angles add to 180°

$y + 50 + 90 = 180$

$y + 140 = 180$

$y = 180 - 140$

$y = 40°$

(c)

Angles add to 180°

$z + 50 + 50 = 180$

$z + 100 = 180$

$z = 180 - 100$

$z = 80°$

Exercise 14H

What angles do these letters represent?

1

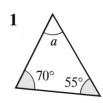

2

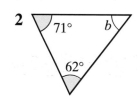

3

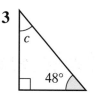

4

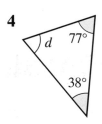

5

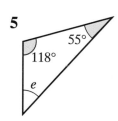

6

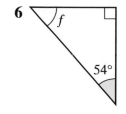

7

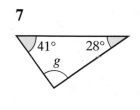

8

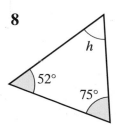

9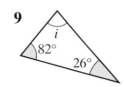

10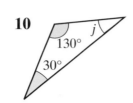

11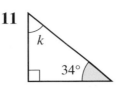

12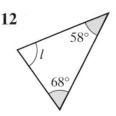

13 Using a pencil and ruler draw a quadrilateral
   on a piece of paper.
   Cut it out. Colour the four angles.
   Cut out the angles and fit them together.
   What do you notice?

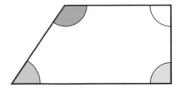

14.9 Isosceles triangles

Isosceles triangles have two sides
the same and two angles the same:

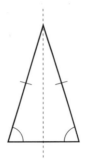

Isosceles means
'same legs'.
Isosceles triangles
always have a line
of symmetry
down the middle.

Example 9

Find the size of angle *a* in
this isosceles triangle.

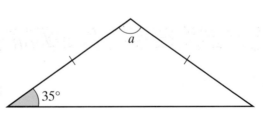

The sum of the angles is 180° so:
$a = 180 - 35 - 35 = 110°$

Exercise 14I

Find all of the missing angles in these isosceles triangles.

1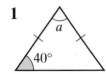

2

3

4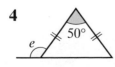

5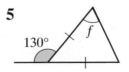

6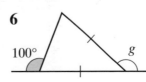

14.10 Drawing angles

You can use a protractor to help you draw an angle.

Example 10

Draw an angle of 67°.

Draw a straight line

Put the protractor on the line like this:

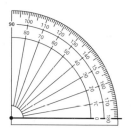

Remember to put the cross at one end.

Use the anticlockwise scale.
Make a mark at 67°

Join up the mark to the end of the line.

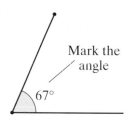

Mark the angle

67°

Exercise 14J

1 Draw these angles using a protractor or angle measurer.

(a) 40°   (b) 65°   (c) 50°   (d) 135°   (e) 15°

(f) 34°   (g) 170°   (h) 75°   (i) 123°   (j) 27°

(k) 164°   (l) 105°   (m) 46°   (n) 82°   (o) 155°

14.11 Constructing triangles

Engineers and architects use triangular shapes in their designs because they are strong.

You can use a ruler and protractor to help you draw triangles and quadrilaterals.

An accurate drawing like this is called a **construction.**

Exercise 14K

Construct accurate drawings from the diagrams.
Measure and write down the unknown sides and angles.

1   **2** 6 cm   **3** 5 cm   **4** 8 cm
 30° 50°   45°   35°   75°
 7 cm   7 cm   6 cm

5 5 cm   **6** 4 cm   **7** 6 cm   **8** 4.5 cm
 110° 80°   35°   20°
      5 cm   75°   8 cm   50° 60°
 120°   6 cm 50°   45°   9 cm
      6 cm

See page 12 for more on constructing parallel lines.

Summary of key points

1 A shape has rotational symmetry if it looks exactly the same <u>two or more times</u> in a full turn.

2 The order of rotational symmetry is the number of times it looks exactly the same in a full turn.

3 An angle is a measure of turn.
   An angle is usually measured in degrees, ° for short.

4 There are 360° in a full turn.

5 $\frac{1}{4}$ turn is 90°   **6** $\frac{1}{2}$ turn is 180°

7 Right angle   Acute angle   Obtuse angle   Reflex angle

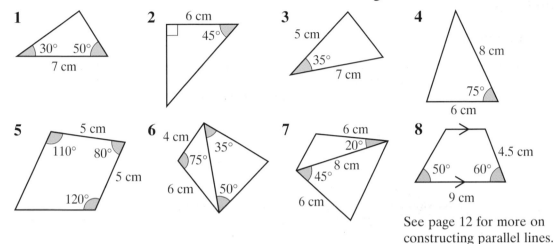

   Exactly 90°   Less then 90°   Between 90° and 180°   Over 180°

8 Angles in a right angle add up to 90°.

9 Angles on a straight line add up to 180°.

10 When two straight lines cross, the opposite angles are equal.

11 Angles at a point add up to 360°.

12 The angles of a triangle add up to 180°.

15 Handling data

You often see information given in charts like these:

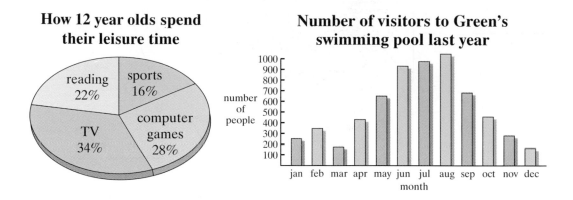

**How 12 year olds spend
their leisure time**

reading 22%
sports 16%
computer games 28%
TV 34%

**Number of visitors to Green's
swimming pool last year**

number of people

jan feb mar apr may jun jul aug sep oct nov dec
month

■ **Another word for information is data.**

Data can come from many different sources. For example:

● from a **survey** – of how people use their leisure time.

● from an **experiment** – to find out how quickly plants grow.

● from a **database** – a store of information such as test results.

This unit shows you some ways of organizing and presenting data that make it easier to work with and to spot patterns.

15.1 Collecting data

The kind of data you need to collect depends on what you want to find out.

■ **You can collect data by:**
  ● doing a survey using a questionnaire
  ● making observations and recording your results
  ● getting information from other places, such as books, newspapers or the internet.

Example 1

Altaf and Hannah were bored one lunchtime.

They decided to do a survey . . .

Is there enough to do at Lunchtime?

Do you think there is enough to do at lunchtimes?

Yes ☐   No ☐

Do you go to lunchtime clubs?

Never ☐   Once a week ☐   More than once a week ☐   Every day ☐

Which of these clubs would you attend?

Badminton ☐	Chess ☐
Aerobics ☐	Music ☐
Maths ☐	Internet ☐
Basketball ☐	Art ☐

Altaf's friend Michael suggested adding these 2 questions:

How often would you go?

Once a week ☐   Everyday ☐

What do you think of school dinners?

Like them ☐   OK ☐   Rubbish ☐

Altaf changed this question because there should also be boxes for students who go more than once or who never go.

Hannah removed this question because it is not relevant to this survey.

Exercise 15A

1 Look at these pairs of questions. Choose whether Question (i) or Question (ii) would be best.

	Question (i)	Question (ii)	To find out:
(a)	What do you usually do in your spare time?	Do you watch TV or read in your spare time?	What they do in their spare time.
(b)	Which flavour of crisps do most people like best?	Which flavour of crisps do you like best?	The most popular flavour.
(c)	How do you usually get to school?	What's the best way to get to school?	How pupils get to school.
(d)	Have you read any books by Charles Dickens?	Have you read *Oliver Twist*?	If they have read *Oliver Twist*.
(e)	What colour are your eyes?	Do you have blue or brown eyes?	The most common eye colour.

2 These questions are not suitable for a questionnaire. For each one give a reason why and write a more suitable question.

(a) It's boring at lunchtime isn't it?

Yes ☐   No ☐

(b) How long does it take you to get to school in the morning?

1 hour ☐ $\frac{1}{2}$ hour ☐

(c) What job do you want to do?

doctor ☐   designer ☐   engineer ☐

(d) Have you ever copied anyone's homework?

Yes ☐   No ☐

15.2 Organizing data

A data collection sheet is a good way of organizing data collected in a survey or experiment.

Ahmed asked 40 people:

'Where did you go on holiday this year?'

He used this table to collect the data:

This is a data collection sheet.

Country	
England	
Wales	
Ireland	

Ahmed made a **tally mark** | for each person's answer on his record sheet:

Country	Tally	Frequency
England	ЖЖ ЖЖ		11
Wales	ЖЖ		6
Ireland	ЖЖ |||	8
Scotland	||||	4
Spain	||	2
Italy	ЖЖ	5
Others	||||	4

This column shows the frequency of each answer – how often each answer occurred.

Remember:
ЖЖ means 5.

This is called a tally chart or a frequency table.

The frequency is the number of times an answer occurs. For example, two people said they went to Spain. The frequency of the answer "Spain" is 2.

■ **You can use a tally chart (or frequency table) to collect and organize data.**

Exercise 15B

1 Copy and complete this frequency table.

Goals	Tally	Frequency
0	ЖЖ ЖЖ ЖЖ ЖЖ	
1	ЖЖ ЖЖ ЖЖ ЖЖ	
2		18
3		11
4	ЖЖ ЖЖ	
5		7
6				

2 This table shows the number of pupils
  in 7C who were late each day during one
  half-term.

Mon.	Tues.	Wed.	Thurs.	Fri.
2	3	1	2	4
3	0	2	3	3
5	1	0	4	2
3	2	0	2	3
1	1	3	2	2
2	1	1	2	3

Copy and complete this frequency table;
Monday is done for you.

Day	Tally	Frequency
Mon.	ЖЖ ЖЖ ЖЖ I	16
Tues.		
Wed.		
Thur.		
Fri.		

3 At breaktime the first fifty sales from the tuck shop were:

crisps, sweets, drink, drink, roll, crisps, roll, cake, roll,
crisps, fruit, roll, sweets, drink, roll, fruit, drink,
sweets, roll, cake, crisps, roll, cake, fruit, roll,
drink, fruit, crisps, cake, crisps, roll, roll,
sweets, crisps, cake, roll, crisps, drink, cake,
cake, crisps, roll, fruit, sweets, roll, drink,
crisps, sweets, roll, cake.

Draw a frequency table for this data.

4 Lester did a traffic survey to find the most popular make of car.

His results were:

Ford, Rover, Ford, Volvo, Nissan, Peugeot, BMW, Ford, BMW, Vauxhall, Nissan, VW, Peugeot, Ford, Nissan, Honda, Rover, VW, Vauxhall, Ford, Daewoo, BMW, Peugeot, VW, Volvo, Vauxhall, Ford, Vauxhall, Rover, Ford, VW, Nissan, Ford, Peugeot, Vauxhall, Ford, Honda, BMW, Ford, VW, Ford, Vauxhall, Rover, Honda, VW, Nissan, Rover, Ford, Nissan, VW, Peugeot, Ford, Nissan, VW, Ford, Rover, Volvo, Honda, Nissan.

Draw a frequency chart for his results.

5 **(a)** Roll a dice.
Record the number shown on the top face.
Repeat 60 times.
Draw a frequency table.

(b) Roll two dice.
Record the difference between the two numbers.
Repeat 60 times,
Draw a frequency table.

Remember:
The difference is the larger number minus the smaller number.

15.3 Pictograms

Reyhana did a survey to find out the way people travelled on holiday. She asked 40 people: 'How did you get to your holiday destination?'

This frequency table shows her data:

Way of travelling	Frequency
Car	16
Plane	14
Train	6
Boat	4

The same information can be shown more visually by using pictures or symbols to represent data:

Way of travelling	Key: ▱ = 4 people
Car	▱ ▱ ▱ ▱
Plane	▱ ▱ ▱ ◿
Train	▱ ◿
Boat	▱

Each ▱ symbol represents 4 people. So 4 × 4 = 16 people travelled by car.

■ **A pictogram uses pictures or symbols to show data.**

Exercise 15C

1 The pictogram shows how much pocket money six people get each week.

🪙 represents one pound (£1).

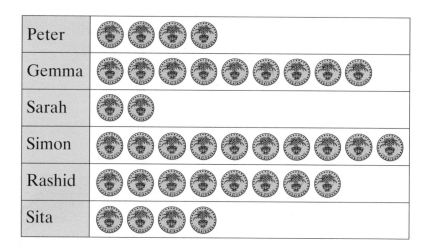

(a) Without counting, who gets the least pocket money each week?

(b) How much money did they get altogether? (Count this time.)

(c) Who gets exactly £8?

(d) How much does Gemma get?

2 This pictogram shows the number of cars using the station car park one week.

🚗 represents 10 cars

Monday	🚗 🚗 🚗 🚗 🚗 🚗 🚗 🚗
Tuesday	🚗 🚗 🚗 🚗 🚗 🚗
Wednesday	🚗 🚗 🚗 🚗 🚗
Thursday	🚗 🚗 🚗 🚗 🚗 🚗 🚗
Friday	🚗 🚗 🚗 🚗 🚗
Saturday	🚗 🚗 🚗 🚗

(a) How many cars used the car park on Wednesday?

(b) How many cars altogether used the car park during the week?

(c) It costs £1.50 to park Monday–Friday but Saturday is free.
How much money was taken that week?

3 This pictogram shows the number of letters delivered to Rachel's Garage in one week.

✉ represents 4 letters.

Monday	✉ ✉ ✉ ✉ ✉ ✉ ✉ ✉
Tuesday	✉ ✉ ✉ ✉ ✉ ✉
Wednesday	✉ ✉ ✉ ✉ ✉ ✉ ✉ ✉ ✉ ✉
Thursday	✉ ✉ ✉ ✉ ✉ ✉ ✉ ✉ ✉
Friday	✉ ✉ ✉ ✉ ✉ ✉ ✉
Saturday	✉ ✉ ✉ ✉ ✉

(a) How many letters were delivered on Tuesday?

(b) How many letters were delivered altogether that week?

15.4 Bar charts

Ahmed's data about the places people went to on holiday is:

Country	Frequency
England	11
Wales	6
Ireland	8
Scotland	4
Spain	2
Italy	5
Others	4

He can display his data on a bar chart.

■ **A bar chart uses bars, blocks or lines to show data.**

Here are three different types of bar charts Ahmed can use to display his data.

1 Horizontal bar chart:

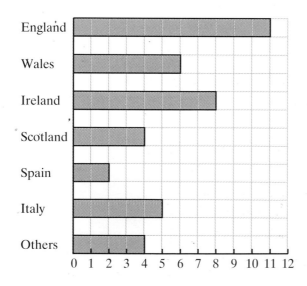

2 Vertical bar chart:

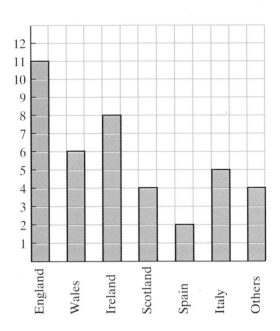

3 Bar-line graph or Stick graph:

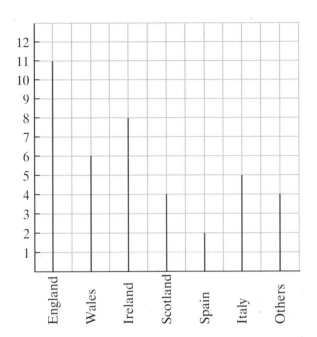

Exercise 15D

1 Gwen asked people 'What is your favourite colour?'
She listed the replies:

green, red, red, blue, yellow, blue, green, white, red,
green, red, yellow, blue, blue, red, green, red, green,
yellow, white, blue, red, orange, blue, red, yellow, blue,
blue, red, green.

Draw a bar chart to show her results. (You may find it
helpful to draw a tally chart first.)

2 Jason emptied a tube of Tasties on a plate and noted
the colours:

Blue	6	Red	8	Mauve	4
Yellow	10	White	3	Brown	7
Pink	2	Orange	5		

Draw a bar chart to represent this data.

3 This table shows the number of goals scored in league matches one Saturday.

Number of goals	0	1	2	3	4	5	6
Number of matches	5	8	11	14	9	3	2

Illustrate this information using a bar-line graph.

4 Employees of a supermarket were asked how they came to work. The results were:

Walk   22   Car   24   Bus   18
Train   10   Cycle   6   Motorcycle   8

(a) Draw a horizontal bar chart to show this data.

(b) Draw a vertical bar-line graph for the same data.

(c) Which did you find easier to draw?
Give your reason.

5 The marks in a spelling test are shown in this table.

(a) Draw a bar-line graph to represent this data.

(b) Which mark did most pupils get?

(c) How many pupils scored 7 or more?

10	6	7	9	5	7	9	3
3	9	8	7	6	10	7	6
9	5	10	3	8	8	5	9
7	8	6	5	9	6	7	5
4	9	8	7	6	8	10	7

15.5 Dual bar charts

■ **Dual bar charts are used to compare two sets of similar data.**

Example 2

The number of students in 7G arriving late for school one week was:

	Monday	Tuesday	Wednesday	Thursday	Friday
Week 1	4	5	2	3	2
Week 2	6	3	4	1	2

Draw a dual bar chart to show this data.

This dual bar chart shows the data for each week in a different colour:

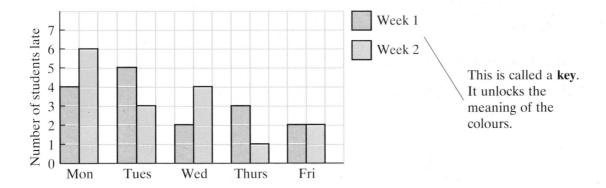

This is called a **key**. It unlocks the meaning of the colours.

Exercise 15E

1   This dual bar chart shows the number of hours of sunshine one week in Margate and Brighton.

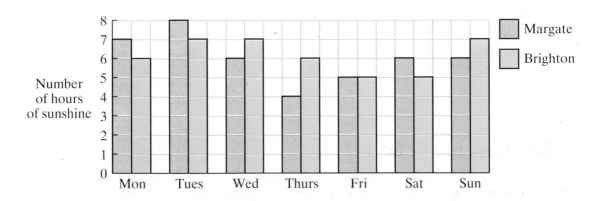

(a) How many hours of sunshine were there in Margate on Saturday?

(b) On how many days were there six hours or more of sunshine in   (i) Margate   (ii) Brighton?

(c) Which day did both resorts have the same number of hours of sun?

(d) On which day did one town have two hours' more sunshine than the other?

(e) Which town had the most sunshine during the whole week?

2 This table shows how many fan letters two boy bands received one week:

	Mon	Tues	Wed	Thur	Fri	Sat
Boys unlimited	5	8	2	11	6	10
Boys 'r' us	7	3	9	4	12	7

(a) Draw a dual bar chart to represent this data.
(b) On which day were most letters received?
(c) How many letters were received altogether?

3 The table shows Judy and Iris' test scores. The tests were marked out of 20.

	English	Maths	Science	History	Geography	French	Art
Judy	16	14	10	15	19	6	8
Iris	12	18	18	7	11	14	10

(a) Draw a dual bar-chart to compare their results.
(b) Use information from your chart to write *two* sentences comparing their results.
(c) If anyone scored less than 10 they had to do the test again. Which tests did Judy have to do again?

4

The chart shows the maximum and minimum temperatures in New York:

	Jan	Feb	Mar	Apr	May	Jun	Jul	Aug	Sep	Oct	Nov	Dec
Max	37	38	45	57	68	77	82	80	79	69	51	41
Min	24	24	30	42	53	60	66	66	60	49	37	29

(a) Draw a dual bar chart to show this data.
(b) In which month was the difference between the maximum and minimum temperature greatest?
(c) Write down three observations from your chart.

An observation is something you notice, like a pattern in the data.

5 This dual bar chart shows the number of cars sold by two garages:

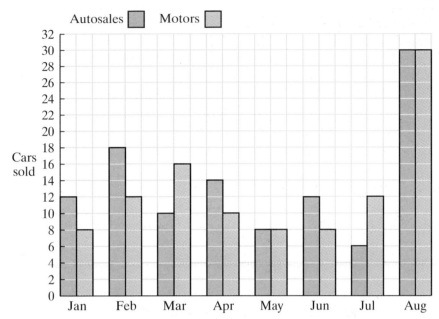

Autosales ▢   Motors ▢

Cars sold

(a) Which garage sold most cars in March?

(b) Autocars sold more cars than Motors did in June.
How many more cars did they sell?

(c) Which garage sold most cars altogether?

(d) Copy and complete this table using data from the
dual bar chart:

	Jan	Feb	Mar	Apr	May	Jun	Jul	Aug
Autosales	12				8		6	
Motors	8	12		10				

15.6 Pie charts

■ **A pie chart is a way of
displaying data to show
how something is
shared or divided.**

This pie shows how much
market share different
soap powders have.

The larger the angle
the more the sector
represents.

Sudso

Bleacho

Dazzlo

Example 3

Denzil counted the number of birds he saw in his garden one morning.

Draw a pie chart to show this data.

Bird	Frequency
Sparrow	9
Blackbird	3
Starling	5
Robin	1
Total	18

Here is how to calculate the angles of the sectors:

18 birds are represented by 360°

1 bird is represented by $\dfrac{360}{18} = 20°$

Bird	Frequency	Angle
Sparrow	9	$9 \times 20 = 180°$
Blackbird	3	$3 \times 20 = 60°$
Starling	5	$5 \times 20 = 100°$
Robin	1	$1 \times 20 = 20°$

To find the angle for a sector multiply the number of birds it represents by 20°

Now draw the pie chart using a protractor:

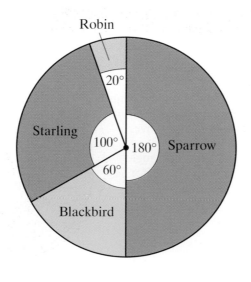

Check that the angle total is 360°:

$180 + 60 + 100 + 20 = 360$

Mark in the angles. Write in what each sector represents.

Example 4

This pie chart shows how 36 pupils usually come to school:

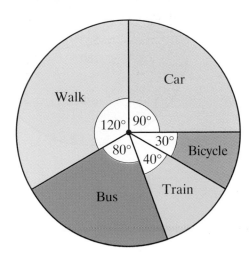

How many pupils walk to school?

The angle of the Walk sector is 120°.

The fraction of pupils who walk to school is $120 \div 360 = \frac{1}{3}$

The number of pupils is $\frac{1}{3}$ of the total

$$\frac{1}{3} \text{ of } 36 \quad \text{is} \quad 36 \div 3 = 12$$

So 12 pupils walk to school.

Exercise 15F

1 This pie chart shows 20 pupils' favourite colours.
   (a) What is the angle of the Red sector?
   (b) How many pupils chose Red?
   (c) How many pupils chose Green?

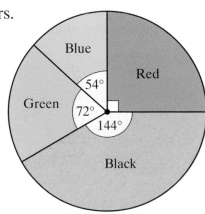

2 Karen earns £30 per week
   baby sitting.
   The pie chart shows how
   she spent it last week.

   Copy and complete this table.

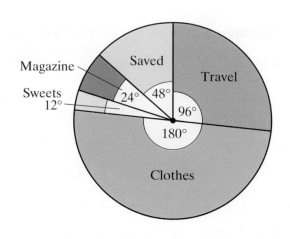

Item	Angle	£
Travel		
Clothes		
Sweets		
Magazines		
Saved		

3 The table shows the number of vehicles in a car park.
   Copy and complete the table.

Type	Number	Angle
Car	45	
Lorry	2	
Motorcycle	3	
Van	10	

   Display this information on a pie chart.

4 This pie chart shows how many letters Vijay
   received last week.

   Measure the angles using a protractor and
   copy and complete the table.

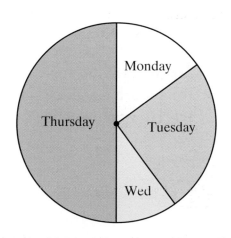

Day	Angle	Number of letters
Monday	54°	3
Tuesday		
Wednesday		
Thursday		

5 Amy asked the 30 pupils in her class
'Which channel do you watch the most?'
The table shows her results.

Draw a pie chart to illustrate this data.

Channel	Frequency
BBC1	10
BBC2	1
ITV	15
Channel 4	2
Channel 5	2

15.7 Different types of data

Some data can be counted:

There are 8 people
in this room

There are 15 sheep
in the pen

20 red cars pass the
school in one hour

■ **Data you can count is called discrete data.**

Some data needs to be measured:

The distance around
the tree trunk is 86 cm

Sue is 1.54 m tall

The temperature is 15.4 °C

■ **Data you measure is called continuous data.**

Exercise 15G

Use one of the words $\boxed{\text{Discrete}}$ or $\boxed{\text{Continuous}}$
To describe each of these forms of data:

1 The length of a field
2 The number of hairs on a person's head
3 The number of budgies in an aviary
4 The ages of your classmates
5 The amount of water in a jug
6 The weights of turkeys in a supermarket
7 The cost of an ice cream
8 The shoe sizes of your classmates
9 The width of a person's foot
10 The time it takes to run 100 metres

15.8 Line graphs

So far all the data shown in charts has been discrete.

■ **You can show continuous data in a line graph.**

Example 5

Verity recorded the temperature in her garden every hour
from 8 am to 5 pm.

Time	8 am	9 am	10 am	11 am	12 pm	1 pm	2 pm	3 pm	4 pm	5 pm
Temp (°C)	7	9	12	16	22	22	21	20	20	18

(a) Draw a line graph to show this data.
(b) Describe any pattern you see.
(c) Use your graph to estimate the
temperature at 11:30 am.

(a) First plot all the points.
Then join them up.
(b) The line graph shows that
the temperature rises then
starts to fall.
(c) At 11:30 am the temperature
is approximately 19 °C.

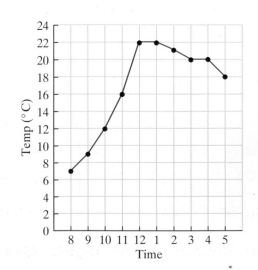

Joining the points on a line graph helps you estimate values in between them.

You cannot do this for discrete data. There are no values 'in between'. For example, there can be 3 people in a car or 4 people, but not 3.7 people.

Exercise 15H

1 A hospital nurse recorded a patient's temperature in degrees Celsius every hour.
   The results are shown in this table.

Time	0600	0700	0800	0900	1000	1100	1200	1300
Temperature (°C)	33	37	39	45	42	43	40	37

   (a) Draw a line graph to show this data.
   (b) What might the patient's temperature have been at
       (i) 0730   (ii) 1130
   (c) What time was the highest temperature recorded?
   (d) Describe what happened to the patient's temperature between 0900 and 1200.

2 Joe kept a record of the mileage on his car as it got older.
   His data is shown in the table:

Age (years)	0	1	2	3	4	5	6
Miles ('000)	0	12	20	30	41	57	65

   (a) Display the data on a line graph.
   (b) Estimate how many miles the car had done when it was $4\frac{1}{2}$ years old.

3 The maximum and minimum temperatures in °F in Llangrannog last year were:

	Jan	Feb	Mar	Apr	May	Jun	Jul	Aug	Sep	Oct	Nov	Dec
Max	45	48	52	55	60	66	72	75	67	56	49	42
Min	34	32	36	39	40	42	44	45	39	37	33	30

   (a) On the same axes draw line graphs to represent this data.
   (b) Make a comment on your results.

4 The table shows the number of ferries leaving
   Fishguard before noon for the last 10 months.

Month	Jan	Feb	Mar	Apr	May	Jun	Jul	Aug	Sept	Oct
Ferries	34	32	38	40	40	45	45	48	44	36

Draw a diagram to represent this data.
Why should you *not* draw a line graph?

15.9 Scatter graphs

Ken is a used car salesman.
He has 10 cars for sale.

He makes a table of the miles
travelled and the age of each
car:

Age (years)	3	5	2	3	1	4	6	6	7	2
Miles ('000)	27	40	15	37	12	58	70	48	80	32

He plots all the points on a **scatter graph**:

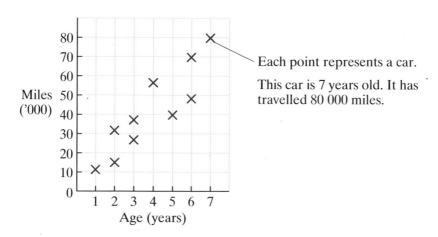

Each point represents a car.

This car is 7 years old. It has
travelled 80 000 miles.

There seems to be a relationship between the age of a car
and the number of miles it has travelled.

In general the number of miles travelled increases as the
age of the car increases.

Ken also makes a table of the value of the car and its age:

Age (years)	3	5	2	3	1	4	6	6	7	2
Value (£)	7400	3500	8200	6100	9900	3000	3000	4200	2200	8500

The scatter graph looks like this:

In general, the price of a car decreases as the age of the car increases.

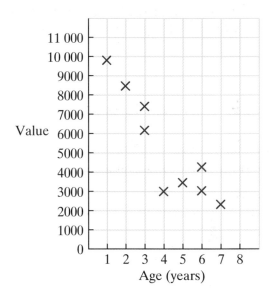

- **A scatter graph (or diagram) can be used to show whether two sets of data are related.**

- **The relationship between two sets of data is called a correlation.**

You need to be able to recognize different types of relationships between two sets of data. Look at these scatter graphs:

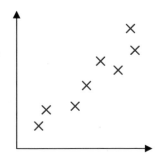

As one value increases the other one also increases. There is a **positive correlation**.

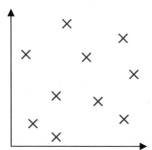

As one value increases the other decreases. There is a **negative correlation**.

The points are randomly and widely spaced out. There is **no correlation**.

Exercise 15I

1 Twelve Year 7 pupils took a reading test and a spelling test.
Their scores out of 100 are shown in the table:

Reading	52	60	82	75	90	30	25	48	63	71	38	20
Spelling	48	60	76	70	74	25	24	51	62	65	43	15

(a) Draw a scatter graph to illustrate this data.
Put spelling on the *x*-axis and reading on the *y*-axis.

(b) Comment on any correlation you see.

2 Owen sells new cars.
The table shows the value and the engine size of 10 new cars.

Value (£'000)	7	9.5	12	9.8	11	17	16.5	15	19	24
Engine size (litres)	1	1.1	1.6	1.1	1.4	2.2	1.8	1.6	2	2.5

(a) Draw a scatter graph to show this data.

(b) Comment on the correlation.

3 The average fuel consumption (in miles per gallon) and the engine size (in litres) of 12 cars is shown in the table:

mpg	30	45	40	32	35	38	28	18	22	36	48	60
litres	2	1.1	1.5	1.2	1.6	1.1	1.6	3	2.5	1.4	1	1.1

(a) Draw a scatter graph to show this data.

(b) Comment on the correlation.

4 In a fitness competition 10 men did as many press-ups as they could in 1 minute. The table shows the number of press-ups each man managed and his age.

Age	40	30	62	21	38	54	31	28	45	58
Press-ups	31	52	8	60	35	20	41	63	18	12

(a) Plot this data on a scatter graph.

(b) Comment on the correlation.

Summary of key points

1   Another word for information is **data**.

2   You can use a tally chart (or frequency table) to collect and organize data.

3   A pictogram uses pictures or symbols to show data.

4   A bar chart uses bars, blocks or lines to show data.

5   Dual bar charts are used to compare two sets of similar data.

6   A pie chart is a way of displaying data to show how something is shared or divided.

7   Data you can count is called discrete data.

8   Data you measure is called continuous data.

9   You can show continuous data in a line graph.

10   A scatter graph (or diagram) can be used to show whether two sets of data are related.

11   The relationship between two sets of data is called a correlation.

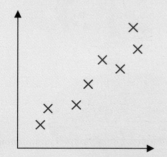

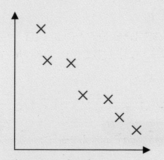

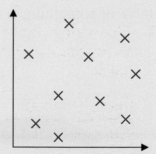

As one value increases the other one also increases. There is a **positive correlation**.

As one value increases the other decreases. There is a **negative correlation**.

The points are randomly and widely spaced out. There is **no correlation**.

16 Percentages

16.1 Understanding percentages

The symbol % means 'per cent'.
Per cent means 'in every 100'.

3% means 3 in every 100.
3% is called a **percentage**.

100% of something is all of it.

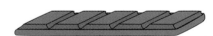

There are 5 pieces of
chocolate in this bar.
Each piece is $100 \div 5 = 20\%$
of the whole.

There are 4 slices of pizza.
Each slice is $100 \div 4 = 25\%$.
3 slices will be $3 \times 25\% = 75\%$

Exercise 16A

1 A rod is cut into five equal pieces. What percentage of
the rod is each piece?

2 A pie is cut into ten equal pieces. What percentage of
the pie is each piece?

3 What percentage of each shape is shaded?

(a)

(b)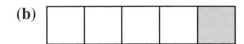

(c)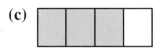

(d)

(e)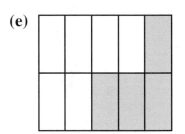

(f)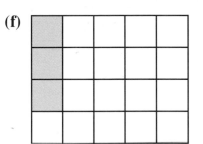

(g)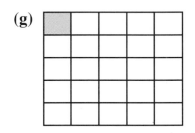

(h)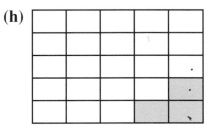

(i)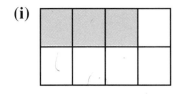

(j)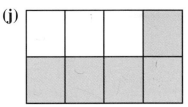

16.2 Writing percentages as fractions

You can write a percentage as a fraction.

3% means 3 out of 100. As a fraction this is $\dfrac{3}{100}$ —— Notice that the denominator is 100

3% and $\dfrac{3}{100}$ represent the same amount.

■ **You can write a percentage as a fraction with the denominator 100.** For example:

$$23\% = \frac{23}{100}$$

These hundred squares show some more fractions and percentages:

$\frac{1}{4}$ shaded

1	2	3	4	5	6	7	8	9	10
11	12	13	14	15	16	17	18	19	20
21	22	23	24	25	26	27	28	29	30
31	32	33	34	35	36	37	38	39	40
41	42	43	44	45	46	47	48	49	50
51	52	53	54	55	56	57	58	59	60
61	62	63	64	65	66	67	68	69	70
71	72	73	74	75	76	77	78	79	80
81	82	83	84	85	86	87	88	89	90
91	92	93	94	95	96	97	98	99	100

25 parts shaded.
25% shaded.

$\frac{1}{2}$ shaded

1	2	3	4	5	6	7	8	9	10
11	12	13	14	15	16	17	18	19	20
21	22	23	24	25	26	27	28	29	30
31	32	33	34	35	36	37	38	39	40
41	42	43	44	45	46	47	48	49	50
51	52	53	54	55	56	57	58	59	60
61	62	63	64	65	66	67	68	69	70
71	72	73	74	75	76	77	78	79	80
81	82	83	84	85	86	87	88	89	90
91	92	93	94	95	96	97	98	99	100

50 parts shaded.
50% shaded.

$\frac{3}{4}$ shaded

1	2	3	4	5	6	7	8	9	10
11	12	13	14	15	16	17	18	19	20
21	22	23	24	25	26	27	28	29	30
31	32	33	34	35	36	37	38	39	40
41	42	43	44	45	46	47	48	49	50
51	52	53	54	55	56	57	58	59	60
61	62	63	64	65	66	67	68	69	70
71	72	73	74	75	76	77	78	79	80
81	82	83	84	85	86	87	88	89	90
91	92	93	94	95	96	97	98	99	100

75 parts shaded.
75% shaded.

Example 1

Write these percentages as fractions in their simplest form:

(a) 20%   **(b)** 5%   **(c)** 40%

(a) 20% means $\frac{20}{100}$ **(b)** 5% means $\frac{5}{100}$ **(c)** 40% means $\frac{40}{100}$

Remember: to find the simplest form, you divide the top and the bottom by the same number.

$$\frac{20}{100} = \frac{1}{5} \quad (\div 20)$$

$$\frac{5}{100} = \frac{1}{20} \quad (\div 5)$$

$$\frac{40}{100} = \frac{2}{5} \quad (\div 20)$$

■ **Remember these percentages and their equivalent fractions:**

Equivalent means they represent the same amount.

$$50\% = \frac{1}{2} \quad 25\% = \frac{1}{4} \quad 75\% = \frac{3}{4}$$

Exercise 16B

1 For each hundred square, write down
- the fraction shaded
- the percentage shaded

(a)

1	2	3	4	5	6	7	8	9	10
11	12	13	14	15	16	17	18	19	20
21	22	23	24	25	26	27	28	29	30
31	32	33	34	35	36	37	38	39	40
41	42	43	44	45	46	47	48	49	50
51	52	53	54	55	56	57	58	59	60
61	62	63	64	65	66	67	68	69	70
71	72	73	74	75	76	77	78	79	80
81	82	83	84	85	86	87	88	89	90
91	92	93	94	95	96	97	98	99	100

(b)

1	2	3	4	5	6	7	8	9	10
11	12	13	14	15	16	17	18	19	20
21	22	23	24	25	26	27	28	29	30
31	32	33	34	35	36	37	38	39	40
41	42	43	44	45	46	47	48	49	50
51	52	53	54	55	56	57	58	59	60
61	62	63	64	65	66	67	68	69	70
71	72	73	74	75	76	77	78	79	80
81	82	83	84	85	86	87	88	89	90
91	92	93	94	95	96	97	98	99	100

(c)

1	2	3	4	5	6	7	8	9	10
11	12	13	14	15	16	17	18	19	20
21	22	23	24	25	26	27	28	29	30
31	32	33	34	35	36	37	38	39	40
41	42	43	44	45	46	47	48	49	50
51	52	53	54	55	56	57	58	59	60
61	62	63	64	65	66	67	68	69	70
71	72	73	74	75	76	77	78	79	80
81	82	83	84	85	86	87	88	89	90
91	92	93	94	95	96	97	98	99	100

2 Write these percentages as fractions.
Write the fractions in their simplest form.

(a) 1%   **(b)** 29%   **(c)** 26%   **(d)** 40%

(e) 42%   **(f)** 48%   **(g)** 44%   **(h)** 60%

(i) 12%   **(j)** 10%   **(k)** 8%   **(l)** 28%

(m) 55%   **(n)** 90%   **(o)** 45%   **(p)** 25%

16.3 Writing percentages as decimals

You can also write a percentage as a decimal:

$$3\% \quad \text{means} \quad \frac{3}{100} \quad \text{means} \quad 3 \div 100 = 0.03$$

■ **To change a percentage to a decimal divide by 100.**
For example: 23% means $23 \div 100 = 0.23$

Remember: to divide by 100 move every digit 2 places to the right.

Example 2

Write these percentages as decimals:
(a) 37%   **(b)** 70%

(a) $37\% = 37 \div 100 = 0.37$
(b) $70\% = 70 \div 100 = 0.70 = 0.7$

Exercise 16C

Change these percentages to decimals:

1 12%   **2** 29%   **3** 66%   **4** 25%

5 8%   **6** 35%   **7** 42%   **8** 3%

9 17%   **10** 1%   **11** 5%   **12** 82%

13 99%   **14** 7%   **15** 16%   **16** 80%

17 Copy and complete this table of equivalent percentages, fractions and decimals.

Percentage	Fraction	Decimal
80%	$\frac{4}{5}$	0.8
70%		
10%		
	$\frac{1}{100}$	
	$\frac{1}{2}$	
		0.25
	$\frac{3}{4}$	
100%		

Hint: to change a fraction to a decimal you divide the top by the bottom, for example
$\frac{3}{5} = 3 \div 5 = 0.6$

16.4 Writing fractions and decimals as percentages

From decimal to percentage

To change a percentage to a decimal **divide by 100.**

$$\overset{\div 100}{\frown}$$
$$22\% = 0.22$$
$$\underset{\times 100}{\smile}$$

Notice that $\div 100$ and $\times 100$ are inverse operations.

There is more about inverses on page 231.

■   **To change a decimal to a percentage multiply by 100.**

From fraction to percentage

■ **To change a fraction to a percentage:**
  - **find an equivalent fraction with denominator 100**
  - **multiply the fraction by 100%**

$$\frac{11}{50} \overset{\times 2}{\underset{\times 2}{=}} \frac{22}{100} = 22\%$$

■ **If you can't find an equivalent fraction with denominator 100:**
  - **change the fraction to a decimal**
  - **change the decimal to a percentage**

$$\frac{6}{15} = 0.4$$
$$0.4 \times 100 = 40\%$$

Exercise 16D

1 Change each of these decimals to percentages:

(a) 0.25   (b) 0.75   (c) 0.16   (d) 0.5   (e) 1.25

(f) 0.05   (g) 0.01   (h) 1.01   (i) 2.25   (j) 1.32

Remember: a percentage can be greater than 100%.

2 Change each of these fractions to percentages:

(a) $\frac{50}{100}$ (b) $\frac{33}{100}$ (c) $\frac{1}{100}$ (d) $\frac{4}{100}$ (e) $\frac{22}{50}$

(f) $\frac{7}{25}$ (g) $\frac{3}{10}$ (h) $\frac{3}{2}$ (i) $\frac{3}{20}$ (j) $\frac{1}{8}$

3 Write each of these as:
  - a fraction in its simplest form
  - a percentage

(a) 0.2   (b) 0.11   (c) 0.03   (d) 1.6   (e) 0.003

4 Convert these fractions to percentages and mark them on this number line:

(a) $\frac{6}{8}$ (b) $\frac{10}{200}$ (c) $\frac{50}{40}$ (d) $\frac{7}{20}$ (e) $\frac{3}{5}$

0%   25%   50%   75%   100%   125%

16.5 Finding a percentage

■ To find a percentage of a number:
- change the percentage to a decimal
- multiply the decimal by the number

Example 3

Find:

(a) 20% of £30　　　　　　　(b) 15% of 60 kg

(a) $20\% = 20 \div 100 = 0.2$　　(b) $15\% = 15 \div 100 = 0.15$

20%	of	£30	15%	of	60 kg

= 0.2 × 30 = £6　　0.15 × 60 = 9 kg

Remember to give units in your answer.

Exercise 16E

Find:

1 10% of £35　　　　　　2 20% of £15

3 50% of 17 kg　　　　　4 25% of 240 g

5 17% of £28　　　　　　6 6% of £22.50

7 53% of £36　　　　　　8 12% of 165 kg

9 15% of 75 kg　　　　　10 30% of 15 m

11 5% of 4.2 m　　　　　12 75% of 18 kg

13 8% of 17.5 kg　　　　14 13% of £62

15 A Hi-Fi system costs £179. Wes wants to buy the
Hi-Fi system on credit. The shopkeeper asks for a
15% deposit.
How much deposit must Wes pay?

16 There are 30 pupils in Class 7M. 60% of them are girls.
How many girls are there in Class 7M?

17 The 75 boys in Year 7 were asked to choose their
favourite sport. 84% of the boys chose football. Work
out how many boys chose football.

18 Of the 950 pupils in Peak School 6% usually cycle to school and 22% usually travel to school by bus. Find:

    (a) the number of pupils who usually cycle to school,

    (b) the number of pupils who usually travel to school by bus.

19 There are 55 seats in a coach. 40% of the seats are vacant. How many seats are vacant?

20 A school raises £2400 during a summer fair. The school gives 35% of the money to charity. How much money is left?

16.6 Percentage increase and decrease

Increases and decreases are often given in percentages.

House prices increased by 5.2% in March

SALE 20% off marked prices

$33\frac{1}{3}$% EXTRA FREE!

Which car? magazine reports that on average a car depreciates in value by **16%** each year.

Example 4

Jane earns £800 per month.
Next month she will get a pay rise of 5%.

(a) How much is her pay rise?

(b) What will she earn next month?

(a) Her pay rise will be 5% of £800

    5% is $5 \div 100 = 0.05$

    So 5% of £800 is $0.05 \times 800 = £40$

(b) Next month she will earn $£800 + £40 = £840$

Example 5

In a sale all prices are reduced by 15%

Find the sale price of a dress that originally cost £24

15% is $15 \div 100 = 0.15$

The dress is reduced by $0.15 \times 24 = 3.6$
$$= £3.60$$

So the sale price is $£24 - £3.60 = £20.40$

■ **To increase an amount by a percentage:**
  ● **find the percentage of the amount**
  ● **add it to the original amount**

■ **To decrease an amount by a percentage:**
  ● **find the percentage of the amount**
  ● **subtract it from the original amount**

Exercise 16F

1 Dara left £150 in her savings account for one year. She was paid interest of 7% per year.

Hint: You can use your calculator to help. To find 10% of £35, press:

| 3 | 5 | × | 1 | 0 | % | = |

  (a) Calculate the amount of interest paid to Dara.

  (b) How much did she have altogether?

2 In a sale *Music Corner* reduced the prices of CDs by 5%. Robert bought a CD which usually cost £12. Work out:

  (a) the reduction in the price

  (b) the new price of Robert's CD

3 A shopkeeper buys polo shirts for £8.40 each and sweatshirts for £12.80 each. He sells them for 45% more than he buys them for. Work out the price at which he sells:

  (a) a polo shirt   **(b)** a sweatshirt

4 In his job as a salesman John is paid a basic rate of £5.20 per hour and a 15% commission on sales. How much is John paid in a week when he works 28 hours and makes sales of £540?

5 Ramana is paid at a basic rate of £3.80 per hour. The hourly rate for overtime is 30% more. During a particular week Ramana worked a basic 40 hours and then four hours overtime. Calculate:

(a) the hourly rate for overtime

(b) the total amount Ramana earned that week

Summary of key points

1 You can write a percentage as a fraction with the denominator 100. For example:

$$23\% = \frac{23}{100}$$

2 Remember these percentages and their equivalent fractions:

$$50\% = \tfrac{1}{2} \qquad 25\% = \tfrac{1}{4} \qquad 75\% = \tfrac{3}{4}$$

Equivalent means they represent the same amount.

3 To change a percentage to a decimal divide by 100. For example: 23% means $23 \div 100 = 0.23$

4 To change a decimal to a percentage <u>multiply by 100</u>.

5 To change a fraction to a percentage:
- find an equivalent fraction with denominator 100
- multiply the fraction by 100%

6 If you can't find an equivalent fraction with denominator 100:
- change the fraction to a decimal
- change the decimal to a percentage

7 To find a percentage of a number:
- change the percentage to a decimal
- multiply the decimal by the number

8 To increase an amount by a percentage:
- find the percentage of the amount
- add it to the original amount.

9 To decrease an amount by a percentage:
- find the percentage of the amount
- subtract it from the original amount.

17 Averages

You often see or hear the word average.
Here are some examples:

- The average number of children in a family is 2.4
- The average rainfall in Britain in June is 50 mm.
- 12-year-olds in Britain spend 4 hours a day watching TV on average.

This box holds 38 matches on average. The number of matches may vary slightly.

The word average means that something is typical, or describes something that typically happens.

In mathematics an average is a single value that is typical of a set of data. It can be used to make general statements about the data.

There are three different averages:

- the mean
- the mode
- the median

This unit describes each average and shows you how to find them.

17.1 The mean

The **mean** is one of the most commonly used types of average.

■ **The mean of a set of data is the sum of the values divided by the number of values.**

$$\text{mean} = \frac{\text{sum of the values}}{\text{number of values}}$$

Ian got these marks for his last 8 Geography homeworks:

7, 5, 8, 3, 1, 8, 10, 6

His mean mark is worked out like this:

$$\frac{7+5+8+3+1+8+10+6}{8} = \frac{48}{8} \quad \text{— add up all the values} \\ \text{— divide by the number of values} \\ = 6$$

Ian's mean mark was 6.

Exercise 17A

1 Calculate the mean of each set of values:
   (a) 5, 9, 4, 6, 8, 4
   (b) 8, 5, 6, 7, 4, 9, 3, 6, 7, 5
   (c) 15, 18, 13, 16, 14, 12, 17
   (d) 21, 34, 26, 40, 22, 44, 35, 30
   (e) 18, 45, 23, 27, 33, 41, 36, 28, 16, 33

2 Here are 8 people's heights:

   172 cm,   178 cm,   170 cm,   171 cm,
   175 cm,   177 cm,   173 cm,   172 cm

   (a) What is their mean height?
   (b) How many people were taller than the mean height?

3 Here are the weekly wages of 15 professional footballers:

   £200, £200, £210, £220, £220, £250, £250, £250, £280, £280, £300, £350, £400, £410, £500

   Work out their mean wage.

4 Ben and Amy did a survey to see how many books pupils in their class had read in the last two months. Here are their results:

   2, 3, 1, 0, 1, 2, 1, 2, 3, 4, 0, 1, 0, 3, 5, 1, 0, 2, 6, 1, 0, 2, 3, 1, 0, 0, 3, 2

   Work out the mean number of books read.

   This is the average number of books read by each pupil.

5 Gordon worked during his holidays and was paid:

	Mon	Tues	Wed	Thurs	Fri	Sat
Week 1	£5.60	£6.20	£2.40	£6.30	£8.60	£10.30
Week 2	£4.40	£6.20	£4.00	£7.24	£8.60	£12.40

   Calculate:
   (a) His mean daily wage for week 1.
   (b) His mean daily wage for week 2.
   (c) Gordon's mean daily wage for the two weeks.

   Hint: you need to find the mean of **all** the values.

6 The average test mark for a group of ten pupils was 42.5

(a) How many marks did the group get altogether?

(b) Two new pupils took the test and joined the group. One scored 33 and the other scored 6. Calculate the new mean for the group.

Hint: if you know the mean and the number of values, how do you find the sum of the values from

$$\text{mean} = \frac{\text{sum of the values}}{\text{number of values}}$$

7 Peter's and Karen's marks in a series of tests were:

Peter	25	36	34	45	37	42
Karen	31	28	43	35	39	28

(a) Who had the higher mean mark and by how much?

(b) If Peter scores 26 in the next test, how many marks must Karen get to have the same mean mark as Peter?

17.2 The mode

■ **The mode of a set of data is the value which occurs most often.**

Ian's marks for his last 8 Geography homeworks were:

7, 5, 8, 3, 1, 8, 10, 6

He scored 7, 5, 3, 1, 10 and 6 once each.
He scored 8 twice.

The mode was 8. You can say the **modal** mark was 8.

Example 1

Find the mode of each set of data:

(a) 1, 5, 3, 2, 7, 4, 3, 2

(b) 23, 43, 25, 66, 41, 24

(c) 11, 13, 11, 13, 14, 15, 11

(a) 1, 5, 7 and 4 all occur once.
2 and 3 occur twice.
There are two modes: 2 and 3.

There is often
more than one
modal value.

(b) Each value occurs only once.
There is no mode.

(c) 14 and 15 occur once.
13 occurs twice.
11 occurs three times.
The mode, or modal value, is 11.

Exercise 17B

1 Find the mode of each set of data:

(a) 5, 2, 8, 2, 6, 8, 4, 2, 6, 9

(b) 7, 3, 3, 6, 8, 1, 4, 7, 5, 2, 7, 8

(c) 6, 8, 2, 7, 3, 7, 5, 2, 4, 7, 3, 2, 6

(d) 13, 16, 11, 14, 17, 15, 10, 19, 12, 11,
17, 15, 19, 17, 14, 18, 13, 10, 15, 17,
10, 18, 14, 12, 15, 10, 16, 12, 19, 16,
12, 15, 11, 13, 18, 16, 15, 13, 11, 14

2 Rachel asked the girls in her class what size shoes they
wore. The results were:

5, 3, 3, 4, 3, 4, 6, 4, 3, 5, 5, 4, 6, 4

(a) What is the mode of this data?

(b) Give a reason why a shoe shop will be interested in
the modal size.

3 These are the numbers of hours of sunshine at a
seaside resort on each day one June.
Find the mode for the numbers of hours of sunshine.

6	10	8	7	5	7	1	0	2	5
7	8	6	6	2	2	0	1	7	9
10	0	4	7	8	7	9	10	5	6

4 Find the mode of the shoe sizes for your class.

5 There are 30 pupils in class 7A.
Their marks in last week's science test are shown on
the bar chart.

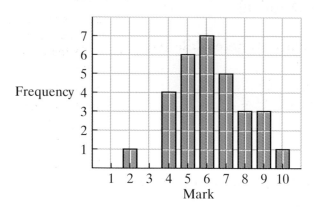

Which mark was the mode?

17.3 The median

The third kind of average is the median.
It is the middle value of a set of data.

To find the middle value you must arrange the data in
order of size.

Example 2

Find the median of each set of data:
(a) 1, 3, 2, 6, 5, 8, 4, 3, 3
(b) 4, 8, 3, 5, 6, 3, 5, 7, 6, 3
(c) 20, 26, 82, 40, 32, 64

(a) Arrange the values in size order:

> 1, 2, 3, 3, 3, 4, 5, 6, 8

The middle value is 3.
The median is 3.

(b) Arrange the values in size order:

> 3, 3, 3, 4, 5, 5, 6, 6, 7, 8

There are two middle values: 5 and 5.
They are the same.
The median is 5.

(c) Arrange the values in order of size:

20, 26, 32, 40, 64, 82

There are two middle values: 32 and 40.
They are not the same.
The median is the average (mean) of the middle two numbers:

$$\text{median} = \frac{32+40}{2} = \frac{72}{2} = 36$$

The median is 36.

Notice that this median value is not in the original list.

Because there is an even number of marks there are two 'middle' values.

The median is calculated from these.

■ **The median of a set of data is the middle value when the data is arranged in size order.**
When there is an even number of values the median is the average (mean) of the middle two values.

Exercise 17C

1 Find the median of the following sets of data:

(a) 6, 2, 9, 1, 4, 8, 5, 9, 7
(b) 12, 18, 10, 14, 17, 13, 12, 18, 15
(c) 31, 45, 16, 38, 36, 42, 29, 40, 37
(d) 8, 3, 5, 11, 4, 9, 4, 7
(e) 26, 16, 23, 14, 18, 22, 25, 10

2 The number of people sitting in the first nine rows of a cinema were:

on Tuesday: 15, 26, 19, 32, 36, 25, 30, 17, 23
on Friday: 17, 11, 28, 34, 23, 32, 19, 20, 16

(a) Find the median for (i) Tuesday (ii) Friday.
(b) Find the median for both days together.

3 A class of 30 pupils was asked to estimate the length of an exercise book (in pages). Here are their results:

65, 70, 80, 50, 80, 75, 95, 60, 45, 65, 60,
85, 100, 90, 95, 95, 90, 60, 80, 100, 45,
50, 65, 85, 90, 70, 75, 65, 80, 85

Find their median estimate.

17.4 The range

Ian's Geography homework marks were:

> 7, 5, 8, 3, 1, 8, 10, 6

His highest mark was 10. His lowest mark was 1.

The range of his marks was: $10 - 1 = 9$

■ **The range of a set of data is the difference between the highest and lowest values:**

> **range = highest value − lowest value**

Exercise 17D

1 Calculate the range for each set of data:
   (a) 6, 8, 3, 9, 7, 2, 5, 5, 3
   (b) 12, 6, 13, 21, 9, 16, 8, 15, 11
   (c) 21, 18, 15, 26, 17, 11, 14, 23, 19
   (d) 36, 23, 41, 17, 45, 19, 31, 26, 35
   (e) 53, 27, 72, 54, 33, 25, 34, 70, 49

2 Here are Ailsa's times in minutes for her journeys to and from school one week.

> 22, 21, 24, 28, 23, 24, 21, 26, 23, 25

Find the range of her times.

3 The range of a set of data is 12.
  If the smallest value is 33, what is the largest value?

4 The average daily sales for 3 car showrooms are shown in the table.

	Jan	Feb	Mar	Apr	May	Jun	Jul	Aug	Sep	Oct	Nov	Dec
Quicksale	12	15	23	11	21	18	14	48	23	18	24	20
Motormove	24	27	10	15	18	22	14	38	21	16	19	18
Carseller	17	19	16	34	26	18	22	52	30	25	19	24

Calculate the range for each month.

5 Six tennis racquets are priced as follows:
  £85, £72, £106, £80 and ☐
  If the range is £38 what could ☐ be?

17.5 Averages and range from frequency tables

Data is often shown in a frequency table.
You can use the table to work out the mean, mode and
range of the data.

There is more about
collecting data in
frequency tables on
page 295.

Example 3

This frequency table shows the number of pets the students
in class 7B own:

Number of pets	Frequency
1	1
2	16
3	10
4	3

Find the mean, mode and range of this set of data.

The table shows that   1 student owns 1 pet
16 students own 2 pets
10 students own 3 pets
3 students own 4 pets

The mean

The mean number of pets is: $\text{mean} = \dfrac{\text{total number of pets}}{\text{total number of students}}$

You could work it out like this:

$$\frac{1+2+2+2+2+2+2+2+2+2+2+2+2+2+2+2+2+3+3+3+3+3+3+3+3+3+3+4+4+4+4}{30}$$

But it is quicker to see that

$$\text{Mean} = \frac{(1 \times 1) \;+\; (16 \times 2) \;+\; (10 \times 3) \;+\; (3 \times 4)}{30} = \frac{75}{30}$$
$$= 2.5$$

The mean number of pets is 2.5

The mode

The mode is easy to spot.
It is the number of pets with
the highest frequency.
The modal number of pets is 2.

> A common mistake is to say the mode
> is 16 because it is the largest number.
> Here the highest frequency shows you
> which **number of pets** is the mode.

The range

The range of pets is:

range = highest number of pets − lowest number of pets

The highest number of pets is 4
The lowest number of pets is 1
The range is $4 - 1 = 3$

Exercise 17E

1 The number of goals scored by
   teams in the Premier League one
   week is shown in the table:

Number of goals	Frequency
0	6
1	2
2	8
3	3
4	1

   (a) Work out the mean number of goals scored.
   (b) What was the modal number of goals scored?
   (c) Find the range of this data.

2 The ages of 100 students in a primary school are given
   in the table.

Age	4	5	6	7	8	9	10	11
Frequency	10	12	13	11	14	16	14	10

   (a) Work out the mean age.
   (b) What is the modal age?

3 The table shows the weekly wages of people working in a garage:

Job	Number of people	Wage
Owner	1	£850
Foreman	1	£250
Mechanic	5	£175
Clerk	2	£150
Cleaner	1	£135

(a) Calculate: (i) the mean wage   (ii) the range.

Each person is given £100 per week pay rise.

(b) Calculate the new mean and range.

(c) Comment on the new results.

17.6 Making comparisons

You can use the average and range to compare two or more sets of data.

Jenny and Aleisha are both Goal Shooters in Netball.

In her last 5 games, Jenny scored 4, 5, 10, 7 and 9 goals. Aleisha scored 12, 12, 0, 11, 0 in her last 5 games.

Which player should be picked for the school team?

Their average scores are:

Jenny: $\dfrac{4+5+10+7+9}{5} = \dfrac{35}{5} = 7$

Aleisha: $\dfrac{12+12+0+11+0}{5} = \dfrac{35}{5} = 7$

Both players score an average of 7

The range of Jenny's scores is $10 - 4 = 6$
The range of Aleisha's scores is $12 - 0 = 12$

The range of Jenny's scores is lower: her results are less spread out. Aleisha has some high scores but also some 'no scores'. Jenny is probably the best choice for the school team.

Exercise 17F

1 The students in class 7D took a spelling test.

The mean mark for the girls was 12.
The range of marks for the girls was 10.

The mean mark for the boys was 10.
The range for the boys was 12.

Overall who did better in the test, the boys or the girls? Justify your answer.

Justify means give a reason to support your answer.

2 A politician said that the average wage in England is higher than the average wage in Germany.
Does this mean the English are better off than the Germans?
Explain your answer.

3 Make up a set of data which shows that left handed people are better at darts than right handed people.

Summary of key points

1 The mean of a set of data is the sum of the values divided by the number of values.

$$\text{mean} = \frac{\text{sum of the values}}{\text{number of values}}$$

2 The mode of a set of data is the value which occurs most often.

3 The median of a set of data is the middle value when the data is arranged in size order.
When there is an even number of values the median is the average (mean) of the middle two values.

4 The range of a set of data is the difference between the highest and lowest values:

$$\text{range} = \text{highest value} - \text{lowest value}$$

18 Transformations

This chapter introduces three types of **transformation**: reflection, rotation and translation.

■ **A transformation moves a shape to a new position:**
  - **The starting shape is called the object.**
  - **The transformed shape is called the image.**

18.1 Reflection

These symmetrical shapes are all made from a shape and its reflection:

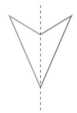  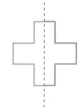

There is more about shapes with reflective symmetry on page 4.

You can draw the reflection of any shape using a line of symmetry.

Example 1

Reflect this shape in the line of symmetry:

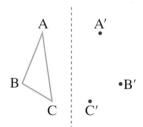 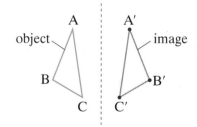

Draw the reflections of the points …

… and join them up.

The reflection of the point A is the point A′. You say 'A prime'.

Note that each point of the reflection is the same distance from the line of symmetry as the original point.

Exercise 18A

1 Copy and complete each diagram by drawing the reflection in the line of symmetry.

(a)

(b)

(c)

(d)

(e)

(f)

(g)

(h)

2 Copy and complete each diagram using the two lines of symmetry.

(a)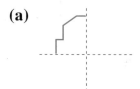

(b)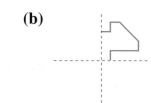

3 Copy this shape.
   (a) Reflect it in the vertical line, then the horizontal line.
   (b) Reflect it in the horizontal line, then the vertical line. Compare your results.

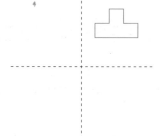

18.2 Rotation

This shape has rotational symmetry of order 3. It looks the same three times in one full rotation.

There is more about rotational symmetry on page 276.

  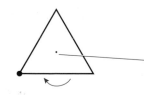

The shape rotates around this point. The point is called **the centre of rotation**.

You can rotate a shape around any point:

Example 2

Draw each shape after a rotation of 90° anticlockwise.

(a) 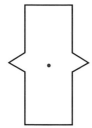 **(b)**

(a) Rotate the shape around the centre:

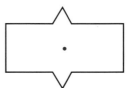

(b) Rotate each point in the shape around the centre of rotation:

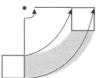

■ **In a rotation, every point of a shape moves through the same angle around a centre of rotation.**

Exercise 18B

1 Copy each shape and then draw it after it has been rotated about the centre of rotation by the amount stated.

(a)

90° anticlockwise

(b)

90° clockwise

(c)

180°

(d)

90° anticlockwise

2 Describe the rotation from A to B.

(a)

(b)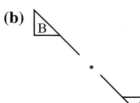

(c)

(d)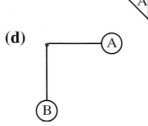

18.3 Translations

Bhavna is designing a treasure map:

She moves the castle 4 spaces up . . .   . . . and 3 spaces to the right.

 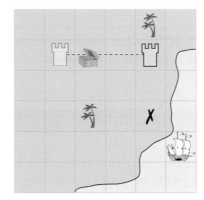

■   **A sliding movement like this is called a translation.**

Example 3

Describe the translation when
shape A moves to A′.

Each point on the shape has moved
4 squares to the right so the
movement is a translation of
'4 squares right'.

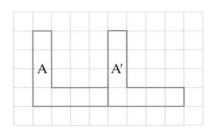

Example 4

Translate the triangle ABC 2 squares left and 4 squares up.

First translate each point: Join them up to complete the image:

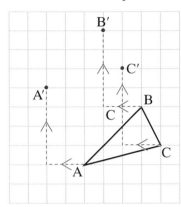   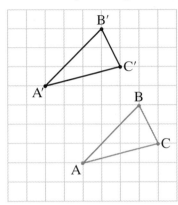

The triangle ABC is
the object.
The triangle A′B′C′
is the image.

Exercise 18C

1   Draw these shapes on squared paper and translate
    them by the amount shown.

    (a)   **(b)**   **(c)**

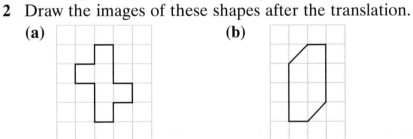

    5 squares right   3 squares down   3 squares up

2   Draw the images of these shapes after the translation.

    (a)   **(b)**

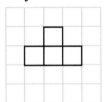   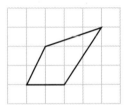

    2 squares down   2 squares down
    and 4 squares left   and 2 squares right

    (c)   **(d)**

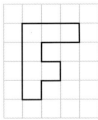   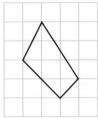

    2 squares left   5 squares up and
    and 2 squares up   2 squares down

3 Describe the translation for each object-image pair:

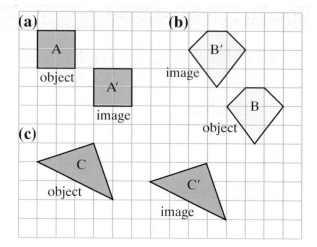

4 Think of at least one other way to describe each translation in question **3**.

18.4 Tessellations

■ **A pattern of shapes which fit together without leaving gaps or overlapping is called a tessellation.**

Rectangles can tessellate in a number of ways:

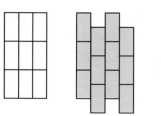

You can tessellate any triangle or quadrilateral by using transformations.

Example 5

Make tessellations with each of these shapes:

(a)

(b)

(a) Rotate the original shape 180° to get this shape.

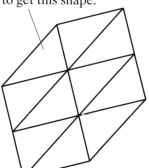

(b) Reflect the original shape in a horizontal line to make this shape.

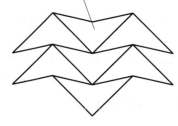

Exercise 18D

1 Make tessellations with each of these shapes:

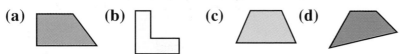

(a) (b) (c) (d)

2 Which of these regular polygons will tessellate?

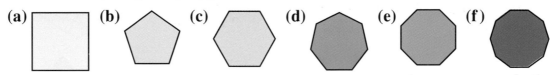

(a) (b) (c) (d) (e) (f)

(g) Which other shape can you tessellate with an octagon?

18.5 Congruence

These shapes all look different but
they are the same shape and size.
If you cut them out they would all
fit on top of each other exactly.

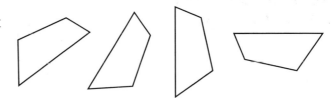

■ **Shapes that are exactly the same shape and size are
congruent.**

Example 6

Which of these shapes are congruent:

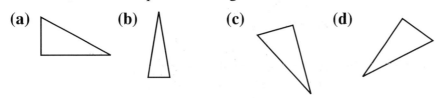

(a) (b) (c) (d)

(c) is the same as (a) after a rotation, a reflection and a
translation.
(d) is the same as (a) after a rotation and a translation.
(b) is smaller than the others and doesn't have a right angle.

So (a), (c) and (d) are congruent.

■ **For any reflection, rotation or translation, the object
and the image are always congruent.**

Exercise 18E

Write down the letters of the shapes which are congruent:

1 (a) (b) (c) (d)

2 (a) (b) (c) (d)

3 (a) (b) (c) (d)

4 (a) (b) (c) 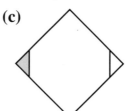 (d)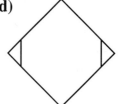

5 Draw as many triangles and quadrilaterals as you can on Activity sheet 10.
Match up any which are congruent.

Use the dots as vertices for your shapes:

Summary of key points

1 A transformation moves a shape to a new position:
 • The starting shape is called the object.
 • The transformed shape is called the image.

2 In a rotation, every point of a shape moves through the same angle around a centre of rotation.

3 A sliding movement is called a translation.

4 A pattern of shapes which fit together without leaving gaps or overlapping is called a tessellation.

5 Shapes that are exactly the same shape and size are congruent.

6 For any reflection, rotation or translation, the object and the image are always congruent.

19 Using and applying mathematics

This unit shows you how to use mathematics to **investigate** a problem.

The problem

Hop and Step

Lucy and her friends are playing a game called Hop and Step.

They have put a green hoop and a red hoop on the floor with some blue hoops in between.

To play the game, Lucy starts in the green hoop. She must finish in the red hoop.

There are three rules to the game:

Rule 1 She can only move forwards towards the red hoop.

Rule 2 She can take a step. This moves her one hoop forward.

Rule 3 She can take a hop. This moves her two hoops forward.

Investigate the number of different ways of getting from the green hoop to the red hoop as the number of blue hoops changes.

Understand the problem

The first thing to do is make sure you understand the problem.
The best way to do this is just have a go.

Example 1

Suppose there are four blue hoops.
Find three different ways of getting from the green hoop to the red hoop.

Remember to follow the rules.

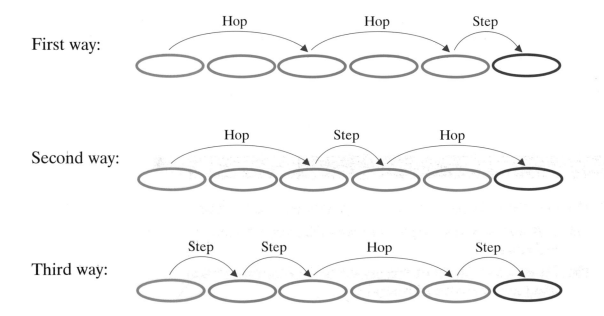

Exercise 19A

Show that there are 8 different ways of getting from the green to the red hoop when there are 4 blue hoops.

Make the problem as simple as you can

Once you understand the problem try to make it as simple as you can.

The simplest game is when there are **zero** blue hoops:

There is only one way of getting to the red hoop: one step.

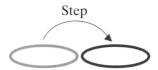

The next simplest game is when there is **one** blue hoop:

There are two ways of getting to the red hoop: one hop or two steps.

Exercise 19B

1 Put two blue hoops between the green and red hoops.
   (a) List all the ways of getting from the green to the red hoop.
   (b) How many different ways are there of getting from the green to the red hoop?

2 Put three blue hoops between the green and red hoop. Show that there are five different ways of getting from the green to the red hoop.

Organize your approach

As the number of blue hoops increases, you need to organize your approach to be sure you find all the ways of getting from the green to the red hoop.

An organized approach to a problem is called a **strategy**.

Here is one strategy you could use:

Do as many hops as you can.

Reduce the number of hops by one.

There will be more than one way of getting from the green to the red hoop with one hop.

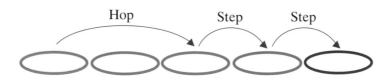

Reduce the number of hops by one again.

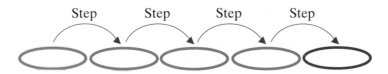

Using a strategy means you are more likely to find **all** the ways of getting from green to red.

You can shorten the words like this:

Let   S   stand for Step

And H stand for Hop.

The moves for three blue hoops are:

HH   2 Hops   0 Steps

HSS ⎫
SHS ⎬ 1 Hop   2 Steps
SSH ⎭

SSSS   0 Hops   4 Steps

When there are three blue hoops there are
5 different ways of getting from green to red.

Notice how the H
appears to move
along a diagonal:

H   S   S
S   H   S
S   S   H

The strategy helps
you spot patterns.

Exercise 19C

Use your strategy to show that there are 8 different ways of
getting from the green to the red hoop when there are
4 blue hoops.

Record your results

So far you should know that the number of ways of getting
from the green to the red hoop is:

1 when there are 0 blue hoops

2 when there is   1 blue hoop

3 when there are 2 blue hoops

5 when there are 3 blue hoops

8 when there are 4 blue hoops

A good way to keep your results is in a table:

Number of blue hoops	Number of ways of getting from green to red
0	1
1	2
2	3

Exercise 19D

Copy and complete the table:

Number of blue hoops	Number of ways of getting from green to red
0	1
1	2
2	3
3	
4	

Make predictions

Once you have some results and have recorded them in a table you can try to predict what will happen next.

Use your table of results to see if you can spot a pattern:

Number of blue hoops	Number of ways of getting from green to red
0	1
1	2
2	3
3	5
4	8

You should be able to see that:

The number of ways increases as the number of blue hoops increases.

You can predict that there will be more than 8 ways when there are 5 hoops.

If you just look at the number of ways you might spot that there is a pattern:

Number of blue hoops	Number of ways of getting from green to red	Even or odd?
0	1	Odd
1	2	Even
2	3	Odd
3	5	Odd
4	8	Even

You can predict that the pattern will continue like this:

Odd, Even, <u>Odd, Odd, Even</u>, Odd, Odd, Even, Odd, Odd, Even ...

This part repeats.

Your prediction could be:
There are an odd number of ways when there are 5 hoops.
There are an odd number of ways when there are 6 hoops.

Exercise 19E

Predict whether there will be an odd or an even number of ways when there are:

(a) 7 blue hoops   **(b)** 10 blue hoops   **(c)** 20 blue hoops

Try to predict the next number

The point of making a prediction is to find the number of ways without having to play the game.

You can predict that there is an odd number of ways when there are 5 blue hoops.
But the best prediction is exactly how many ways there are.

To predict how many ways there are with 5 blue hoops you need to find a pattern in the numbers.

It helps to write the number of ways like this:

| 1 | 2 | 3 | 5 | 8 | ? |

You need to spot that:
To find the next number in the sequence, add the previous two numbers together.

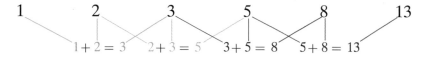

The pattern suggests that the number of ways when there are 5 blue hoops is 13.

You can predict that there are 13 ways when there are 5 hoops.

Hint: if you can't spot a pattern, play the game a few more times to get some more results.

Test your prediction

Now you have a prediction, you must test it to see if it works.

This means you use your strategy to show there are 13 ways when there are 5 blue hoops.

Exercise 19F

1 Show that there are 13 ways of getting from the green to the red hoop when there are 5 blue hoops.

2 Make and test a prediction for the number of ways when there are 6 blue hoops.

Make a generalization

Once you have tested your prediction and it works, you can use your prediction to generalize.
This means giving a rule that always works.

The rule for this sequence of numbers is:

To find the next number in the sequence, add the previous two numbers together.

You can use this generalization to make further predictions if you are still unsure:

Remember: this sequence is called a Fibonacci sequence. You can find out more on page 73.

Number of blue hoops	Number of ways of getting from green to red
0	1
1	2
2	3
3	5
4	8
5	13
6	21
7	34

$8 + 13 = 21$

$13 + 21 = 34$

Exercise 19G

Use your generalization to work out the number of ways when there are:

(a) 8 blue hoops

(b) 9 blue hoops

(c) 10 blue hoops

(d) 15 blue hoops

Trying out some investigations

Here are some investigations to help you practice recording your results, looking for patterns, testing your predictions and making generalisations.

Example 2

These tiles are arranged in a pattern:

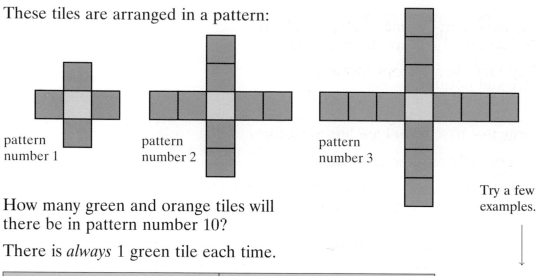

pattern
number 1

pattern
number 2

pattern
number 3

How many green and orange tiles will
there be in pattern number 10?

There is *always* 1 green tile each time.

Try a few
examples.

pattern number	orange tiles
1	4
2	8
3	12
⋮	⋮

Record your
results.

$\times 4$ →

So, for pattern number 4, there
should be $4 \times 4 = 16$ orange tiles:

Look for a
pattern.

Make a
prediction.

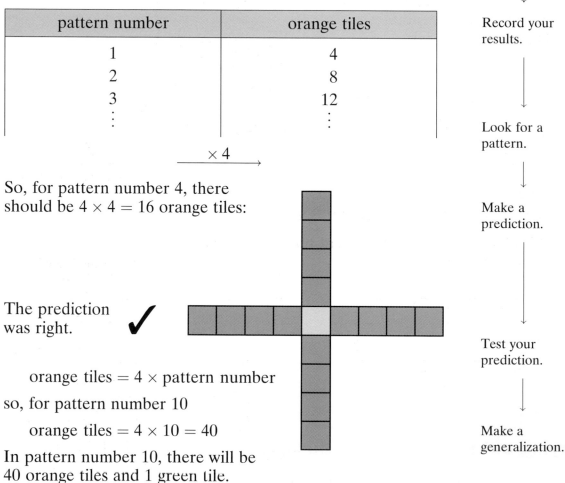

The prediction
was right. ✓

Test your
prediction.

orange tiles = 4 × pattern number

so, for pattern number 10

orange tiles = $4 \times 10 = 40$

In pattern number 10, there will be
40 orange tiles and 1 green tile.

Make a
generalization.

So

total number of tiles = (4 × pattern number) + 1

Exercise 19H

1 Lucy plays a new game of Hop and Step.
   This time the rules are the same except:

   a hop takes her 3 hoops forward.

   - Investigate the number of different ways of getting from the green hoop to the red hoop as the number of blue hoops changes.

   - Try to find a new generalization.

   - Use your generalization to find the number of ways when there are 10 blue hoops.

2 Carlo is designing a restaurant.
   He is investigating how many
   chairs can fit around tables:
   He starts with **1 table**:

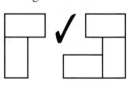

This symbol stands
for a chair

The restaurant
only has
rectangular tables

A maximum of **6 chairs** can fit here.

With **2 tables** there are 3 possible arrangements.
Two of them are:

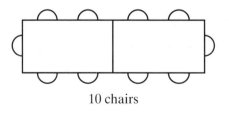

10 chairs

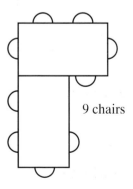

9 chairs

Tables must fit edge
to edge like this:

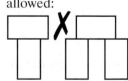

These are not
allowed:

Investigate the maximum number of chairs that can
fit around different numbers of tables.
How many chairs will fit around 100 tables?

3 Tessa is gardening. She wants to surround her square flowerbeds with triangular tiles:

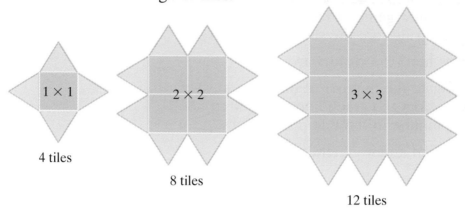

How many tiles would Tessa need for a

12 × 12 flowerbed?

75 × 75 flowerbed?

Investigate how many tiles Tessa would need for different sized flowerbeds.

Summary of key points

For any investigation

- Understand the problem – have a go
- Make the problem as simple as you can
- Organize your approach – use a strategy
- Record your results – use a table
- Make predictions – try to predict the next number
- Test your prediction
- Make a generalization

20 Calculators and computers

This unit shows you some ways of using scientific calculators, graphical calculators and computers to help solve mathematical problems.

The examples will work on Casio calculators and most computers. Your teacher will tell you if you need to change any of the instructions.

20.1 Using your memory

You can use the memory on a scientific calculator to help you with money or lists.

Example 1

Janet's money box contains twenty three 1p coins, seventeen 2p coins, nine 5p coins, and thirteen 10p coins. How much money has she saved?

Press

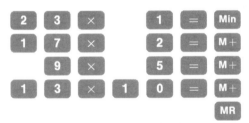

Answer: 232 pence which is £2.32

Exercise 20A   Scientific calculator

1 Lucy buys these stamps from the Post Office: 8 second class stamps at 20p, 22 first class stamps at 26p, 3 stamps at 37p, and 2 stamps at 43p. Find the total cost and the change she receives if she pays with a £10 note.

2 In one week a school tuck shop sold 83 bars of chocolate at 42p each, 229 cans of squash at 35p each and 355 packets of crisps at 15p each. Find the total takings for the week.

Find these keys on your scientific calculator:

Min this key puts a new number into memory

M+ adds a number to the memory

M− subtracts a number from the memory

MR recalls (brings back) from memory

AC clears the calculator display

AC **Min** clears the memory

3 Michael bought 17 Christmas cards at 5p each, 12 cards at 9p each and 5 cards at 14p each. How much did he spend on Christmas cards?

4 Suwani does a 6 mile sponsored walk. Twenty nine people sponsor her at 2p per mile, thirteen people at 5p per mile, and twelve people at 10p per mile. How much will she collect if she completes the whole distance?

20.2 Square numbers and number chains

You can find square numbers using the key x^2

The x^2 key multiplies a number by itself.

Multiplying a number by itself gives a **square number**

Example 2

Find **(a)** 5^2 **(b)** 7^2 **(c)** 13^2

(a) Press `5` `x²` `=`   Answer: 25

(b) Press `7` `x²`   Answer: 49

(c) Press `1` `3` `x²`   Answer: 169

$5 \times 5 = 25$

A short way to write 5×5 is 5^2

You say '5 squared'

Exercise 20B

1 Calculate 9^2

2 Calculate 12^2

3 Calculate 17^2

4 Calculate $5^2 + 12^2$

5 Calculate $6^2 + 8^2$

Number chains

You can make number chains by using simple rules.

Example 3

Start with 44   Follow this rule:

'square each digit and add them together'.

STOP when you get a number which is already
in the chain or you reach 1.

$$44 \rightarrow 4^2 + 4^2 = 16 + 16 = 32$$
$$32 \rightarrow 3^2 + 2^2 = 9 + 4 = 13$$
$$13 \rightarrow 1^2 + 3^2 = 1 + 9 = 10$$
$$1 \rightarrow 1^2 = 1$$

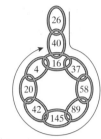

This chain
becomes a
circle unless
you stop.

Number chain: $44 \rightarrow 32 \rightarrow 13 \rightarrow 10 \rightarrow 1$

Exercise 20C

Make number chains using these rules. Stop when you
reach a number which is already in the chain.

1 Square and add the digits starting with 19

2 Square and add the digits starting with 49

3 Square and add the digits starting with 82

4 Square and add the digits starting with 15

20.3 Money and your calculator

You need to be able to interpret your calculator's display
when you do money calculations.

You can press
[C] to cancel an
incorrect entry

[AC] to clear the
display

Example 4

Add £1.27 to £4.23

Press [1] [·] [2] [7] [+] [4] [·] [2] [3] [=]

Answer: £5.50

Your calculator will
display 5.5

When you write
down the answer you
must include:

● the £ sign
● the zero

Example 5

Find the sum of £6.56 and 45p

Press [6] [·] [5] [6] [+] [·] [4] [5] [=]

Answer: £7.01

Enter .45 for 45p – the
calculator may display
the zero for you.

Example 6

Write down the value in **pounds** if your calculator displays

Remember
Your calculator
will not display the
zero.

Answer: £10.60

Example 7

Write down the value in **pence** if your calculator displays

£1.06 = 100p + 6p
      = 106p

Answer: 106p

Example 8

How many 26p stamps can be bought for £9.10?

Press: [9] [.] [1] [÷] [.] [2] [6] [=]

You do not need
to enter the zero
of the 10p since 9.1
is £9 and 10p.

If you do enter the
zero it may
disappear from the
display when you
press the ÷ sign.

Answer: 35 stamps

Example 9

A bottle of cola costs £2.59 for 1.5 litres. Calculate the price
per litre, to the nearest penny.

Press: [2] [.] [5] [9] [÷] [1] [.] [5] [=]

to display:

The first 6 rounds
the 1.72 up to give
1.73.

There is more on
rounding decimals
on page 134.

Answer: £1.73 to the nearest penny.

Exercise 20D   Scientific calculator

1 Write down the amount in words if your calculator
displays these amounts in **pounds**:

(a) [4.6]   (b) [0.38]

(c) [126.08]   (d) [50.04]

2 Show how your calculator will display these amounts in **pounds**:

(a) £12.50   (b) £0.39

(c) 79p   (d) 7p

3 Find the value in **pounds** of:

(a) £3.65 − £1.87

(b) £65 − £0.99

(c) £4 − 65p

4 Find the value in **pence** of:

(a) £4.89 + 36p

(b) £12.80 × 13

(c) £61.94 ÷ 19

(d) £100 − £3.26 + £18.76

In question **4(a)**, enter £4.89 as 489p so that both entries are in the same units.

To change a calculator answer from pounds to pence press:

5 Find the cost, in pounds, of 18 chocolate bars costing 26p each.

6 Find the total cost, in pounds, of 8 scientific calculators at £5.39 each, 6 protractors at 56p each and two mathematics textbooks at £8.99 each.

7 ACE Cosmetics bought some cars for its sales staff. The cost of each car was £14 658.27 and the total bill was £175 899.24. How many cars did the company buy?

Ignore the spaces in the numbers when entering the values into your calculator.

8 A pack of 6 roller ball pens costs £2.59. Calculate the cost per pen, to the nearest penny.

9 Last Monday David and Lynne's weekly supermarket bill was £124.16 for 86 items. Calculate the cost per item, to the nearest penny.

10 Multiply your written answer to question **9** by 86. Find the difference between this answer and the supermarket bill of £124.16.

20.4 Metric measure and your calculator

You need to be careful with units when you use a calculator with metric measures.

There is more on metric units in Chapter 7.

Example 10

Work out 654 cm + 13 cm 45 mm.
Give your answer in centimetres.

Write 13 cm 45 mm in centimetres as a decimal number:

13 cm 45 mm = 13.45 cm

Press: 6 5 4 + 1 3 · 4 5 =

13 cm 45 mm in cm

Answer: 667.45 cm

Example 11

Shamim bought a leg of lamb weighing 1 kg 213 g.
The lamb lost 54 g in weight while it was cooking.
Calculate the weight of the cooked lamb in kilograms and grams.

Write each weight in kilograms as a decimal number:

To change grams into kilograms on your calculator press:

÷ 1 0 0 0 =

1 kg 213 g = 1.213 kg
54 g = 0.054 kg

Press: 1 · 2 1 3 − · 0 5 4 =

Answer: 1.159 kg = 1 kg 159 g

Example 12

1300 sheets of paper weight approximately 1.3 kg. Stefan picked up $\frac{1}{3}$ of the sheets. What was the weight, to the nearest gram, of the paper Stefan was carrying?

Press: 1 · 3 ÷ 3 =

The calculator will display:

This is the weight of Stefan's paper in kilograms.

0.43333333

To change this value from kilograms into grams press:

The calculator will now display:

| 433.3333333 |

Answer: 433 grams, to the nearest gram.

This is the weight of Stefan's paper in grams.

Exercise 20E   Scientific calculator

1 Write these four values in kilograms and find their total weight:

  12 kg 457 g   7894 g   6 kg 26 g   322 g

2 Subtract 123 mm from 85 cm 4 mm. Give your answer in:

  (a) centimetres   **(b)** millimetres

3 A lorry has a maximum weight limit of 3 tonnes. What is the maximum number of each of these items of office furniture it can carry?

1 tonne is 1000 kg

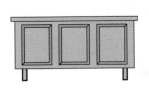  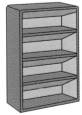

  Desk 24 kg   Cabinet 8.92 kg   Bookcase 7.363 kg

4 Calculate the mean height, to the nearest centimetre, of:

  Jim   164 cm
  Paulo   1 m 78 cm
  Georgia   1 m 65 cm
  Mina   157 cm
  Ted   153 cm
  Celia   1 m 67 cm

There is more on averages in Chapter 17.

When the six heights have been added on the calculator, remember to press ▭ *before* dividing by 6.

Section 20.12 shows another way of calculating the mean on a calculator.

20.5 Time on your calculator

You need to be careful using your calculator with time as the units are divided into 60, not 100.

Example 13

Write down these calculator displays in hours and minutes:

(a) $\boxed{3.25}$ **hours** **(b)** $\boxed{10.66666667}$ **hours**

Remember: $\frac{1}{4}$ of an hour is 15 minutes.

(a) Think of the decimal part as a fraction: $0.25 = \frac{1}{4}$
So 3.25 is 3 hours and 15 minutes.

(b) .6666666... is the decimal equivalent of $\frac{2}{3}$
So 10.66666667 is 10 hours and 40 minutes.

On your calculator display the last 6 in .6666666... has been rounded up to a 7.

Example 14

How would your calculator display these times:

(a) 7 hours and 30 minutes **(b)** 4 hours and 18 minutes

(a) 30 minutes is half an hour so your calculator would display 7.5 hours.

(b) To find the decimal part you need to know how many hours are in 18 minutes:

$$60\overline{)18.0} = 0.3$$

Divide by 60 as there are 60 minutes in one hour.

On your calculator press:

$\boxed{1}\ \boxed{8}\ \boxed{\div}\ \boxed{6}\ \boxed{0}\ \boxed{=}$

to get the answer.

So your calculator would display 4.3 hours.

Example 15

Add 3 hours 45 minutes to 2 hours 24 minutes, and give your answer in minutes.

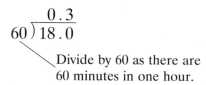

$$3\,\text{hr}\,45\,\text{min} \quad + \quad 2\,\text{hr}\,24\,\text{min}$$
$$\frac{45}{60} = 0.75 \qquad\qquad \frac{24}{60} = 0.4$$
$$3.75 \quad + \quad 2.4 \quad = \quad 6.15 \text{ hours}$$

To get the time in minutes you just multiply by 60:

$\boxed{6}\ \boxed{\cdot}\ \boxed{1}\ \boxed{5}\ \boxed{\times}\ \boxed{6}\ \boxed{0}$ $= 369$ minutes

Example 16

Akram travels 41 km at 12 km per hour. How long was Akram cycling for?

Press:

to display:

| 3.416666667 | hours

Multiply your answer by 60 to give:

| 205 | minutes

Answer: 3 hours 25 minutes.

To calculate the time for the journey divide the distance by the speed:

$$time = \frac{distance}{speed}$$

There is a different version of this formula on page 221.

Exercise 20F   Scientific calculator

1 Write down the time in **hours and minutes** if your calculator displays the following number of **hours**:

(a) | 4.75 | **(b)** | 4.333333333 |

(c) | 10.16666667 | **(d)** | 0.7 |

2 How will your calculator display, in hours:

(a) 5 hours 15 minutes?   **(b)** 8 hours 20 minutes?
(c) 1 hour 54 minutes?   **(d)** 12 minutes?

3 Joshua travelled from Folkestone to Manchester to visit his Grandma and Grandpa in half term.
This table shows the stages of his journey and how long they took:

Stage	From...	... to	Time taken:
1 Train	Folkestone	London	1 hour 40 minutes
2 Tube	London	London	18 minutes
3	Wait		36 minutes
4 Train	London	Manchester	2 hours 40 minutes
5 Car	Station	Grandparents	24 minutes

How long was Josh's journey in minutes?

4 Calculate the time it takes to travel 80 km at 15 km per hour. Give your answer in hours and minutes.

5 Calculate the time in hours and minutes and seconds to travel 340 miles at 45 miles per hour.

20.6 Percentages and your calculator

You can also use your calculator to change percentages into fractions or decimals and to calculate the percentage of a value.

There is more on percentages in Chapter 16.

Example 17

Change 35% into a fraction in its simplest form.

Press: 3 5 a$^{b/c}$ 1 0 0 =

to display ⌐⌐20

Answer: $\frac{7}{20}$

Example 18

Change 8.6% into a decimal.

Press: 8 · 6 ÷ 1 0 0 =

Answer: 0.086 m

Example 19

Find 28% of 2.45 m.

Press: 2 · 4 5 ÷ 1 0 0 × 2 8 =

Answer: 0.686 m

Dividing by 100 gives 1% and then multiplying by 28 gives 28%.

Exercise 20G   Scientific calculator

1 Change the following percentages into fractions or mixed numbers in their simplest form:

(a) 64%   **(b)** 85%   **(c)** 146%   **(d)** 215%

2 Change these percentages into decimals:

    (a) 17%   **(b)** 304%

    (c) 6%   **(d)** 7.25%

3 Find 39% of £43.78, giving your answer to the nearest penny.

4 Which is the bigger, 36.2% of 45 kg or 33.2% of 51 kg and by how many grams?

5 Jasmin was earning £32 456 per annum when she was given a pay rise of 3.2%. What is her new salary, to the nearest penny, following the increase?

per annum is the amount earned in one year

20.7 Arithmetic with brackets and your calculator

Exercise 20H   Scientific calculator

1 Write down the answer to these questions and then check them on your calculator:

Remember: Calculate the inside of the bracket first.

    (a) $12 - 2 + 4$ **(b)** $12 - (2 + 4)$

    (c) $12 - 2 - 4$ **(d)** $12 - (2 - 4)$

    (e) $12 + 2 - 4$ **(f)** $12 + (2 - 4)$

When using a calculator in the above question, enter the data in the order it appears in the sum.

For example for part **(b)** $12 - (2 + 4)$ key in:

When the bracket button is pressed the display may look like this:

$$[01 \qquad\qquad 0.$$

2 Write down the answer to these questions and then check them on your calculator:

    (a) $8 \times 4 + 2$ **(b)** $8 \times (4 + 2)$

    (c) $8 + 4 \times 2$ **(d)** $8 + (4 \times 2)$

    (e) $8 - 4 \times 2$ **(f)** $8 - (4 \times 2)$

20.8 Adding and subtracting negative numbers on your calculator

To enter a negative number enter the number and press [+/-] .

So to enter -7 press: [7] [+/-]

There is more on adding and subtracting negative numbers in Chapter 12.

Example 20

Work out:

(a) $-4 + 7$ (b) $-4 + -2$

(a) Press: [4] [+/-] [+] [7] [=]

Answer: 3

(b) Press: [AC] [4] [+/-] [+] [2] [+/-] [=]

Answer: -6

Always press

[AC]

to clear the screen before the next calculation.

Example 21

Work out: $-4 - -2$

Press: [AC] [4] [+/-] [−] [2] [+/-] [=]

Answer: -2

Example 22

Work out: $12 - (-2 - -4)$

Press: [1] [2] [−] [(...] [2] [+/-] [−] [4] [+/-] [...)] [=]

Answer: 10

On a V.P.A.M. calculator like the Casio *fx-83WA*, you can still enter the data in the order it appears:

Exercise 20I Scientific calculator

1 Work out:

  (a) $8 + -2$ (b) $-7 - 2$ (c) $-6 + -7 - 5$
  (d) $5 - -3$ (e) $-4 - -3$ (f) $7 - 4 - -2$
  (g) $-7.2 + -3.7$ (h) $8.4 - -4.8$
  (i) $2.78 - 6.23 + -1.7$ (j) $-1.2 - -6.54 - -5$

Don't forget to press

before each new calculation.

2 Work out:

    (a) $9 - (-7 + 8)$ **(b)** $-3 + (5 - -2)$ **(c)** $(4 - 7) + (-6 - 2)$

    (d) $6 - (3 - -8)$ **(e)** $9.12 - (4.8 - 2.7)$ **(f)** $-5.1 - (4.6 - -3.98)$

20.9 The constant function

This section shows you a quick way to work out number sequences.

Example 23

Find the next three terms in this sequence:

    2, 4, 6, 8, …

The rule for the sequence is 'add 2'.

Press: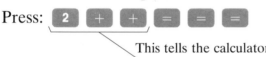

On a V.P.A.M. calculator press:

This tells the calculator to add 2 each time you press =

The sequence is 2, 4, 6, 8, 10, 12, 14, …
so the missing terms arc 10, 12 and 14

Example 24

Find the next three terms in this sequence:

    5, 15, 45, 135, …

The rule for the sequence is 'multiply by 3'.

Press:

On a V.P.A.M. calculator press:

This multiplies each term by 3   The first term is 5

The sequence is 5, 15, 45, 135, 405, 1215, 3645
so the missing terms are 405, 1215 and 3645

Exercise 20J   Scientific calculator

Use your calculator to create the next 6 terms of these sequences:

  1 5, 10, 15, 20, …   **2** 4, 7, 10, 13, …   **3** 3, 6, 12, 24, …   **4** 60, 55, 50, 45, …

  5 60, 30, 15, 7.5, …   **6** 40, 30, 20, 10, …   **7** 10, 50, 250, 1250, …

Exercise 20K   Graphical calculator

Write down the first five numbers in each of these sequences:

1 [4] [EXE] [Ans] [×] [2] [−] [3] [EXE] [EXE] ...

2 [2] [EXE] [Ans] [×] [3] [+] [1] [EXE] [EXE] ...

3 [7] [EXE] [Ans] [×] [2] [−] [1] [EXE] [EXE] ...

4 [7] [8] [4] [EXE] [Ans] [÷] [2] [+] [8] [EXE] [EXE] ...

5 What two step machine produces the sequence:

   5,   13,   29,   61,   125   ... ?

6 What two step machine produces the sequence:

   13,   21,   37,   69,   133   ... ?

20.10 Planning in MSWLogo

This section uses your knowledge of symmetry, turning and angles to produce the digits from 1 to 9 on a computer.

There is more on symmetry in Chapter 1.
There is more on turning and angles in Chapter 14.

Planning ahead

On a sheet of 1 cm square paper, use straight lines to draw all the digits from 1 to 9. Make the maximum height of each digit 4 centimetres.

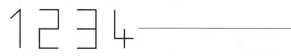

These four digits were drawn in MSWLogo where you must provide the instructions to move the 'turtle' around the screen.

Exercise 20L

In MSWLogo
● Type:

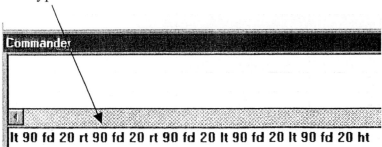

The turtle begins this way round

△

rt 90
will turn it 90° clockwise

▷

fd 40
will move it forward '40' places and draw a line '40' units long

──────▷

and press the Enter Key to produce:

Other useful code is:

lt 90 – to turn the turtle 90° left

bk 20 – to bring the turtle back 20 units

pu – to stop the turtle drawing lines if moved forwards or backwards

pd – to start drawing lines again

ht – to hide the turtle

st – to bring the turtle back

- Bring the turtle back, pick up the pen and move the turtle to a suitable position and type the necessary code to produce the digit 3.
- Continue this way until all the digits have been drawn.

Extension

Produce the code to create a sum such as $7 - 1 = 6$

20.11 Charts and graphs from data using a spreadsheet

Computer spreadsheets can produce a selection of different charts and graphs, so it can be very useful to use a spreadsheet for storing your data.

Find out how to produce bar charts and line graphs from data in your computer spreadsheet.

Look for horizontal bar charts, vertical bar charts and line graphs.

Exercise 20M

1 The daily temperature (minimum and maximum) and monthly rainfall figures for Monkey Bay in Malawi are shown below. Type this data into your spreadsheet and save it.

	A	B	C	D
1	**Month**	**Min Temp °C**	**Max Temp °C**	**Rainfall mm**
2	Jan	23	28	325
3	Feb	22	28	315
4	Mar	21	29	400
5	Apr	20	29	140
6	May	18	26	40
7	Jun	16	25	10
8	Jul	15	25	5
9	Aug	16	26	2
10	Sep	18	29	3
11	Oct	21	32	5
12	Nov	24	32	60
13	Dec	23	30	225

2 Display the rainfall data in a line graph like this:

Hint: Use the ctrl key to highlight columns that are not next to each other.

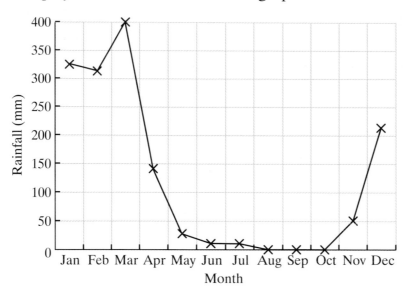

3 Display the maximum and minimum temperature data in a bar chart like this:

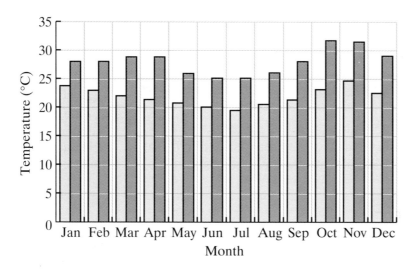

20.12 Finding the sum and mean of data

You can use your calculator to find the sum and mean of data.

You must first change your calculator into *statistics mode*.

To do this press

Some Casio calculators require you to press

to get in to statistics mode.

Check your manual for the correct keys to press.

Your calculator will display the letters SD when you are in statistics mode.

Example 25

Find the sum of 2, 5, 8 and 9.

Press: **2** **M⁺** **5** **M⁺** **8** **M⁺** **9** **M⁺** **SHIFT** **5**

The sum of the data is 24.

Now press **SHIFT** **AC** to clear the data from your calculator's memory.

You can check your total at any time then continue to add more data.

The symbol to find the sum of data is the Greek letter Σ, pronounced 'Sigma'.

In these examples, the calculator displays the Sigma above the 5 key:

Example 26

Find the sum of 5, 9 and 4. Then add 3 and 6 and find the overall total.

Press: **5** **M⁺** **9** **M⁺** **4** **M⁺** **SHIFT** **5**

A sub total of 18 will appear in your display. Now press:

3 **M⁺** **6** **M⁺** **SHIFT** **5**

to give the final total of 27.

Example 27

Find the mean of 12, 6, 9, 6 and 3.
Clear your memory of the previous data and press:

The mean is 7.2.

You can check the mean at any time and then continue adding further data before finding the overall mean.

The symbol on your calculator to find the mean of data is displayed as letter $\bar{x}$, pronounced 'x bar'.

In these examples, the calculator displays $\bar{x}$ above the 7 key:

Example 28

Find the mean of 8, 3 and 7. Add further data of 9 and 6 and find the overall mean of the 5 numbers.

Clear your memory of the previous data and press:

When entering data, press:

to see how many entries you have made so far.

The mean of the first three number is 6.

Then press:

The mean of all the data is 6.6.

Exercise 20N   Scientific calculator

When necessary:
- **give any answers correct to 1 decimal place of accuracy**
- **do not forget to clear data from your calculator's memory.**

1 For the following sets of data find:
   - the sum
   - the mean
   - (a) 6, 5, 11, 9, 17   (b) 3, 9, 6, 11, 14, 21, 2, 5
   - (c) 36, 56, 98, 21, 33, 45   (d) 78, 67, 121, 33, 122, 678

2 In 5 games of netball Anna-Natasha scored 6, 7, 0, 3 and 4 goals.

   (a) What was her mean number of goals per game?

   In her next 5 games she scored a further 6, 1, 0, 3 and 5 goals.

   (b) What is her mean number of goals for all 10 games?

When each set of data has been entered the sum can be displayed by pressing:

The mean can be displayed by pressing:

It is important to enter values of zero to calculate the mean correctly.

Can you explain why?

3 Find the total and mean of the following amounts of money:

£345.78, £1022.34, £6532.27 and £9385.85

4 Find the mean average attendance of these 6 soccer games played at Maine Road, Manchester.

29 653, 31 033, 32 789, 28 456, 32 598 and 31 501

5 Imran is captain of his school cricket team.
In 12 innings he scored the following runs:

12, 145, 78, 33, 19, 0, 0, 122, 97, 56, 111 and 107

(a) What is his total number of runs for the 12 innings?

(b) What is his current batting average?

(c) How many runs must he score in his next two innings to increase his batting average to 70?

Hint: The batting average is the mean number of runs.

6 In 10 mathematics tests Joshua scored

96%, 98%, 65%, 76%, 88%, 77%, 100%, 76%, 68% and 89%

Write down his mean percentage score after

(a) 2 tests

(b) 5 tests

(c) 7 tests

(d) 10 tests

Index